The Future of Social Protection

WHAT WORKS FOR NON-STANDARD WORKERS?

OECD
BETTER POLICIES FOR BETTER LIVES

Please cite this publication as:
OECD (2018), *The Future of Social Protection: What Works for Non-standard Workers?*, OECD Publishing, Paris.
https://doi.org/10.1787/9789264306943-en

ISBN 978-92-64-30693-6 (print)
ISBN 978-92-64-30694-3 (pdf)

Photo credits: © ProStockStudio/Shutterstock.com
© Helga Khorimarko/Shutterstock.com
© Inspiring/Shutterstock.com

Corrigenda to OECD publications may be found on line at: *www.oecd.org/publishing/corrigenda*.

Foreword

Globalisation, technological progress and demographic change profoundly affect OECD labour markets, influencing both the quantity and quality of jobs that are available, as well as how and by whom they are carried out. Policy makers need to strengthen the resilience and adaptability of labour markets so that workers can manage the transition with the least possible disruption, while reaping as much as possible its benefits. Against this backdrop, the OECD Future of Work initiative looks at how demographic change, globalisation and technological progress are affecting job quantity and quality, as well as labour market inclusiveness - and what this means for labour market, skills and social policy.

New technologies lower transaction costs, making it easier for firms to outsource tasks, and for individuals to offer and market their services and to compete with firms, blurring the lines between dependent work and self-employment. This challenges traditional social protection systems, which, in many countries, were built with a stable employer-employee relationship in mind.

Non-standard work and self-employment, in particular, are not recent phenomena. It is therefore interesting to take a closer look at existing programmes in OECD countries that provide social protection to non-standard workers, and to learn from the practical experiences with such approaches. This volume contains seven case studies that shed light on different aspects of the social protection of non-standard workers (the self-employed, those at the border between self- and dependent employment, temporary workers, and workers on flexible or on-call contracts). The first chapter brings together some key policy insights from these case studies, and discusses other recent policy initiatives across the OECD. It also looks at the special challenge of providing social protection to platform workers, and offers policy options to increase the income security of on-demand and flexible hours workers.

The seven case studies in this volume were prepared by independent national experts in cooperation with the Social Policy Division of the Directorate for Employment, Labour and Social Affairs under the supervision of Monika Queisser (Senior Counsellor, Head of the OECD Social Policy Division). The first chapter was written by Monika Queisser and Raphaela Hyee. The volume benefitted from many useful comments provided by Stefano Scarpetta (Director for Employment, Labour and Social Affairs) as well as by staff in the Directorate's Skills and Employability Division. Steve Whitehouse edited the seven case studies, and Liv Gudmundson and Lucy Hulett provided editorial support.

The financial support provided by Germany's Ministry for Labour and Social Affairs is gratefully acknowledged, as well as the inputs of speakers and participants of the Workshop on the Future of Social Protection, held in June 2017 in Berlin.

Table of contents

Foreword 3

Acronyms and abbreviations 11

Executive summary 13

Key insights 14

Chapter 1. Ensuring social protection for non-standard workers 17

1.1. Introduction 18
1.2. Independent and contingent workers in contributory social protection systems 22
1.3. Potential avenues for reform 24
1.4. Offering voluntary protection to non-standard workers 27
1.5. Social security contributions as a driver of non-standard work 28
1.6. Special schemes for non-standard workers 29
1.7. Social protection of platform workers 32
1.8. Policy lessons 35
Notes 37
References 38

Chapter 2. Australia: Providing social protection to non-standard workers with tax financing. 43

2.1. Introduction 44
2.2. Overview of the Australian system of social protection 44
2.3. Labour market and work arrangements in Australia 50
2.4. Access to social protection 58
2.5. The incomes and assets of the self-employed 63
2.6. Discussion and conclusions 65
Notes 68
References 70

Chapter 3. Austria: How social protection rules affect self-employed and independent contractors 75

3.1. Introduction 76
3.2. Definitions of self-employment and independent contractors/freelance contractors 76
3.3. Institutional setting: social protection schemes and self-employment / independent contractors 77
3.4. Quantitative development and assessment of effectiveness and efficiency 82
3.5. Conclusions 93
Notes 94
References 96

Chapter 4. France: Social protection for the self-employed 99

4.1. Introduction 100

4.2. An overview of the French social protection system 101
4.3. The characteristics of self-employed workers 103
4.4. The social contributions paid by self-employed workers 105
4.5. Social benefits for self-employed workers........ 110
4.6. The financial situation and management of the social security regime for self-employed workers........ 114
4.7. The specific situation of the "intermittents du spectacle"........ 115
4.8. Conclusion 118
Notes 120
References........ 122

Chapter 5. Germany: Social insurance for artists and writers 123

5.1. Overview of the German social security system........ 124
5.2. Artists' social security insurance 126
5.3. Efficiency and effectiveness 134
5.4. Conclusion and assessment........ 138
Note........ 141
References........ 142

Chapter 6. Italy: Para-subordinate workers and their social protection 145

6.1. Introduction........ 146
6.2. Welfare entitlements for para-subordinate workers........ 148
6.3. Para-subordinate workers: the extent of the phenomenon 152
6.4. The main characteristics of para-subordinate workers 155
6.5. Earnings distribution by contractual arrangements........ 158
6.6. Para-subordinate workers' working lives: a dynamic perspective........ 160
6.7. Actual accumulation of pension contributions by para-subordinate workers since 1996........ 163
6.8. Concluding remarks 165
Notes 168
References........ 170

Chapter 7. Netherlands: non-standard work and social protection 171

7.1. Introduction........ 172
7.2. The incidence of various forms of non-standard employment 172
7.3. Which groups work on a non-standard work arrangement? 174
7.4. Incentives created by the system and implications for the financing of social protection........ 184
7.5. Conclusions........ 189
Notes 193
References........ 195

Chapter 8. Sweden: Voluntary unemployment insurance........ 197

8.1. Introduction........ 198
8.2. The general architecture of the Swedish unemployment insurance system........ 201
8.3. Non-standard workers and the Swedish social protection system 205
8.4. Theory on unemployment insurance and non-standard workers 209
8.5. How does the Swedish UI system work for non-standard workers? 210
8.6. The importance of union-run and collectively bargained benefit schemes........ 212
8.7. Willingness to pay for UI in a voluntary UI system 213
8.8. Concluding remarks 218
Notes 220

References 222

Tables

Table 3.1. Social protection coverage of self-employed and independent contractors by benefit type 78
Table 3.2. Compulsory social insurance contribution rates by employment type 79
Table 4.1. Minimum contributions for craftsmen/traders with annual income below the minimum income threshold, 2017 (EUR) 107
Table 4.2. Social security contributions rates for craftsmen/traders with annual income below the minimum income threshold, 2017 107
Table 4.3. Social security contribution for dependent employees 109
Table 5.1. Artists and writers only pay half of their total contributions for pension, health and long-term care insurance, in line with the system for regular dependent employees 125
Table 5.2. Contribution rates payable by user companies of artistic services fluctuate to cover 30% of overall costs 130
Table 5.3. Government subsidies to the Artists' Fund are increasing 131
Table 5.4. Distribution of insured in areas of activity and types of insurance (2016) 132
Table 5.5. Declared average earnings of insured people by occupation, gender and age (as of 1 January 2017) 133
Table 5.6. Few self-employed opt in to the public pension system 138
Table 6.1. Labour costs are still lower for para-subordinate workers 148
Table 6.2. Social protection coverage of para-subordinate workers 148
Table 7.1. Non-standard workers are more likely to transition into unemployment-related situations 189
Table 7.2. Inflow rates into various benefit schemes are higher from non-standard contracts 189
Table 8.1. Taxes and collectively bargained contributions for a yearly median wage 205
Table 8.2. Descriptive statistics 216

Figures

Figure 1.1. Non-standard work is widespread in some countries 19
Figure 1.2. Social protection coverage influences the use of non-standard work 29
Figure 2.1. Old-age and disability pension are the quantitatively most important income support payments in Australia 48
Figure 2.2. Benefits are designed to encourage recipients' labour force participation 49
Figure 2.3. One in six Australian workers is self-employed 53
Figure 2.4. Women are more likely to be casual workers than men, but the growth of casual employment is mainly due to its growing prevalence for male workers 55
Figure 2.5. The self-employed have lower incomes, but more assets than employees 64
Figure 2.6. The self-employed benefit slightly less from social spending 65
Figure 3.1. The number of independent contractors is at its all-time low 83
Figure 3.2: Independent contractors are on average better educated than dependent employees 84
Figure 3.3: The majority of *marginal* independent contractors are otherwise insured 85
Figure 3.4: The number of single-person business is growing tentatively 87
Figure 3.5. The number of single-person business of trades- and craftspeople and of "new self-employed" increases progressively 88
Figure 3.6. Many single businesses do not survive the first years of business 89
Figure 4.1. *Micro-entrepreneurs* are driving the recent increase in self-employment 104
Figure 4.2. Self-employment was the main driver of job creation during the recovery 104
Figure 4.3. Above the minimum wage, the tax wedge is lower for the self-employed 110

Figure 4.4. More and more people are using the *intermittent du spectacle* scheme 117
Figure 5.1. Artists' fees have quadrupled over the last two decades 130
Figure 5.2. The public subsidy should cover 20% of the scheme's overall costs 131
Figure 5.3. Membership in the Artists' Social Security Fund is increasing, especially in music and visual art 134
Figure 6.1. Contribution rates for para-subordinates mostly rose since the 1990s 150
Figure 6.2. The number of para-subordinate collaborators follows an inverted U-shape 153
Figure 6.3. The number of exclusive para-subordinate collaborators fell in recent years 154
Figure 6.4. The number of vouchers increased rapidly, and incomes on vouchers are low 155
Figure 6.5. Para-subordinate workers are well educated on average 156
Figure 6.6. Para-subordinates report working under conditions similar to those of employees 157
Figure 6.7. Para-subordinates are less likely to work year-round than dependent employees 158
Figure 6.8. Para-subordinate earnings are lower and more dispersed than those of employees 159
Figure 6.9. Among para-subordinates, both high and low earners are overrepresented 160
Figure 6.10. The number of labour market entrants working as para-subordinates peaked in 2009 ... 161
Figure 6.11. Those who start their careers as para-subordinates often continue on this path 162
Figure 6.12. Those who start as para-subordinates do not work less than others 163
Figure 6.13. Many have low pension contributions, but para-subordinates are more vulnerable 164
Figure 6.14. Low pension accruals are mainly driven by disrupted employment histories 165
Figure 7.1. Forms of non-standard employment in the Netherlands 172
Figure 7.2. Employment has shifted from standard to non-standard employment relations 173
Figure 7.3. Nonstandard work most strongly associated with age 175
Figure 7.4. The tax wedge is significantly higher for dependent employees 184
Figure 7.5. Those working on standard contracts enjoy the highest incomes 188
Figure 8.1. Voluntary UI provides higher replacement rates 202
Figure 8.2. Union- and Unemployment Fund membership are closely related 204
Figure 8.3. Union top-ups counteracted cuts in publicly provided UI 212
Figure 8.4. Low-risk UI funds subsidize high-risk UI- funds 214
Figure 8.5. The 2007 reform introduced an experience rating via unemployment fees 215
Figure 8.6. The UI fund membership among self-employed and the total workforce 217

Boxes

Box 1.1. Key terms 18
Box 1.2. Improving unemployment benefit access to the self-employed 24
Box 2.1. Definition of employment income taken into account for income tests for pensions and allowances, Australia 2017 59
Box 8.1. Terminology on unemployment insurance in Sweden 200

Follow OECD Publications on:

http://twitter.com/OECD_Pubs

http://www.facebook.com/OECDPublications

http://www.linkedin.com/groups/OECD-Publications-4645871

http://www.youtube.com/oecdilibrary

OECD Alerts http://www.oecd.org/oecddirect/

Acronyms and abbreviations

ALMP	Active labour market programmes
ANF	Italian family allowance – *Assegno per il Nucleo Familiare*
CLA	Collective Labour Agreement
CPS	US Current Population Survey
DBA	Dutch Deregulation Labour Relations Assessment Law – *Wet Deregulering Beoordeling Arbeidsrelatie*
GDP	Gross Domestic Product
IAF	Swedish Unemployment Insurance Board
INPS	Italian Social Security Institute – *Istituto Nazionale della Previdenza Sociale*
IOAW	Dutch income provisions for older and partially disabled unemployed employees
IOAZ	Dutch benefit act for elderly self-employed people with a low income – *Wet Inkomensvoorziening oudere en gedeeltelijk arbeidsongeschikte gewezen zelfstandigen*
IOW	Dutch Act on Income Provisions for Older Unemployed – *Wet Inkomensvoorziening Oudere Werklozen*
ISFOL	Italian Institute for developing workers' lifelong learning – *Istituto per lo sviluppo della formazione professionale dei lavoratori*
KSVG	German Artists' Social Security Act – *Künstlersozialversicherungsgesetz*
LFS	Labour force survey
NASPI	*Nuova assicurazione sociale per l'impiego* – Italian unemployment benefit for employees
NDC	Italian notional defined-contribution public pension
PES	Public Employment Service
RSI	French social security scheme for self-employed workers – *Régime Social des Indépendants*
SBSE	Canadian Special Benefits for Self-employed Workers scheme
TFR	Italian form of severance pay that can be used to finance contributions to private pension funds – *Trattamento di Fine Rapporto*
UI	Unemployment insurance
UWV	Dutch Employee Insurance Agency
WAADI	Dutch law on the provision of employees by intermediaries – *Wet Allocatie Arbeidskrachten door Intermediairs*
WIA	Dutch Work and Income (Capacity for Work) Act
WW	Dutch Unemployment Insurance Act
WWZ	Dutch Work and Security Act – *Wet Werk en Zekerheid*
ZW	Dutch Sickness Benefits Act – *ZiekteWet*
ZW	Dutch sickness benefit – *Ziektewet-uitkering*

Executive summary

Most social protection systems were designed with the archetypical full-time dependent employee in mind. Work patterns deviating from this model – be it self-employment or online 'gig work' – can lead to coverage gaps. This is not a marginal issue. Across the OECD on average, 16% of all workers are self-employed, and a further 13% of all dependent employees are on temporary employment contracts. Temporary workers often struggle to accumulate minimum contribution periods, and the self-employed are often covered only by the most basic of benefits.

Rising numbers of non-standard workers also threaten to erode the contribution base and thus revenues of social protection systems. If only some categories of workers are covered by social protection – and liable to pay social contributions – while others are not, firms have an incentive to shift work onto those workers who enjoy the least protection.

New technologies and the new forms of work they create bring the incomplete social protection of non-standard workers to the forefront of the international policy debate. Non-standard work is not new to OECD economies, however, and there are lessons to be learned from strategies that countries already employ to provide social protection to such workers.

This volume presents seven case studies that shed light on different aspects of the social protection of non-standard workers (the self-employed, those at the border between self- and dependent employment, temporary workers, and workers on flexible or on-call contracts). The case studies analyse:

- the implications of a tax-financed social protection system on non-standard workers (Australia);
- voluntary social protection schemes for self-employed workers (Sweden);
- the effects of differing social protection coverage of standard and non-standard workers on the incidence of non-standard employment in the Netherlands, Italy and Austria;
- special schemes for non-standard workers – the French *Régime Social des Indépendants* (RSI) and programmes that provide social protection to special subgroups in the creative industries (the German *artists' insurance scheme* and the *intermittent du spectacle scheme* in France).

The introductory chapter to this volume brings together key policy insights of these case studies, and discusses other recent policy developments across the OECD. It also looks at the special challenge of providing social protection to platform or gig-workers and offers policy options to increase the income security of on-demand and flexible hours workers.

Key insights

Social security contributions should be harmonised across forms of employment as much as possible

Including workers that sit on the border between dependent and independent forms of work in the standard social protection scheme closes coverage gaps and helps ensure that social protection systems cover those who are most at risk.

It can also curb the scale of non-standard employment, and thus limit the erosion of the contribution base of social protection systems, as shown by the policy reform experiences in Italy and Austria. Raising non-wage labour costs, of course, comes at the risk of decreasing employment, just like for standard workers. If certain forms of employment are subject to lower non-wage labour cost, this should be a deliberate policy choice.

Voluntary schemes do not seem to work well for non-standard workers

Any insurance depends on risk sharing across members. If insurance is voluntary, those at highest risk have the greatest incentive to join. Unless a voluntary scheme achieves a very high coverage rate, this adverse selection either leads to a downward spiral of rising premia and falling coverage, or to additional costs in the system. High coverage rates, in turn, may require public subsidies, as the willingness to pay voluntarily for social protection appears to be low, as evidenced by the Swedish example.

Platform work

Online labour platforms have been experiencing spectacular growth in recent years. They make it easier and cheaper to offer and find work online, and have the potential to disseminate the advantages of self-employment – flexibility in working time and place, and autonomy in the organisation of work. Platforms can also offer both employed and non-employed individuals an easy way to smooth temporary income shocks.

Some platforms, however, go beyond a mere "facilitator" or "marketplace" role in determining prices, working times, or details of service provision, undermining the flexibility and autonomy associated with genuine self-employment. Thus, gig workers may end up enjoying few of the advantages of self-employment, but suffer many of its drawbacks, including the risk of demand fluctuations, unpaid down- or waiting times, and patchy social protection coverage. Minimum wages do not typically apply to them. Some platforms intervene in gig-workers' price setting, working time and work organisation to such an extent that they have been found to be the *de facto* employers by national courts. In cases of straightforward misclassification, labour law (when properly monitored and enforced) may be sufficient to ensure the adequate protection of workers.

There is no obvious difference in the need for social protection between self-employed workers who operate on traditional markets, and those who offer their services on platforms, but retain entrepreneurial control over their work. What does distinguish labour platforms from conventional markets is that all transactions are digital and hence completely traceable. This raises the potential for increasing social protection coverage and tax compliance by shifting activities from the informal to the formal economy.

Increasing income security for those working flexible hours

Independent contractors – whether they do work mediated by online platforms or not – as well as workers on on-call or flexible hours contracts lack the income security provided by regular employment relationships while enabling firms to cheaply adjust to demand fluctuations. One way to redress this imbalance is to introduce a wage premium for flexible work as a compensation for assuming part of the entrepreneurial risk. The idea of requiring employers to pay higher rates to those who assume part of the entrepreneurial risk has been gaining traction both in the context of platform work as well as flexible hours work contracts. In Australia, *casual workers* are already entitled to a wage premium. Minimum earnings floors may also be applied to independent contractors.

Chapter 1. Ensuring social protection for non-standard workers

This chapter sets out by presenting the main challenges of covering non-standard workers in contributory social protection systems. It then discusses the advantages and pitfalls of two basic ways in which social protection systems could adapt to these challenges: by tying entitlements to individual workers rather than employment relationships or by doing the opposite and untying benefits from contributions. The chapter offers theoretical considerations and practical country experiences in offering voluntary social protection to non-standard workers, and looks at how social security contributions themselves can be a driver of non-standard work. It then presents two examples of special schemes for non-standard workers, and discusses the emerging challenge of improving the social protection and job quality of platform workers. Finally, it draws policy lessons on improving the social protection of non-standard workers and enhancing the income security of the increasing number of on-demand and flexible hours workers.

The statistical data for Israel are supplied by and under the responsibility of the relevant Israeli authorities. The use of such data by the OECD is without prejudice to the status of the Golan Heights, East Jerusalem and Israeli settlements in the West Bank under the terms of international law.

1.1. Introduction

Social protection systems are often still designed with the archetype of full-time, permanent work for a single employer in mind. Deviations from this pattern – be it self-employment or the combination of different income sources – can lead to coverage gaps or loss of accumulated entitlements.

This is not a marginal issue. Across the OECD on average, 16% of all workers are self-employed (Figure 1.1), and a further 13% of all dependent employees are on temporary employment contracts. Temporary workers often struggle to accumulate minimum contribution periods, and the self-employed are often only covered by the most basic of benefits – only 6 out of 28 European Union member states insure the self-employed in the same way as standard employees (Spasova et al., 2017[1]).

Box 1.1. Key terms

Standard workers

Regular, open-ended dependent employment with a single employer. The definition often also specifies full-time hours; however, since social protection systems typically treat part-time workers like standard workers as long as they meet the minimum income requirements, part-time workers are included in this definition throughout this chapter.

Temporary workers

Workers on a fixed-term contract. Since social protection systems typically do not differentiate between standard- and temporary workers as long as they achieve the minimum contribution periods, this chapter concentrates on the self-employed, and those on the border between self- and dependent employment, as well as those on flexible or on-call contracts.

Flexible or on-call contracts

These are employment contracts that do not require the employer to offer a minimum of working hours, while the employee is not required to accept hours offered; however, times of availability for the worker may be agreed.

Platform workers

Are workers who offer and find their work through online labour platforms.

Para-subordinate workers

In Italy, para-subordinate workers are self-employed, but highly dependent on one or very few clients. They are mandatorily enrolled in a special public fund called *Gestione Separata.*

Independent contractors

Independent contracts (*freie Dienstverträge*) is a form of labour contract between self- and dependent employment. Independent contractors have no or little "personal dependence" on their employer and control their own working time and workflow, but they are contracted for their time and effort (that is, they do not carry entrepreneurial risk).

Figure 1.1. Non-standard work is widespread in some countries

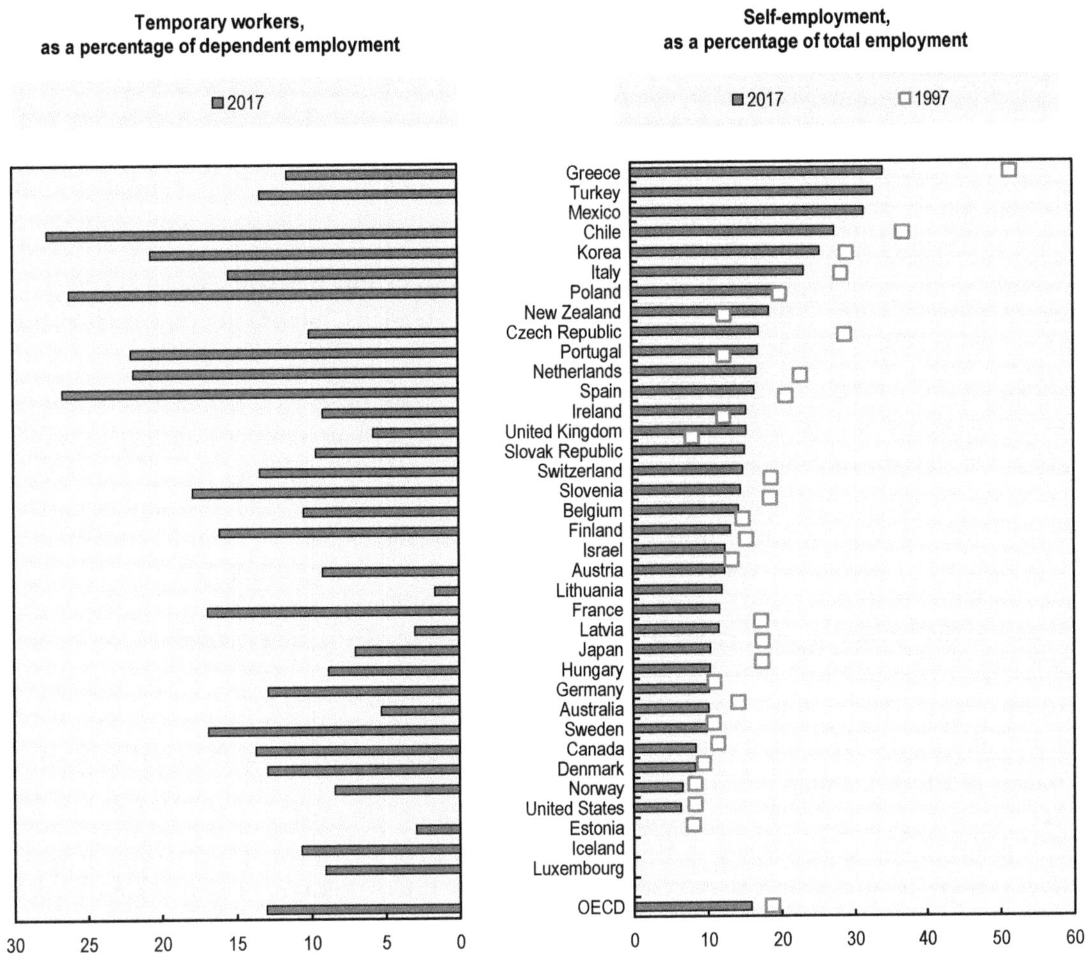

Note: There is no data on temporary employment for Israel, New Zealand or the United States, no data on self-employment for Iceland and Luxembourg; no data on France before 2003, on Lithuania and Mexico before 2005 and on Switzerland before 2010. Data on self-employment for Austria refer to 1999, for Spain to 1998, for Turkey and the United Kingdom to 2000, for the Slovak Republic to 2000 and 2015, for Latvia to 1998 and 2014

Source: OECD (2018), "Labour Force Statistics: Summary tables" and OECD Employment and Labour Market Statistics (database).

Rising numbers of non-standard workers also threaten to erode the contribution base of social protection systems. If tax and social protection systems are designed such that only some categories of workers are covered by social protection – and liable to pay social contributions – while others are not, firms have an incentive to shift work onto those workers who enjoy the least protection. But also low-risk workers (e.g. younger and better-educated workers) may self-select into self-employment and other non-typical or new employment forms. This undermines risk pooling that is crucial to any form of insurance.

Global trends such as globalisation and digitalisation are likely to make the divergence between the ideal of dependent, full-time employment and labour market realities more salient. New technologies make it easier and cheaper to offer and find work online, and online intermediaries (work platforms) have experienced spectacular growth in recent years, although they still account for a very small share of workers in OECD countries (e.g., Katz and Krueger (2016[2]), Pesole et al. (2018[3])).

These new technologies lower transaction costs, allowing firms to outsource more and more, pushing the boundaries of the firm (OECD, 2016[4]). This offers valuable flexibility to many who have previously been excluded from the labour market, such as those with caring responsibilities, or those in remote areas.

But it also exposes workers to new risks: since these *gig* or *crowd workers* are hired for specific tasks only, they can be instantly dismissed if demand drops. They cannot rely on the insurance function of the standard employment contract, as the first line of defence against demand fluctuations (Parsons, 1986[5]). At the same time, they have less access to income replacement payments than other workers. While firms may thus have a dual cost advantage of avoiding both social contributions as well as having to pay employees during down-times, workers incur a double risk.

Shifting low-paid work onto independent contractors, regardless of whether it is through online platforms or traditional markets, also threatens the effectiveness of minimum wage floors. This applies to flexible hours contracts as well: while minimum wages guarantee minimum *hourly* payments, the lack of fixed working hours introduces income insecurity on the working time margin. Firms may use flexible forms of employment to circumvent minimum wage increases: Datta et al. (forthcoming[6]) show that while the hourly wage rate of UK domiciliary care workers paid at the minimum wage went up by 7.5% following the introduction of the National Living Wage in 2016, their probability of being on a zero hours contract increased by 4.7%. Thus, workers may suffer from decreasing incomes despite minimum wage increases.

New technologies and the new forms of work they create bring the incomplete social protection of non-standard workers to the forefront of the international policy debate (see, for example, the European Commission's initiative on Access to social protection (European Commission, 2018[7]; European Commission, 2018[8])). It is hardly a new phenomenon, however: across the OECD on average, self-employment as a share of total employment decreased by 4 percentage points over the past 20 years, although trends have been very uneven across countries (see Figure 1.1). Recent US-census data show that the share of workers who are independent contractors decreased slightly between 2005 and 2017 (from 7.4% to 6.9% of total employment), while the share of on-call and agency workers stagnated over this period (BLS, 2005[9]; BLS, 2018[10]).

But labour force surveys likely underestimate the actual extent of self- and contingent employment. Abraham et al. (2017[11]) show that nearly two-thirds of all workers who have self-employment income in US tax data do not report having self-employment income in labour force surveys – half of them have incomes as both self-employed and dependent employees, and are thus likely omit their second job, while the other half report being employed, indicating misclassification – and this gap is widening. As a consequence, levels and trends in self-employment appear much lower in survey data estimates than indicated in the tax data.

As non-standard work is not generally new to OECD economies, there are lessons to be learned from strategies that countries already employ to provide social protection to such workers. In fact, as Prassl (2018[12]) argues, even gig work, while enabled by new technologies, shares many traits with historical on-demand work such as 19th century dock labour. Policy solutions that were and are applied to non-standard workers therefore deserve attention as possible remedies to current challenges.

The diversity of social protection systems across the OECD means that some policy solutions that are currently discussed have already been implemented in practice. For example, untying social protection from the employment relationship, and instead offering benefits on a means-tested basis, is often brought forward as a solution to the problem of closing coverage gaps. Australia's largely general revenue-financed social protection system (supplemented by 'Pay-As-You-Go' financed and income tax subsidised compulsory superannuation) provides an example of such a system. Similarly, some countries extend coverage to non-standard workers by establishing voluntary schemes; the Swedish unemployment insurance system offers lessons on how such schemes work in practice.

This volume collects seven case studies that shed light on different aspects of the social protection of non-standard workers. The case studies analyse

- the implications of a general revenue-financed social protection system on non-standard workers (Chapter 2 on Australia);
- voluntary social protection schemes for self-employed workers (Chapter 8 on Sweden);
- the effects of differing social protection coverage of standard and non-standard workers on the incidence of non-standard employment in the Netherlands (Chapter 7), Italy (Chapter 6) and Austria (Chapter 3), including reforms to increase the coverage of non-standard workers on para-subordinate workers in Italy the integration of independent contractors into the Austrian social protection system;
- special schemes for non-standard workers, specifically the French *Régime Social des Indépendants* (RSI) in France (Chapter 4), and programmes that provide social protection to special subgroups in the creative industries (the German *artists' insurance* for artists and writers (Chapter 5) and *the intermittent du spectacle scheme* for performing artists and some stage technicians in France (Chapter 4).

This chapter brings together some key policy insights from these case studies, as well as recent policy initiatives across the OECD. It also looks at the special challenge of providing social protection to platform or gig-workers and offers policy options to increase the income security of on-demand and flexible hours workers.

The chapter sets out the main theoretical and practical considerations that complicate social protection for non-standard workers (Section 1.2), and discusses the advantages and pitfalls of two basic ways to reform social protection systems to facilitate the inclusion of non-standard workers (Section 1.3). It goes on to synthesise policy lessons from voluntary social protection schemes (Section 1.4), the incorporation of non-standard workers into the standard social protection system (Section 1.5) and discusses two country experiences of special schemes for artists and workers in the entertainment industry (Section 1.6). Section 1.7 discusses the special situation of workers in the platform economy. Section 1.8 offers policy lessons on improving social protection for non-standard workers.

1.2. Independent and contingent workers in contributory social protection systems

Independent and contingent workers do not easily fit into the framework of contributory social protection systems: who should be liable for their employer contributions, and how should contributions and benefit entitlements be calculated with highly fluctuating earnings? Providing unemployment insurance for the self-employed, in particular, also raises significant moral hazard problems.

First, in contributory systems, employers and employees share the contribution burden – who should be liable for the employer contributions if an employer is not easily identified? This is the so-called *double contribution issue.*

Requiring the self-employed to pay both employer and employee contributions is the straightforward solution to this problem. This would effectively force them to raise their prices, bringing their labour cost more in line with that of dependent employees. In the United States, self-employed workers pay both employer and employee contributions to social insurance; the difference in the non-wage labour cost between dependent employees and self-employed workers at the average wage is only 1.6 percentage points, compared to 30 percentage points in the Netherlands, and mainly due to employer contributions to unemployment and work-injury insurance that do not cover the self-employed (OECD, forthcoming[13]; SSA and ISSA, 2018[14]).

Not all self-employed workers have the bargaining power to shift these costs onto consumers however. Self-employed earnings are typically dispersed, with a high share of low earners (see the articles in this publication for non-standard workers in selected OECD economies, and Berg (2016[15]) for crowd workers). For example, one in-four self-employed workers in France earns less than EUR 12 000 per year (Chapter 4). Minimum wages typically do not apply to them, and their scope for collective bargaining is often limited by competition law (BMAS, 2017[16]). Raising labour costs for the self-employed also comes at the risk of pushing economic activities into the informal economy, especially for *peer-to-peer* transactions that are difficult to monitor for tax authorities (OECD, 2018[17]).

Charging clients directly is a possible approach to address this challenge, but this is not straightforward from an administrative perspective. The German artists' insurance scheme is an example of this approach (Section 1.6.1): firms and public entities who contract artists, writers or journalists pay a fixed contribution to a special fund administering social protection for artists and writers. The German pension fund monitors these contributions in the course of their regular social security compliance inspections; a significant advantage considering that monitoring of individual self-employed earnings can be difficult for tax authorities, compared to taxes on employee earnings which are often withheld at the source (OECD, 2018[17]).

The government could also heavily subsidise schemes for the self-employed, which raises concerns about equal treatment and may create adverse incentives for both employers and employees. Where they exist, such schemes are therefore often limited to occupations that are thought to create special value for the public, such as the arts. The German government funds half of employer contributions in the artists' insurance scheme (Chapter 5); in the French *intermittents du spectacle* scheme for performing artists and related occupations contributions cover less than 20% of total benefit expenditure (Chapter 4).

Second, the self-employed often have fluctuating earnings – because they are paid at irregular intervals, because there are time-lags between work and payment, or because demand for their services is erratic (ISSA, 2012[18]). Thus, contributions are difficult to calculate – even if they are annualised, contributors might struggle to pay in bad years; contributors also have some control over the timing of payments, and could time them to circumvent means-tests.

Third, the self-employed do not meet several conditions that typically limit moral hazard in unemployment insurance: fluctuations in demand are hard to distinguish from voluntary idleness. Income fluctuations complicate the calculation of benefit entitlements, even if income is annualised. There is no employer to confirm a layoff, and job search efforts are even more difficult to monitor than for dependent employees. Also, because downward wage rigidity does not apply to the self-employed, they are more likely to have lower present than past earnings, and therefore a stronger incentive to become and remain unemployed (Chapter 8).

As a consequence, unemployment is generally the least-covered risk for self-employed workers: only 8 of all 28 European Union member states fully cover self-employed workers for unemployment insurance, and nine do not offer any form (even partial or voluntary) insurance. In contrast, self-employed women are covered for maternity benefits in all but 6 European Union member states (Avlijas, 2018[19]).

Where the self-employed are covered by unemployment insurance, they often face more stringent eligibility conditions:

- In Sweden, self-employed workers have to close down their business before claiming benefits. Because setting up a business has a significant administrative cost, this is an expensive check, which seems to work: over the 2004-2016 period, the average unemployment rate among insured self-employed workers was 4%, compared to 7% among dependent employees (Chapter 8).
- In Austria, self-employed workers have six months to decide whether to opt-into voluntary unemployment insurance upon starting their business – this decision is binding for eight years (Chapter 3).[1] This check is designed to prevent those whose business is winding down to opt in just before collecting benefits. It has the drawback, however, that it asks start-ups to commit to a long-term fixed cost just as their finances are the tightest. In 2015, only 0.3% of all eligible self-employed persons opted into this insurance.
- In Belgium, self-employed workers who have been declared bankrupt, are in a collective debt settlement, or who have been forced to interrupt their business activities, as well as self-employed workers in economic difficulties who cease all their self-employed activities may (under certain conditions) be entitled to a monthly benefit and health care without paying social contributions.

Box 1.2. Improving unemployment benefit access to the self-employed

The Danish unemployment insurance reform

In 2018, Denmark implemented a reform designed to make unemployment benefits more accessible to the self-employed and other non-standard workers. Before the reform, self-employed applicants had to produce documentation not only on earnings, but also revenue and tax declarations, proof of orders etc., while employees only needed to prove that they met the minimum earnings requirements. Benefit entitlement was therefore less predictable for the self-employed than for standard workers. Also, enrolees could only be insured as either dependent employees or self-employed, which made it harder for those combining dependent and self-employment to meet the minimum earnings requirements

The reform intends to harmonise benefit receipt rules: eligibly will solely be based on reaching a minimum (taxable) income over a three-year period and will not be conditioned on the type of employment. This should make eligibility more predictable for workers, as they can verify that they reached the required earnings-threshold on their tax return. As all income from work will be considered together, the reform should also improve eligibility for those who combine income from various sources. It also aims to simplify the administrative process of proving that a company has in fact closed down. To avoid that the self-employed continue working while receiving benefits, it also introduces a six-month "job search" period, during which benefit recipients have to look for dependent employment and are not allowed to start their own business. The implementation and effectiveness of this reform needs to be followed closely and could provide interesting policy lessons to other countries.

Source: Report from the working group of self-employed persons in the unemployment insurance system (Arbejdsgruppen om selvstændige i dagpengesystemet, (2017[20])); Kvist (2017[21])).

1.3. Potential avenues for reform

Social protection systems could adapt to these challenges in two basic ways: tie entitlements to individual workers rather than to specific employment relationships or do the opposite and untie benefits from contributions. This section briefly discusses each of these options.

1.3.1. Individualisation of social protection

This approach ties social protection entitlements to individuals, not employment relationships, by recording all social protection contributions made by workers themselves, employers or the state on their behalf in one account. As the timing and the provenance of contributions are irrelevant, such individual activity accounts would solve the problems of high earnings variability as well as of combining incomes from different sources. Recording all contributions in one place would also preserve entitlements during job changes and career breaks, supporting increasingly uneven employment patterns and labour market flexibility. This is why this idea, while not new, has been gaining popularity in recent years, especially among advocates for workers in new and emerging employment types such as "gig work" and micro-entrepreneurship (e.g. Etsy (2016[22])).

In theory, individual activity accounts could accommodate contract work and short-time, contingent employment and collect the entitlements of multiple job holders in one place.

Several OECD countries are currently planning to introduce such "*individual activity accounts*", which also allow beneficiaries to withdraw funds for causes not previously insured by social protection, such as education and vocational training, or starting a business. Depending on the specific model, individuals might also use them to take time out for caring responsibilities, or to retire early.

As individual accounts collect individual contributions for individual use, in their purest form, they do not incorporate risk-sharing, which is fundamental to any insurance. Thus, they would be unable to protect even high-earning individuals against catastrophic risks such as disability. Any other, implicit redistribution in the system – such as from those with very stable jobs to those who become unemployed frequently, or between those whose work carries health risks and those who can work healthily until retirement – has to be made explicit.

Individual activity accounts *per se* do not solve the *double contribution problem* (see above), and as such, meaningful benefits for the self-employed will remain elusive unless ways are found to levy social contributions from customers. Also, without substantial subsidies, they would be worthless to many low-income and part-time workers – though governments could of course decide to pay into accounts directly, e.g. by giving "starting endowments" to young people.

Making social protection entitlements more fungible for beneficiaries is moreover not without risk, as myopia can lead individuals to spend their entitlements too early, leaving them poor in old age. The experience of the Dutch Life Course Savings Scheme shows that many chose to use their funds to retire early instead of using them for further training or caring for family members (Delsen and Smits, 2014[23]).

1.3.2. Making social protection more universal

Untying social protection from the employment relationship – that is, granting individual entitlements to tax-financed benefits based on need rather than on earnings or contributions – would extend coverage to non-standard workers and get around the problem of tracking entitlements across jobs and over the lifecycle. Some benefits – such as health insurance and maternity or parental leave – are already universal in a number of OECD countries, and most countries have social assistance *benefits of last resort*, that provide basic assistance to those in need who are not entitled to any other benefits.

Depending on how exactly means-tests are implemented, non-standard workers may be *more, not less likely* to receive them, because they have less stable careers, are more likely to work part-time, and because their median earnings tend to be lower (Chapter 2). In the Netherlands, for example, the inflow rate into social assistance is nine times higher for non-standard workers than for dependent employees (Chapter 7). In Austria, on the other hand, only 0.2% of social assistance recipients are self-employed, while they make up about 12% of total employment. This is likely due to the fact that the means-test generally asks for business assets to be liquidated (Chapter 3).

However, in making entitlements more universal, policy makers should consider the risk of crowding out employer contributions. Australia and New Zealand are examples of general revenue-financed social protection systems that do not condition eligibility on previous contributions. In Australia, benefits are income- and assets-tested, although targeting has been relaxed incrementally over the past 50 years. The Australian story is complicated, however, by the social protection system's interaction with a system of workplace benefits and entitlements, including paid holidays and sick and carer's leave, that *casual* workers (about a quarter of all workers) as well as independent contractors (a further 9% of total employment) are not entitled to. Casual workers do not receive notice of termination or redundancy pay, which leaves them less time to search for other work. As a consequence, they end up unemployed more frequently than standard employees (although they are also more likely to work in high-unemployment sectors). This lack of workplace entitlements contributes to their more frequent receipt of general revenue - financed benefits and is the biggest source of cost-savings for firms in choosing this employment form (Chapter 2). In decoupling entitlements from jobs, policy makers have to think about how to ensure that employers continue to contribute, and that the government does not just take over parts of normal compensation from employers.

While means-testing benefits solves the problem of coverage gaps, it does *not* remove the need for tracking self-employment income, but rather makes it more salient: the problem of highly fluctuating earnings among the self-employed makes overpayments more likely, which is arguably an issue in a general revenue-financed system where benefits are not balanced out by contributions. This problem has no straightforward technical solution.

Abolishing means-testing altogether (that is, moving in the direction of a *basic income*) would remove all compliance issues and could easily incorporate non-standard workers. But it would be a budgetary challenge: replacing all existing working-age benefits by a flat-rate amount (without raising general revenue) in a budget-neutral way would lead to benefit levels below the poverty line in all OECD countries. It would also imply sometimes significant losses for disadvantaged groups such as the disabled, as benefits would no longer be targeted (OECD, 2017[24]). This raises substantial fairness concerns, as some individuals, such as the disabled, have greater needs than others (Piachaud, 2016[25]).While a basic income scheme could incorporate top-ups for specific groups, this would undermine the appeal of simpler (and cheaper) administration and complete predictability of basic income.

A basic income can also reduce work incentives, although individual labour supply is determined through a complex interplay of individual preferences, labour market characteristics and institutional and societal factors, leading to income and substitution effects, and thus depends on a range of factors, including the overall design of the tax system including basic-income payments, local labour demand, and the availability of child care. Thus, the effects of basic income schemes have to be assessed empirically.

Experiments with basic income schemes are currently under way in several OECD countries. Finland started paying randomly selected unemployment benefit recipients a basic income in January 2017. Payments are not conditional on work and participants are not required to seek employment. With a trial run of two years, the pilot will end in 2018, and first results of the experiment will be published in late 2019 to early 2020. The Finnish government has recently rejected the proposal to expand the experiment to a sample of employees (Peter, 2018[26]). Ontario, Canada, started a randomised experiment, the *Ontario Basic Income Pilot* in 2017. Exclusively targeted at low-income households, the pilot was supposed to run for three years. Payments were not unconditional, but were withdrawn against labour income at a rate of 50%. The Canadian government has however decided to end the programme prematurely as early as autumn 2018 (Kassam, 2018[27]).

1.4. Offering voluntary protection to non-standard workers

In extending social security coverage to non-standard workers, several countries opt for voluntary schemes: e.g. Austria introduced a voluntary unemployment insurance option for the self-employed in 2009 (Chapter 3), and Spain made its *protección por cese de actividad de los trabajadores autónomos* (unemployment benefit for the self-employed) voluntary in 2014 (Moral-Arce, Martí-Román and Martí-Román, 2018[28]).

Voluntary insurance schemes risk adverse selection of members: those self-employed workers with the highest risk have the biggest incentive to join. If the scheme is entirely self-funded, this can lead to a vicious circle of contribution hikes and low-risk members leaving.

When an experience rating was introduced in the Swedish unemployment insurance scheme in 2007/08, raising average premiums by 300%, membership in the voluntary Unemployment Insurance Funds dropped by around 10 percentage points. The two groups of workers who generate the lowest overall unemployment insurance expenses were most likely to leave the funds: workers over the age of 60 who have the lowest unemployment risk of all age-groups, and those under the age of 25 who, despite a high unemployment risk, have very low unemployment durations and low earnings (Chapter 8).

Partly general revenue-funded schemes can result in high public subsidies. Since 2010, self-employed workers in Canada have the option of voluntarily contributing to the Special Benefits for Self-employed Workers (SBSE) scheme to gain access to maternity and parental benefits, sickness benefits and care benefits for ill family members. Benefit entitlements and contribution rates are equal to those of dependent employees; that is, employer contributions are covered by a public subsidy. An evaluation of this programme (Employment and Social Development Canada, 2016[29]) found strong indications of adverse selection: Over three quarters of claims were for maternity and parental benefits, and two-thirds of opt-ins were women (who represent only 43% of all self-employed workers), while two-thirds were between the ages of 25 and 44 (compared to just one third of all self-employed). Opt-ins also had significantly lower incomes than other self-employed workers. In 2011, the first year benefits were paid out, premiums covered less than one-third of benefit payments.

In Austria, self-employed workers can opt into an income replacement programme in case of short-term illness, and about 8% of all eligible self-employed do. In 2016, nearly half of those who were covered received a benefit, and the average benefit duration was 22 days, nearly twice the average duration of sick-leave among (compulsory insured) dependent employees. In response to the deficits this scheme was running, the minimum benefit was cut significantly in 2017 (Chapter 3).

Thus, for voluntary schemes to be financially viable, they have to reach very high coverage rates, which can be tricky to achieve as workers seem to have a very low willingness to pay for social protection: the increase in Swedish UI fund premiums, while high in relative terms, only amounted to about 1% of median net-wages in 2008; at the same time, a tax credit was introduced that raised net earnings by about 5% for the median worker, so most workers could have paid the increased premiums and still experienced an increase in take-home pay. Still, one in eight members left the Unemployment Insurance Funds (Chapter 8). While the reform has since been largely reversed, membership rates have not yet recovered to their pre-reform levels.

A recent survey among European non-standard workers also found a low willingness to pay for social protection: only one in five non-standard workers who are presently not covered by social protection would be willing to pay 5% or more of their income for unemployment insurance; only a third would be willing to pay over 5% to be covered by old-age benefits (European Comission, 2018[30]). In designing effective voluntary contribution schemes, policy makers will thus have to accept substantial public subsidies if they want to achieve high coverage rates and avoid adverse selection (Chapter 8).

1.5. Social security contributions as a driver of non-standard work

Incomplete social protection coverage of non-standard workers can also increase non-standard work as employers seek to minimise non-wage labour costs. This is particularly the case for work arrangements that sit on the border between self- and dependent employment, and can therefore serve as substitutes for standard employees.

In the Netherlands, for example, the total "payment wedge" (including personal income tax, social security contributions and other compulsory payments) between hiring a dependent employee and an independent contractor at the average wage is 30%, 21pp of which are employer social security contributions (OECD, forthcoming[13]). This cost difference may be claimed by the employer or the employee, depending on their respective bargaining power on the labour market. In the Netherlands, research indicates that for low-wage employees, this payment wedge is almost entirely captured by employers, while at the upper end of the wage distribution, workers do capture part of it (Ministry of Finance (2015[31]) and Chapter 7).

In Italy, *para-subordinate* workers are self-employed, but highly dependent on one or very few clients. They used to pay lower pension contribution rates and were not covered for unemployment or sickness benefits. This resulted in significantly lower non-wage labour costs, and rising numbers of para-subordinate workers: in 2007, para-subordinates made up over 11% of all dependent employment. Recent labour market entrants were especially likely to work as para-subordinates: almost a third of new university graduates started their careers this way in 2011. As pensions directly depend on lifetime contributions, lower pension contribution rates imply lower pension entitlements.

In response to the growing number of para-subordinate workers, Italy gradually increased their social security contribution rates (and thus welfare guarantees) from the late 1990s, and accelerated this process from 2007 to an annual increase of one percentage point, until they reached the contribution rate of employees. As the total social security contribution rate increased by seven over a decade, the number of para-subordinate workers more than halved (Figure 1.2, Panel A). The onset of the decline in the number of para-subordinate collaborators predated other measures, such as the tightening of the regulation of para-subordinate arrangements (2012) and the abolition of some types of para-subordinate arrangements (2015), supporting the idea that the widespread use of para-subordinate collaborations was mainly driven by their lower cost. Further measures to persuade employers to hire workers on permanent contracts – such as a significant reduction in employer social security contributions for new hires through the 2015 Jobs Act – further contributed to the decline of para-subordinate contracts (Chapter 6).

Similarly, in Austria, independent contractors (*freie Dienstnehmer*) control their own working time and workflow but are contracted for their time and effort. Concerns that employers might use this form of employment to evade the compulsory social protection system drove their gradual integration into the system: since 2008, independent contractors are liable for the same (employer and employee) social security contributions as standard employees.[2] While their number had been steadily growing until early 2007, it began to fall following the reform's announcement, and was at its all-time low in 2016 (Figure 1.2, Panel B, Chapter 3).

The fall in the number of independent contractors was mainly driven by the falling number of workers taking up jobs as independent contractors, rather than by the dissolution of existing independent contracts – which is why their number continues to fall six years following the reform.

However, the likelihood of being in standard employment within one month of transitioning out of an independent contract increased from 11% before the reform's announcement in 2006 to 13% after the reform's implementation. In addition, the share of workers who transitioned out of the labour force upon exiting an independent contract dropped significantly, in line with the fact that prior to the reform, independent contractors were not covered by unemployment insurance. Unemployment insurance coverage proved important for former independent contractors during the Financial Crisis (Hofer, Hyee and Titelbach, 2018[32]).

Figure 1.2. Social protection coverage influences the use of non-standard work

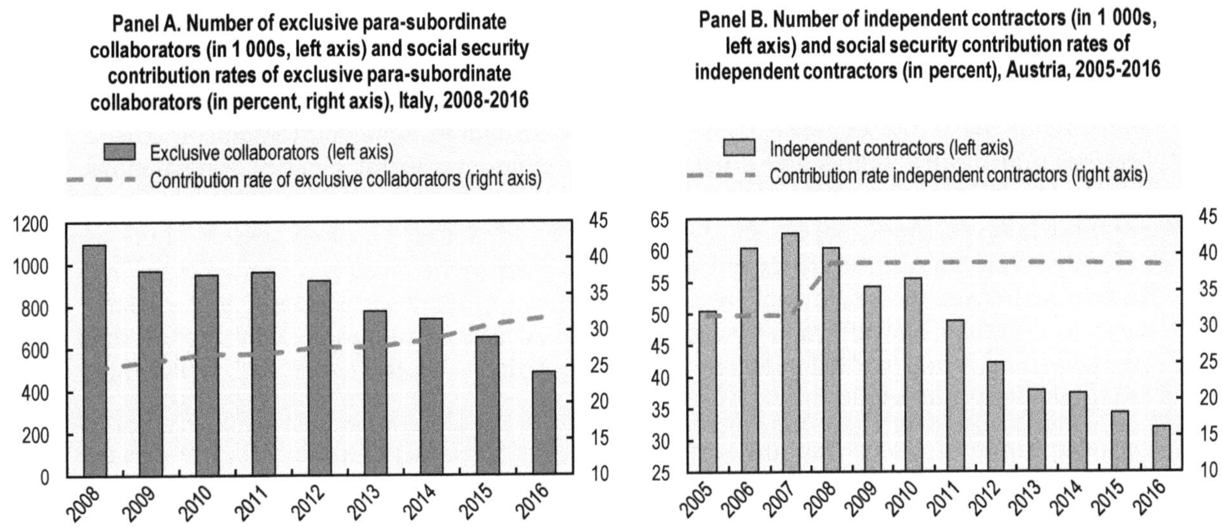

Note: Exclusive para-subordinate collaborators collaborate on short- or long-term projects and are neither retired nor do they have income from dependent employment. They are the biggest group of para-subordinates, making up roughly 60% of all para-subordinates in 2008 and 40% in 2016.
Source: Panel A: Adapted from Chapter 6. Panel B: Adapted from Chatper 3, contribution rates from Hauptverband der Österreichischen Sozialversicherungsträger.

1.6. Special schemes for non-standard workers

Where self-employed workers are covered under a completely separate social protection regime, the reasons are often more historic than pragmatic. In France, for example, the self-employed initially opposed their integration into the general social insurance system. Instead, occupational schemes were established, the scope of which varies across professions. This led to very unequal coverage of dependent employees and the self-employed: while compulsory, occupational retirement schemes have existed since the 1960s, self-employed workers have only been entitled to sickness benefits since 2016.

They remain uncovered for some risks including occupational accidents and unemployment, although voluntary options have been introduced in recent years (Chapter 4). This interplay of several autonomous schemes and a complex system of contribution rates and entitlements obscure the relationship between gross and net wages and hinder the mobility of workers across jobs and occupations.

To lower administration costs and improve service delivery, several independent schemes were merged into the *Régime social des indépendants* (RSI). The RSI remained autonomous in that it was run by elected representatives of its members. It does not have the administrative capacity to collect contributions itsself, but delegates this to URSSAF, a network of private bodies that collect social contributions for dependent employees.[3] This requires intense coordination between the two bodies, which could not be achieved, resulting in insufficient collection of contributions, erroneous overcharging of members and delayed payments. These major malfunctions led to the dissolution of the RSI; it is set to be completely absorbed by the general social security system by 2020 (Chapter 4).

Some countries also have special, more generous schemes for artists and other creatives who often have unstable employment patterns and may thus struggle to accumulate the contribution periods necessary to receive social protection benefits. This section discusses two of these schemes: the German artists' insurance, which charges consumers employer contributions, and the French *intermittents du spectacle* scheme.

1.6.1. Customers contribute to social protection: the German artists' insurance

The German writers' and artists' insurance scheme directly addresses the *double contribution issue* by levying social security contributions upon customers of artistic services. Qualifying writers and artists only pay employee social security contributions that make up half of the scheme's total budget. A public subsidy, justified by private households' consumption of art and writing, covers 20% of the overall cost. Institutions that rely on the services of artists and writers (e.g. publishers, theatres, libraries or private companies) cover the remaining 30%, proportional to their use of artists' and writers' services – the Ministry of Employment and Social Affairs calculates the contribution rate annually, depending on the number of insured artists and the artist and writer fees reported by institutions.

Membership is mandatory but low-earning artists and those with high incomes or private insurance can be exempted. Customer contributions are levied on *all* expenditure on services commissioned from artists and writers, however, in order to not create distortions on the market for artistic work. This also mitigates some of the cost savings of contracting instead of hiring artists and writers.

Compliance and administrative costs seem comparable to those in the general system. Companies are required by law to declare their expenditure on artistic and writing services. The German Pension Fund is in charge of company inspections for the artists' insurance, which it carries out in the course of every regular social security compliance inspection since 2015. This keeps administrative costs low and led to a jump in contributing companies by 50 000 within two years. Employers' associations claim that costs for administering fund contributions can run as high as 70-100% of overall contributions, but it is not clear whether these estimates are realistic, or how they compare to administering social security contributions for regular employees.

Fund membership has continually risen over the past twenty years and stands at 0.5% of total employment in Germany. In line with an increase in Fund membership, the public subsidy has almost quadrupled. While there are no data on how many self-employed artists' and writers would qualify for the scheme if they applied – admittance is based on reaching a minimum required income in a listed profession – labour force survey estimates based on the number of self-employed artists indicate a coverage rate of about one-third.

While the artists' insurance scheme seems effective in securing customers' contributions to artists' social protection, providing artists with adequate pension entitlements remains challenging. Declared earnings are very low: in 2016, on average, male artists earned just 54% and female artists just 40% of overall average gross earnings in Germany. Combined with the unstable career patterns of many artists and writers, pension contributions on these incomes do not give rise to pensions sufficient to prevent old-age poverty.

Most self-employed artists and writers combine their artistic work with other income, and those at the low end of the income distribution seem to self-select into the fund. A high share of enrolees report incomes just above the minimum threshold for eligibility, which may indicate that they mainly join the fund to gain access to health and long-term care insurance (even minimum contributions guarantee full health- and long-term care coverage, while pensions depend on earnings).

Hence, many insured artists enjoy full access to health insurance while paying only minimum contributions, which leads to a concentration of bad risks in the fund. Low declared earnings may be a result of weak demand and low prices for art-work, but it might also be the result of under-declaration of earnings. Incentives to declare income above the minimum contribution thresholds are weak if individuals either have other, private pension insurance, or their true earnings are still so low that they cannot expect a pension above the poverty line. Many fund members might therefore have to rely on general revenue-financed social assistance in retirement age (Chapter 5).

1.6.2. Intermittents du spectacle

In France, artists and technicians on fixed-term contracts in the entertainment industry benefit from shorter contribution periods for eligibility to the unemployment insurance system under *intermittents du spectacle* scheme. This special scheme was set up to accommodate the fact that performers and stage and film technicians are hired for productions on a short-term basis and would otherwise struggle to qualify for benefits

The short contribution periods make this scheme very attractive: to qualify for benefits, only 507 hours of work over the past 12 months are required, and spells of employment increase the benefit receipt duration. Thus, claimants can receive the benefit indefinitely, if they work at least two to three months per year.

The number of qualifying workers rose from 50 000 to over a quarter of a million from 1980 to 2015, and about 40% of them claim unemployment benefits. Many claimants become unemployed once they reach the minimum contribution period to qualify for the benefit, and many cycle back and forth between unemployment benefit receipt and working for the same employer, suggesting that some companies adapt their workforce management to the regulations of the scheme (Cour des Comptes, 2012[33]). In 2012, expenditures on benefits exceeded contributions by a factor of more than five. The net cost of the scheme – defined as expenditure on benefits minus contributions to the scheme – was roughly EUR 1 billion in 2012, for a scheme covering about 250 000 workers (Chapter 4). In comparison, that same year the deficit of the general unemployment system in France, covering around 24 million dependent employees, was EUR 2.7 billion (OECD, 2018[34]).

1.7. Social protection of platform workers

Online labour platforms experienced spectacular growth in recent years. According to data provided by the Oxford Internet Institute, the five largest online facilitators of work carried out exclusively online (from low-skilled "click work" to high-skilled freelance jobs) grew by over a third between May 2016 and April 2018 (Oxford Internet Institute, 2018[35]). Standard Labour Force surveys often do not separately capture work facilitated through online platforms, and might underestimate the true incidence where they do, given that platform work is often in the informal economy (OECD, 2018[36]). A recent dedicated survey of internet users in 15 European Union member states suggests that 8% of the working age population of these countries performs work over an online platform at least once a month, and about 2% have platform work as their main source of income (Pesole et al., 2018[3]).

Online platforms have the potential to enable individuals to compete with firms and opt for entrepreneurship instead of employment. They lower transaction costs by providing consumers with information on service quality and monitoring and enforcing transactions, making it less risky for consumers to choose an individual instead of an established firm (Choudary, 2018[37]; OECD, 2016[4]). They also offer individuals access to a network of potential consumers as well as tools to facilitate the sale of goods or services, reducing barriers to market entry. Through online platforms, individuals can achieve a reputation and client base that would have required the resources of a firm in traditional markets.

In lowering the barriers to self-employment, online platforms can disseminate its advantages – flexibility in working time and place, autonomy in the organisation of work – to those who were previously excluded from the labour market, including parents and others with caring responsibilities, or individuals living in areas with weak local labour markets. Platforms can also offer both employed and non-employed individuals an easy way to smooth temporary income shocks.

However, some platforms go beyond a mere "facilitator" or "marketplace" role in determining prices, working times, work attire or details of service provision such as how costumers should be greeted (Choudary, 2018[37]). These controls and regulations guarantee that costumers receive a consistent and standardised service, but undermine the flexibility and autonomy associated with genuine self-employment. Platforms also limit workers' entrepreneurial decision making in more subtle ways, e.g. by withholding key information, exemplified by rideshare app Uber's practice of not letting drivers know the rider's destination before accepting a fare, meaning the driver cannot judge the profitability of the ride (Prassl, 2018[12]).

Thus, gig workers may end up enjoying few of the advantages of self-employment, but suffer many of its drawbacks, including the risk of demand fluctuations and unpaid down- or waiting times, and the lack of employee benefits such as paid vacation, sick-leave or severance pay. As with other self-employed workers, employment protection and minimum wage regulations do not apply to them, and they are often not or not as well covered by social protection.

Some platforms intervene in gig-workers' price setting, working time and work organisation to such an extent that they have been found to be the *de facto* employers by national courts. Many jurisdictions have "primacy of facts" principles that allow workers to be classified as employees if they meet minimum standards of dependency on and accountability; examples include FedEx in the United States or Uber in the United Kingdom, and several other cases are pending in other OECD countries (Prassl, 2018[12]). In cases of straightforward misclassification of dependent employees as independent contractors, labour law (when properly monitored and enforced) may thus be sufficient to ensure the adequate protection of workers.

Policy makers who want to improve the employment quality and social protection of gig-workers have to look carefully at the individual case of both worker and platform. Platform workers are a very heterogeneous group. While the majority seem to use platforms to top-up income from other sources, some do rely on platforms for most of their income: a recent survey of platform workers in seven European countries showed that platform work was the only source of income for about 10% of platform workers (Huws, Spencer and Holts, 2017[38]). Thus, while most platform workers are likely to be covered by social protection through a first job or a spouse, a significant minority may be at risk of being unprotected in the event of unemployment, illness or disability.

Similarly, while flexibility in working time and location is the main reason for choosing platform work for many,[4] there is a significant minority who work for platforms because no other work is available – in a 2018 survey, nearly one in five Italian and one in ten UK gig-workers stated that platform work was their only option (Boeri, Giupponi, Krueger, & Machin, 2018). Workers who perform gig-work as a last resort, as well as low-skilled workers performing tasks that are highly substitutable for platforms, are more likely to receive low pay and suffer from social protection gaps.

In contrast, there is no obvious difference in the need for social protection between self-employed workers who operate on traditional markets, and those who operate on platforms, but retain entrepreneurial control over their work, such as designers or translators who market their services through online platforms.[5]

What does distinguish labour platforms from conventional markets is that all transactions are digital and hence completely traceable. This raises the potential for increasing social protection coverage and tax compliance by shifting activities from the informal to the formal economy.

Payments to individual contractors can be difficult to monitor for tax authorities, and underpayments are often not pursued given the low amounts at stake (Prassl, 2018[12]). Unlocking platform payment data for the purpose of the collection of social security contributions and taxes can also lower the administrative burden on individuals, which can be substantial, especially when they derive only occasional or low incomes from self-employment. For example, Indonesia has introduced a compulsory accident insurance scheme for motor-taxies hailed through an online app – a portion of the fare is automatically deducted to insure both driver and passenger for the duration of the trip (ILO and OECD, 2018[39]).

Countries may require platforms to share payment and identification data for tax compliance purposes – e.g. Finland has introduced legislation to access data from peer-to-peer and crowdfunding platforms located in Finland. Requiring platforms to withhold taxes is also a possible tool to increase compliance. However, if the platform is located in a different jurisdiction than the worker, domestic legislation might not be enough to ensure compliance by the platform. Countries may still reach agreements directly with platforms, but data transmission might require user consent because of data protection legislation (OECD, 2018[17]).

Estonia, for example, already collaborates with ridesharing apps Uber and Taxify for income tax purposes: drivers can permit the platforms to transmit income and deduction data to the tax authorities, who pre-fill a tax return for self-employment income to ease the administrative burden on drivers (Loite, 2016[40]). In 2017, drivers declared nearly half a million euros in earnings, over five times as much as in 2016, the first year that earnings information was directly submitted by platforms (Tax and Customs Board, Republic of Estonia, 2017[41]). While such measures are likely to increase compliance by reducing compliance costs for drivers, their reach is limited by the need to obtain drivers consent to share their data.

Thus, there is a strong case for international co-ordination. Through the OECD's Forum on Tax Administration, 50 tax administrations are currently exploring which data on platform users would be required to match payments to tax records, and how and with which periodicity such data should be transmitted. A common and standardised solution, underpinned by an agreement on information exchange between tax authorities, would reduce burdens both for national tax authorities and platforms, who would not have to handle individual requests by different tax administrations, in different formats and periodicities. Results of these consultations are expected in 2018 (OECD, 2018[17]).

Some countries have developed dedicated schemes for the administration of social security contributions of platform workers. In Sweden, gig-workers are legally required to register with an umbrella company, a private entity who nominally acts as the employer of the gig-worker in administering their payroll tax and social security payments in exchange for a fee. They are thus covered by the general public social protection system, but they are excluded from important components of the social protection system that are part of collective agreements, including additional pension, sickness and accident insurance covers; and they do not have access to union-run unemployment insurance.

These are important limitations: about 25% of all currently paid pensions in Sweden come from occupational schemes as part of collective agreements. This share is expected to grow, as public pensions grow slower than labour earnings. Also, the threshold for pensionable income is indexed to the average wage, and therefore, the net replacement rate for higher-earners falls as wage inequality increases in Sweden. The same effect lowers the net replacement rates for above-average earners in the public sickness and accident insurance, increasing the importance of collectively bargained benefits.

Platform workers also struggle to access the main pillar of the Swedish unemployment insurance, provided by Unemployment Insurance Funds: while they may join a fund for standard workers, in practice, funds have been reluctant to pay out benefits to platform workers, because they have no employer to confirm that they have been laid off (Chapter 8).

In Belgium offers a simplified tax treatment to platform workers who only earn "occasional" income (below EUR 6 130 per year in 2018) from platform work is exempt from social security contributions and income tax. This exemption only applies to services provided to individuals (not firms) and excludes the provision of goods, letting of property and movables (including car-sharing). It is limited to a number of platforms based in the European Economic Area who fully disclose their workers and their remuneration.

Platforms themselves could also provide social protection to workers – e.g. Uber will offer basic medical, accident, maternity and paternity insurance to regular drivers in some European countries starting in mid-2018 (Uber, 2018). Platforms have been reluctant to participate in workers' social protection, however, to avoid the appearance of an employment relationship.

1.8. Policy lessons

This section summarises some key policy insights from the country studies collected in this publication, and suggests policy options for increasing the income security of on-call workers or those on flexible hours contracts.

1.8.1. Social security contributions should be harmonised across forms of employment as much as possible

Including workers that sit on the border between dependent and independent forms of work in the standard social protection scheme closes coverage gaps and helps ensure that social protection systems cover those who are most at risk.

It can also curb the extent of non-standard employment, and thus limit the erosion of the contribution base of social protection systems, as shown by the policy reform experiences in Italy and Austria. Raising non-wage labour costs, of course, comes at the risk of decreasing employment, in the same way as this can be the case for standard workers. If certain forms of employment are subject to lower non-wage labour costs, this should be a deliberate policy choice.

1.8.2. Voluntary schemes do not seem to work well for non-standard workers

Any insurance depends on risk sharing among members. With a voluntary insurance scheme, those who have the highest risk have the greatest incentive to join. Unless a voluntary scheme achieves a very high coverage rate, this adverse selection either leads to a downward spiral of rising premia and falling coverage, or to additional costs in the system. High coverage rates, in turn, may require public subsidies, as the willingness to pay voluntarily for social protection appears to be low in some cases, as seen, for example, in Sweden where voluntary unemployment insurance coverage fell after a moderate rise in contribution rates in 2007/08.

Adverse selection in voluntary schemes is not limited to unemployment insurance but can be observed for sickness benefits (voluntary sickness benefits for self-employed workers in Austria) and even maternity and carers' benefits (evidenced by the Canadian Special Benefits for Self-employed Workers scheme).

1.8.3. Making entitlements portable supports mobility across jobs and forms of employment

Untying entitlements from specific relationships with employers, and tying them to individual contributions instead, not only makes it easier for workers to switch jobs, but it also makes it easier for them to switch between self- and dependent employment. Furthermore, it facilitates the harmonisation of entitlements across contractual arrangements. Individualised forms of social protection, however, can only offer protection if sufficient contributions are paid by or on behalf of the beneficiary.

Austria offers an interesting policy lesson in this respect when, in 2003, its severance pay scheme was replaced by company-based pension accounts. While the old severance pay entitlements benefitted only laid-off employees, all dependent employees now have a company-based pension account, which is portable across jobs. This measure increased job mobility for workers in distressed firms (where a plant closure or mass layoff will take place in the near future, Kettemann et al. (2016[42])). As the pension accounts are tied to the individual, and employers contribute a fixed rate of individual earnings, it was easy to extend the programme to independent contractors in 2008.

1.8.4. Increasing income security for those working flexible hours

Independent contractors – whether they do work mediated by online platforms or not – as well as workers on on-call or flexible hours contracts lack the income security provided by regular employment relationships while enabling firms to cheaply adjust to demand fluctuations. One way to redress this imbalance is to introduce a wage premium for flexible work as a compensation for assuming part of the entrepreneurial risk. The idea of requiring employers to pay higher rates to those who assume part of the entrepreneurial risk has been gaining traction both in the context of platform work (Chapter 8) as well as flexible hours work contracts (Taylor, 2017[43]).

In Australia, casual workers, who may be terminated on short notice and do not receive some benefits like paid holidays or paid sick leave that are provided to permanent employees, are already entitled to a *casual loading* of 25% for each hour worked compared to a worker doing the same job on an ongoing basis (Chapter 2).[6]

On-call or other flexible workers would also benefit from minimum hours guarantees: in Australia and the Netherlands, for example, employers already have to pay on-call workers at least three hours of work each time they call on the employee (Chapter 7).

Minimum earnings floors may also be applied to independent contractors: the New York Taxi and Limousine Commission is currently considering introducing a *minimum driver pay* standard for drivers for ride-hailing apps. The proposal would set an earnings floor at roughly 115% of the minimum wage and increase driver earnings after expenses by 22.5% on average (Parrott and Reich, 2018[44]). The Netherlands plans to introduce a payment floor of EUR 15-18 per hour for independent contractors who are paid below 125% of the statutory minimum wage or the lowest wage in the relevant collective agreement (Government of the Netherlands (2017[45]) and Chapter 7).

Notes

[1] Those who were already self-employed upon the introduction of the programme in 2009 had one year to decide whether to opt-into the programme.

[2] They have to contribute to pension, health and accident insurance since the late 1990s; in 2008 they were incorporated into the unemployment insurance system, the insolvency remuneration fund, the chamber of labour and the severance pay scheme *Abfertigung neu* (a form of portable employer-funded pension account).

[3] The URSSAF (*Unions de recouvrement des cotisations de sécurité sociale et d'allocations familiales*) are private bodies collecting employees' and employers' contributions to the general social security system, see Chapter 4.

[4] In a 2015 survey, around 30% of gig-workers performing work exclusively online on the Amazon Mechanical Turk and Crowdflower platforms named a preference to work from home, or only being able to work from home as the main reason for choosing this type of work (Berg, 2016[15]).

[5] Indeed, most social protection systems do not seem to make such a difference: a survey conducted by the European Social Insurance Platform, an association of European statutory social insurance organisations (ESIP, 2017[46]) found that in all twelve participating European Union and EEA member countries, workers providing "virtual tasks" (graphic design, translation etc.) would be considered as self-employed. While there are differences in statutory coverage by the pension insurance across the surveyed countries, they are the same as for other self-employed persons.

[6] Empirical evidence suggests, however, that casual workers do not in fact receive higher wages and might even suffer a wage penalty compared to similar permanent workers (see Chapter 2 for an overview of recent evidence). Thus, monitoring is crucial (as in the case of minimum wages).

References

Abraham, K. et al. (2017), *Measuring the Gig Economy: Current Knowledge and Open Issues*, U.S Census Bureau, http://aysps.gsu.edu/files/2016/09/Measuring-the-Gig-Economy-Current-Knowledge-and-Open-Issues.pdf (accessed on 10 December 2017). [11]

Arbejdsgruppen om selvstændige i dagpengesystemet (2017), *Et nyt dagpengesystem for fremtidens arbejdsmarked. Report from the working group on self-employed persons in the unemployment benefit system*, http://www.bm.dk. [20]

Avlijas, S. (2018), "The dynamism of the new economy: Non-standard employment and access to social security", *Research note*. [19]

Berg, J. (2016), "Income security in the on-demand economy: Findings and policy lessons from a survey of crowdworkers", *Conditions of Work and Employment Series*, No. 74, ILO, Geneva, http://www.ilo.org/wcmsp5/groups/public/---ed_protect/---protrav/---travail/documents/publication/wcms_479693.pdf (accessed on 12 December 2017). [15]

BLS (2018), *Contigent and alternative employment arrangements - May 2017*, http://www.bls.gov/cps (accessed on 11 June 2018). [10]

BLS (2005), *Contingent and alternative employment arrangements, February 2005*, http://www.bls.gov/cps/ (accessed on 11 June 2018). [9]

BMAS (2017), *White paper work 4.0*, German Federal Ministry of Labour and Social Affairs, http://www.arbeitenviernull.de. [16]

ILO (ed.) (2018), *The architecture of digital labour platforms: Policy recommendations on platform design for worker well-being*, http://www.ilo.org/global/topics/future-of-work/publications/research-papers/. [37]

Cour des Comptes (2012), *Le régime des intermittents du spectacle: la persistance d'une dérive massive*, Cour des comptes. [33]

Datta, N., G. Giupponi and S. Machin (forthcoming), "Zero Hours Contracts and Labour Market Policy", *mimeo*. [6]

Delsen, L. and J. Smits (2014), "The Rise and Fall of the Dutch Savings Schemes", *SSRN Electronic Journal*, http://dx.doi.org/10.2139/ssrn.2414546. [23]

Employment and Social Development Canada (2016), *Evaluation of the Employment Insurance Special Benefits for Self-employed Workers*, http://canada.ca/publicentre-ESDC. [29]

ESIP (2017), *Statutory Pension Insurance of Digital Platform Workers - a comparative perspective*, ESIP, https://www.esip.eu/images/pdf_docs/Mapping---Statutory-pension-coverage-of-platform-workers.pdf. [46]

Etsy (2016), *Economic Security for the Gig Economy*, https://extfiles.etsy.com/advocacy/Etsy_EconomicSecurity_2016.pdf. [22]

European Comission (2018), *Behavioural study on the effects of an extension of access to social protection for people in all forms of employment*, European Commission, http://dx.doi.org/10.2767/180611. [30]

European Commission (2018), *Commission Staff Working Document, Impact Assessment accompanying the Proposal for a Council Recommendation and Access to social protection for workers and the self-employed, SWD(2018)71*, https://eur-lex.europa.eu/legal-content/EN/TXT/?uri=CELEX%3A52018SC0070. [8]

European Commission (2018), *Proposal for a Council Recommendation and Access to social protection for workers and the self-employed, COM(2018)132*. [7]

Government of the Netherlands (2017), *Confidence in the Future - 2017-2021 coalition agreement*, https://www.government.nl/. [45]

Hofer, H., R. Hyee and G. Titelbach (2018), *Where did all the independent contractors go?*. [32]

Huws, U., N. Spencer and K. Holts (2017), *Work in the European Gig Economy*, FEPS, http://www.feps-europe.eu/. [38]

ILO and OECD (2018), *Promoting adequate social protection and social security coverage for all workers, including those in non-standard forms of employment*, Paper prepared for the G20 (Argentinian presidency). [39]

ISSA (2012), *Handbook on the extention of social security coverage to the self-employed*, http://www.issa.int. [18]

Kassam, A. (2018), "Ontario's new Conservative government to end basic income experiment", *The Guardian*, https://www.theguardian.com/world/2018/aug/01/ontarios-new-conservative-government-to-end-basic-income-experiment. [27]

Katz, L. and A. Krueger (2016), "he Rise and Nature of Alternative Work Arrangements in the United States, 1995-2015", *NBER Working Papers*, p. No. 22667. [2]

Kettemann, A., F. Kramarz and J. Zweimüller (2016), "Beyond Severance Pay: Labor market responses to the introduction of occupational pensions in Austria", *Mimeo, University of Zurich*, http://www.econ.uzh.ch. [42]

Kvist, J. (2017), "Denmark: a new unemployment insurance scheme for the future labour market", *ESPN Flash Report 2017/45*, http://ec.europa.eu/social/main.jsp?catId=1135&langId=en.. [21]

Commission, E. (ed.) (2016), *e-stonian look at: collaborative economy*, http://ec.europa.eu/transparency/regexpert/index.cfm?do=groupDetail.groupDetailDoc&id=26192&no=8 (accessed on 1 July 2018). [40]

Ministry of Finance (2015), *IBO Zelfstandigen zonder personeel*, Ministry of Finance, Netherlands. [31]

Moral-Arce, I., J. Martí-Román and Á. Martí-Román (2018), "Cessation of activity benefit of Spanish self-employed workers: a heterogeneous impact evaluation", *MPRA Paper No. 85111*, https://mpra.ub.uni-muenchen.de/85111/. [28]

OECD (2018), "Policy brief on the future of work", in *Online work in OECD countries*, http://www.oecd.org/employment/future-of-work/. [36]

OECD (2018), *Social Expenditure Database (SOCX)*, https://doi.org/10.1787/socx-data-en. [34]

OECD (2018), *Tax Challenges Arising from Digitalisation – Interim Report 2018: Inclusive Framework on BEPS*, OECD/G20 Base Erosion and Profit Shifting Project, OECD, Paris, http://dx.doi.org/10.1787/9789264293083-en. [17]

OECD (2017), "Basic income as a policy option: Can it add up?", *Policy brief on the future of work* , https://www.oecd.org/els/emp/Basic-Income-Policy-Option-2017.pdf (accessed on 14 September 2017). [24]

OECD (2016), "New Forms of Work in the Digital Economy", *OECD Digital Economy Papers*, No. 260, OECD Publishing, Paris, http://dx.doi.org/10.1787/5jlwnklt820x-en. [4]

OECD (forthcoming), *The tax treatment of non-standard work*, OECD Publishing, Paris. [13]

Oxford Internet Institute (2018), *The Online Labour Index*, http://ilabour.oii.ox.ac.uk/online-labour-index/. [35]

Parrott, J. and M. Reich (2018), *An Earnings Standard for New York City's App-based drivers: Economic Analysis and Policy Assessment. Report for the New York City Taxi and Limousine Commission*, The New School, Center for New York City Affairs, http://irle.berkeley.edu/an-earnings-standard-for-new-york-citys-app-based-drivers/. [44]

Parsons, D. (1986), "The employment relationship: Job attachment, work effort, and the nature of contracts", in Ashenfelter, O. and R. Layard (eds.), *Handbook of Labor Economics*, Elsevier, North-Holland, http://dx.doi.org/10.1016/S1573-4463(86)02004-7. [5]

Pesole, A. et al. (2018), *Platform workers in Europe*, Publications Office of the European Union. [3]

Peter, L. (2018), *No plans to expand Finland basic income trial*, https://www.bbc.co.uk/news/world-europe-43866700. [26]

Piachaud, D. (2016), "Citizen's Income: Rights and Wrongs", *Case*, No. 200, Centre for the Analysis of Social Exclusion (CASE), London, http://sticerd.lse.ac.uk/dps/case/cp/casepaper200.pdf. [25]

Prassl, J. (2018), *Humans as a service - The Promise and Perils of work in the gig economy*, Oxford University Press, https://doi.org/10.1093/oso/9780198797012.001.0001. [12]

Spasova, S. et al. (2017), *Access to social protection for people working on non-standard contracts and as self-employed in Europe*, European Commission, Brussels, http://dx.doi.org/10.2767/700791. [1]

SSA and ISSA (2018), *United States of America*, Social Security Administration, https://www.socialsecurity.gov/policy. [14]

Tax and Customs Board, Republic of Estonia (2017), "Income declared trough Uber and Taxify has overwhelmingly increased", *Press release*, https://www.emta.ee/eng/income-declared-through-uber-and-taxify-has-overwhelmingly-increased (accessed on 1 July 2018). [41]

Taylor, M. (2017), *Good work: the Taylor review of modern working practices*, Her Majesty's Government, https://www.gov.uk/government/publications/good-work-the-taylor-review-of-modern-working-practices. [43]

Chapter 2. Australia: Providing social protection to non-standard workers with tax financing

Peter Whiteford and Alexandra Heron

Changes in the nature of work and labour market regulation pose challenges to social protection systems relying on social insurance contributions. In contrast, the Australian system of social protection relies on general government revenue rather than social security contributions. In this system, some of the vulnerabilities of the social insurance state may not be so salient, but other challenges and trade-offs exist. In particular, Australia has been described as a "wage-earner's welfare state" (Castles, 1985), with social protection linked to employment conditions, including relatively high minimum wages, paid sick, care, parental and holiday leave, workers compensation and mandatory occupational pensions. As in social insurance states, changes in the nature of work could potentially undermine these features of the Australian social protection system. A further difference is that the Australian social security system is highly income-tested, with spending being more targeted to the poor than any other OECD country. Administration of income-testing becomes more complicated if patterns of work become irregular or other circumstances, such as multiple job holding become common. This chapter assesses Australian employment and social security policies and institutions to identify strengths and weaknesses of the Australian approach to social security.

2.1. Introduction

Changes in the nature of work pose challenges to the social security systems of high-income countries, particularly those relying on contributory social insurance systems. These systems are based to varying degrees on workers satisfying contribution conditions that require or assume full-time engagement in paid work for the majority of years that individuals are in the labour force, together with formal arrangements for the payment and recording of contributions by employers and employees. They also often distinguish between employees and the self-employed. As temporary work and changing forms of employment contracts become more prevalent, the assumption of full-time, permanent formal employment threatens to become less representative, potentially undermining welfare state finances as well as the social protection of workers and their families.

This paper discusses the case of Australia, where virtually none of its system of social security is based on contributory social insurance principles. This offers the opportunity to explore a case study where some of the apparent vulnerabilities of the social insurance state may not be so salient, but where other challenges and trade-offs may have arisen in the context of other forms of social protection.

The paper is structured as follows: the next section of the chapter provides an overview of the Australian system of social protection and its guiding principles; this is followed by a brief discussion of how the system has developed over time in terms of its main programmes addressing lifecycle needs and social risks and how these compare with social protection in other OECD countries. The second section of the paper outlines the status of many of these alternative forms of employment within the framework of Australian employment law – which also differs in important ways from the systems of other OECD countries. This is followed by an overview of the current state of the Australian labour market in relation to the trends of concern – part-time employment and under-employment, self-employment and independent contractors, and the "gig economy". The paper also compares the level of non-standard employment in Australia with that in other OECD countries. The third section then discusses the interaction between social protection design and the Australian labour market, identifying how different programmes deal with different risks and lifecycle phases and evaluating how these programmes address the challenges identified above. The fourth section discusses the incomes and assets of the self-employed and how they differ from employees and other households. The paper concludes with an assessment of how well the Australian system deals with the challenges of the changing nature of work.

2.2. Overview of the Australian system of social protection

Social security is only part of a broader system of social protection in Australia (Whiteford and Angenent, 2002). The Australian social security system differs from the social insurance systems common in other OECD countries, both in terms of how benefits are financed and also in terms of how benefits are distributed between income groups. In most OECD countries, the bulk of government benefits are financed by contributions from employers and insured employees, and benefits are often related to past earnings, so that higher income workers receive higher absolute levels of benefits if they become unemployed or incapacitated or when they retire.

In contrast, in Australia, most government benefits are flat-rate entitlements financed from general government revenue, and there are no explicit social security contributions required as a condition of eligibility. While the recently introduced Paid Parental Leave scheme (see Section 2.4.2), uses previous employment as a targeting mechanism to determine eligibility it does not require explicit contributions. In addition, most benefits are income tested and asset tested, so that entitlements reduce as resources increase (Whiteford, 2017). Within these income and assets tests, income from self-employment and business resources are treated differently from other employment or unearned income (see Section 2.4.2). To a very substantial degree, payments are the responsibility of the Commonwealth (national) government, with eligibility conditions and entitlements being uniform across the country.

It is important to note, however, that there are programmes at the level of Australian state governments – notably compensation for work accidents and motor vehicle accidents – that involve contributions of different sorts, and in the case of compensation for accidents or illness arising from work also pay high wage replacement rates. In addition, many public sector employees and some private sector workers also are covered by defined-benefit occupational pension schemes for retirement (although most of these schemes are now closed to new entrants).

Workers may also be entitled to various forms of social protection as part of their employment. Indeed, a famous characterisation of Australia is that it was a "wage-earner's welfare state" (Castles, 1986), where "redistributive efforts were achieved using the instruments of wage regulation rather than traditional tax-and-spend welfare policies" (Deeming, 2013, p.669). This reflected the early introduction of a very high minimum wage, and the extensive regulation of conditions of employment.

Australia's statutory minimum wage is the third highest in the OECD in purchasing power terms (OECD, 2017a), and due to the relatively low level of taxes (and the absence of social security contributions) (OECD, 2017b), the purchasing power of the full-time, after-tax minimum wage is the highest in the OECD (OECD, 2015b).

In 2010, Australia had the equal fifth lowest level in the OECD of in-work poverty among households of working age (4.3%) and the fourth lowest among working age households with all adults in employment (2.4%) (OECD, 2013). The design of the Australian social security system means that relative income poverty in working-age households in Australia is highly concentrated in households where no one is in paid employment (Whiteford and Adema, 2007; Davidson et al., 2018).

The scope of workplace regulation has changed significantly over time but remains important. Apart from very high income-replacement – up to full-replacement – rates for accidents at work, a majority of employed people are entitled to paid sick leave and paid carers' leave of up to ten days a year (combined) paid at the base rate of pay as a minimum, as well as paid annual leave and public holidays.

Since the early 1990s, there has also been a mandatory superannuation savings system – the Superannuation Guarantee – covering most employees, which requires employers to contribute to individual accounts for their employees. These can be supplemented by employee contributions, and are supported by extensive tax concessions.

Because the Australian government income support system is not contributory, eligibility is based on residence and coverage of the population is broadly based. The main criteria for being covered is meeting residence requirements, falling into specific eligibility categories, and satisfying income and assets tests. Duration of payment receipt is not time limited, with income support payments being paid indefinitely subject to the continued meeting of eligibility criteria. Benefits are legal entitlements and recipients have the right to seek merits-based or judicial review of administrative decisions.

While income support payments are means tested, these income and assets tests are more generous than those typically applying in social assistance schemes in many other countries. This combined with Australia's more generous rates of assistance, occurs as the Australian social security system operates as the primary system of support, rather than a residual form of support, for individuals with no or low income. As discussed below, the income tests for income support payments have also changed over time, with the withdrawal rate – the rate at which benefits are reduced as private income increases – in almost all cases being between 40 cents in the dollar and 60 cents in the dollar. In this regard, it can be argued that the Australian system is now more like a set of negative income taxes for eligible groups than a tightly targeted social assistance scheme for the very poor. In this regard, the Australian social security system is a unique form of social assistance, being less "generous" and more targeted than a social insurance system, but more "generous" than other social assistance systems.

In order to be eligible for most income support payments, individuals must fall into defined categories – such as having qualifying Australian residence and being over the relevant age pension age, being sufficiently disabled as to be relieved of an expectation to actively seek work, caring for a person with a disability, caring for young children, being unemployed, or being a student. In addition, each payment has a range of other eligibility conditions, including differing age and residence requirements, domestic circumstances and having income and assets below specified levels. Once these conditions of eligibility are satisfied, the level of benefits to which individuals are entitled will be calculated on the basis of the precise level of the income and assets of themselves and their partners and aspects of their family living arrangements.

According to the McClure Review of the Australian Welfare System (2015) there are around 20 **income support payments** of the types described above and 55 **supplementary payments**, which cover additional costs; the most important of the latter are related to the presence of children and to the housing costs of households, but also include additional support for carers, a range of education expenses and pharmaceutical, energy, transport and telephone costs, among other items. Spending on these cash benefits for children in Australia is the sixth highest in the OECD, and the fourth most progressive in terms of distribution (Stewart and Whiteford, 2018). They thus form a very important part of the income support package for low-income working families, including those in non-standard employment.

The Australian income support system has developed over time in relation to two broad types of need, themselves based on the relationship of individuals to the labour market. 'Social security pensions', initially, old-age and invalid pensions, were provided to those not expected to be in the labour force because of old-age, or disability. 'Social security benefits' (also referred to as 'allowances'), initially, unemployment, sickness and special benefits, were provided to those expected to be in the labour force, but who were not currently in the workforce (because of unemployment, short-term illness or injury, or some other 'special' circumstance anticipated to be of short duration). However, the slow dissolution of the "wage earners' welfare state" model in the 1970s and into the 1980s rendered these types of need increasingly irrelevant[1]; so that, by the mid-1990s, a number of new 'social security benefits' (i.e. Partner Allowance, Parenting Allowance, Widow Allowance, Mature Age Allowance) had been designed around long-term receipt of income support, in anticipation of being outside the labour force, or having minimal attachment to it. Developments since the mid-1990s have further blurred the distinctions between 'social security pensions' and 'social security benefits'[2]. Legislative benchmarking of 'social security pensions' to a measure of average wages (from 1997), combined with indexation of pensions to the higher of the Consumer Price Index and a specially constructed 'living costs' index for pensioners and beneficiaries (2009), has resulted in a large (and still increasing) divergence between maximum rate packages structured around pensions versus benefits (where once, in the early 1990s, pensions and benefits packages were paid at close to the same maximum rates)

Overall, Australia is the sixth lowest spender on public social security cash benefits of 35 OECD countries, spending 8.6% of GDP in 2014 (Whiteford, 2017). However, it has the highest level of spending on income-tested benefits of any OECD country – 6.5% of GDP in 2012, with the next nearest countries being Ireland, Iceland and Canada (OECD, 2014). It also has the highest share of cash spending devoted to income-tested payments – nearly 80% of total benefit spending in 2012.[3] As a result, Australia also has the most progressive distribution of all cash benefits in the OECD, with more than 40% of benefit spending being directed to the poorest 20% of the population (OECD, 2008).

Income support payment receipt is fairly common in Australia. In total, there are around 2.5 million people receiving Age Pension, and around 2.5 million people receiving working-age income support (Figure 2.1). In 2016, 27.5 % of the adult population were receiving an income support payment, comprising 76% of the population aged 65 and over and 16% of the population of working age.

Interpreting coverage of social security in an income-tested system will necessarily be different from coverage in a contributory system. On the whole, with the exclusion of those not residentially qualified for payment, the people not receiving income support payments will be those whose incomes and assets are high enough to exclude them from payments; that is, they will be better off than those who claim payments with limited or no private resources. The non-contributory nature of the Australian system will therefore tend to favour many of the groups who are not covered by social insurance in other countries, including those with interrupted work histories, secondary earners and part-time casual and seasonal workers, older working-aged migrants and people with lifetime disability, for example.

A further indicator of the different way in which the Australian system operates is the estimates of very high take-up of benefits among those eligible. For example, Baker (2010) estimated that take-up of Parenting Payments in 2008 was 94%, while take-up of Disability Support Pension was 98%, well above the levels found in many other OECD countries (Hernananz et al., 2004).

Figure 2.1. Old-age and disability pension are the quantitatively most important income support payments in Australia

Number of Income Support recipients by benefit programme, June 2018

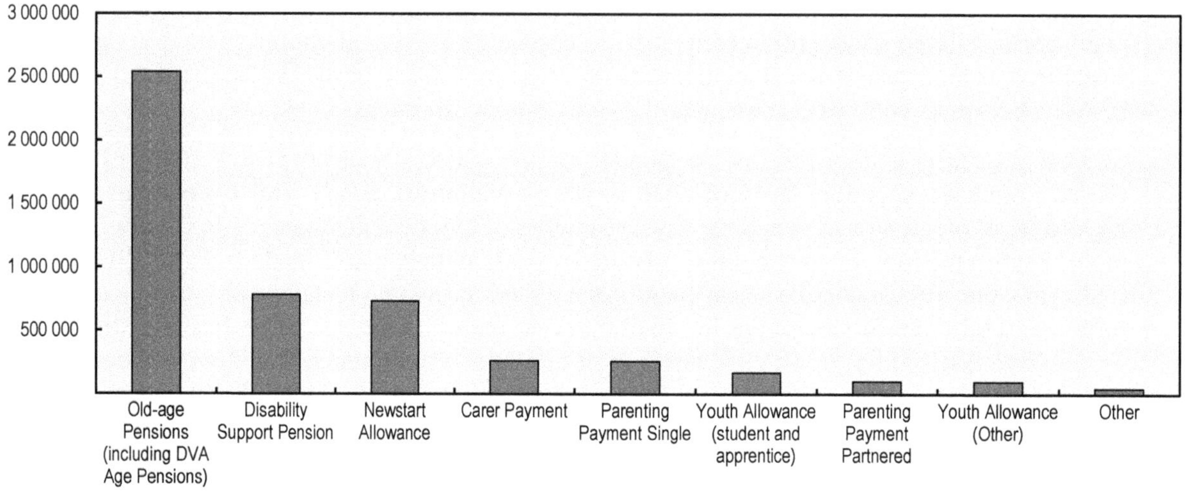

Source: DSS Payment Demographic data https://data.gov.au/dataset/dss-payment-demographic-data

As noted earlier, over time the Australian system of income support has evolved from a tightly income-tested social assistance system to a set of payments that are more like a set of negative income taxes for people who fall into the specific categories noted above. Since the late 1960s, the withdrawal rate on adult income support payments has been reduced from 100% to between 40% and 60%, with "free areas" of income below which payments are not reduced[4]; these are more generous for social security pension recipients than for recipients of social security benefits/allowances, with the exception of student payments. The free areas for student payments are particularly generous, however, this design in part reflects that maximum rates for students without children (both youth and adult) are well below those paid to unemployed adults.[5] In addition, the system of payments for families with children seeks to provide support to families in part-time or casual or otherwise low-paid work, with taper rates on 'adjusted taxable income' (once income exceeds the income free area) of between 20% and 30%. However, this support is undermined to some extent, particularly for families with variable incomes throughout a financial year, by the need for recipients of fortnightly payments to 'estimate' their 'adjusted taxable income' for a full financial year; see Whiteford, Mendelson and Millar, (2003).

Figure 2.2. Benefits are designed to encourage recipients' labour force participation

Number of Income Support recipients and share of recipients with earnings from employment, by benefit programme, June 2

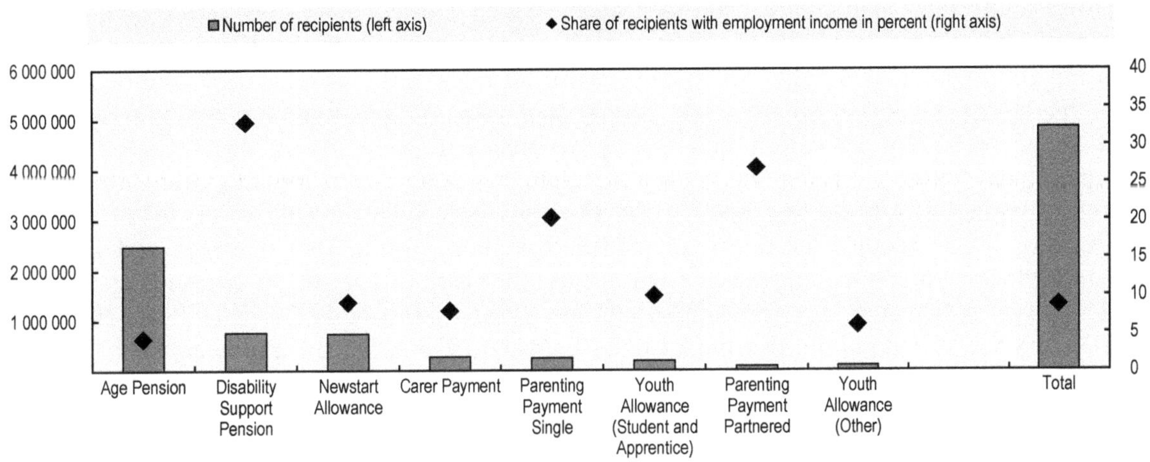

Source: DSS Payment Demographic Data - Datasets - https://data.gov.au/.

These changes particularly for social security benefits/allowances were designed to encourage part-time work by recipients with, for those with full-time job search obligations, the objective of facilitating the transition into full-time work. For members of a couple, the changes were accompanied included the provision of income free areas and lower taper rates for both members of a couple, ensuring that a second earner was rewarded for taking up work. There are also a range of provisions designed to smooth transitions between the income support system and employment, or back into the income support system. For example, there are abridged reclaim procedures if a person loses qualification for a payment or benefit and reapplies for that payment or benefit within 13 weeks of the cancellation. These have the effect of reducing the incidence and severity of breaks in receipt of government benefits following 'peaks' in receipt of private income. A related feature is Working Credits, which accumulate when the total income of the recipients is less than their "free area" of AUS 48 per fortnight (including paid work and investments). Working credits can accumulate up to a maximum of 48 each fortnight, to a maximum of 1 000 Working Credits, which can then be run down if a recipients gains more substantial earnings, so that they do not immediately lose their entitlements.

Overall around 11% of income support recipients have earnings from work with these levels being lowest for Age Pensioners and Disability Support Pensioners (Figure 2.2). For those of working age, around 17% have earnings as well as their income support payments. The highest level of earnings is received by those receiving Youth Allowance for students (38%) who have the highest income test free area, single parents receiving Parenting Payment (Single) (27%) who have the lowest taper rate (40%), followed by those receiving unemployment payments (Newstart Allowance at 21% and Youth Allowance Other at 20%). Overall, in June 2016, there were close to 450 000 people both working and receiving social security payments, which was equivalent to around 12% of all part-time workers in Australia. In addition to these people receiving income support and working part-time, there are also many low and middle income families with children simultaneously receiving family payments and working; in most cases, there is a full-time worker in these households.

2.3. Labour market and work arrangements in Australia

Since the 1970s, Australia – like other OECD countries - has experienced significant structural changes in its labour market, including an initial fall in male labour force participation rates particularly at older ages (which subsequently recovered) and an increase in prime-age female participation rates, mainly an increase in part-time and casual employment. There have also been major changes in the processes of youth entry to the labour market – where once young men took on full-time employment after finishing secondary education and young women had a relatively short period of employment before marrying and having children, now longer educational participation – both in terms of finishing high school and attending university or other forms of tertiary education – has become the norm for men and women. Age at first marriage and first childbirth for women has increased from around 20 years of age, to 30 years of age, or older. Age at first marriage for women has increased from around 21 in 1975 to 28 in 2013 and age at first childbirth from 24 to 31 between 1975 and 2014. Between the 1970s and the 1990s employment and labour force participation also fell significantly at older ages, although these declines were partly reversed between the 1990s and 2008.

At the same time as these changes in the labour market were under way, Australia also carried out significant reforms to its system of labour market regulation (and social security, as discussed above). These changes in labour market regulation therefore potentially have significant implications for social security policy. As a result, understanding how social security policies deal with an individual's work status requires an understanding of the interaction between employment conditions and entitlements and social security entitlements.

This section sets out the main components of the Australian workplace relations system, and then discusses the main employment types and how they have quantitatively evolved in recent years. It also puts non-standard work in Australia in the OECD context.

2.3.1. Overview of the Australian workplace relations system [6]

Although it was influenced by the British common law legal system, Australia nevertheless developed a very different industrial relations model where federal and state governments, employers and unions all played a role in regulating employment relations at a national and industry level (Owens et al., 2011). The past 30 years or so have witnessed radical changes, however, with the decentralisation and individualisation of what was "a relatively centralised framework of wages [and conditions] determination" (Wright and Lansbury, 2015, p. 9).

These changes have enabled workplace-level collective negotiation of pay and conditions (agreement is contained in enforceable enterprise agreements) whilst retaining industry/occupation specific legal minima (called modern awards) which enterprise agreements may diverge from if they leave employees better off overall. Modern awards set minimum wages as well as other working conditions such as overtime payments and additional leave conditions. Their overall contents are specified in the Fair Work Act 2009 (FWA), Australia's principal employment rights statute, and each award is set and reviewed by an independent statutory body, the Fair Work Commission (FWC). Neither modern awards nor enterprise agreements may undercut the National Employment Standards, a minimum statutory safety net of minimum employment conditions contained in the Fair Work Act that applies to all national system employees (Stewart et al., 2016).

Compared with other English-speaking countries employment relations remain quite regulated, albeit less than in many European nations. The most significant employment protections which exist for employees are largely provided by the Fair Work Act, as described above. The self-employed are significantly less protected.

The most relevant employment standards relating to social security risks are ten days paid personal sick leave which may also be taken as carer's leave. This accumulates each year, as long as a permanent employee remains working for the same employer. This means that long-term workers could be entitled to long-duration, fully paid sick leave at older ages when they may require this support.

In contrast, government-provided Sickness Allowances are payable to people aged 22 or older, but under age pension age, and who either have a job or are receiving Austudy Payment (an income support payment for students or Australian Apprentices aged 25 or older) or ABSTUDY living allowance as a full-time student. Apart from meeting the income and assets tests and residency rules, claimants must provide a valid medical certificate, and have work or study to return to when their health improves. However, in June 2016 only around 7 700 people received Sickness Allowance – or roughly 0.3% of all working-age social security recipients – primarily because permanent employees would generally be entitled to paid sick leave as a condition of employment, and recovery times for most episodically experienced illnesses and injuries affecting work attendance do not exhaust statutory sick leave entitlements.

In terms of costs of employment, full-time permanent employees are also entitled to 20 days (25 days for regular shift workers) paid annual leave plus around eight paid public holidays per year, with paid annual leave rights also accumulating whilst working with the same employer. A rough calculation is that paid annual holidays add 10.1% to normal salary costs, with paid public holidays adding a further 3.4%. If a worker took all of their personal sick and compassionate leave each year this would add a further 4.3%, so that the total potential cost of these leaves is equivalent to nearly 18% of the cost of days actually worked.

These paid leaves are unavailable to casual workers (some unpaid leaves are however), although casuals do receive a loading of between 15% and 25% on their pay, partly to compensate for this.

The most recent (2016) figures (Department of Employment, 2017) indicate that a total of 60.5% of those working had their pay set by awards (24%) or collective agreements (36.5%), with a growing proportion covered by awards which only set minimum pay and conditions (see above). Workers were in individual agreements in 37.3% of cases and 3.6% were owner managers of incorporated enterprises (OMIEs).

Whether a worker is an employee or an independent contractor significantly affects the worker's employment rights but does not directly affect their social security entitlements. Employment entitlements broadly defined, however, may impact on how well a worker is protected against social risks such as time off work due to accidents, ill health and caring, and income in old age. Thus, where a worker's status impacts on employment entitlements it may also indirectly support or undermine the functions of the public social security system.

Deciding in a contested case which status a worker has can be complex and depends on many different aspects of the worker/employer relationship (for example, control of how work is done, a worker's freedom to substitute another to do the work). These have been discussed extensively by labour lawyers (Stewart et al., 2016; Owens et al., 2011).

Independent contractors should operate genuinely independent businesses providing "services in freely negotiated commercial contracts" whilst employees on the other hand are "subordinate" to their employers (Owens et al., 2011, p. 153).

Differences in interpretation may depend on whether a court views its role as being to determine the extent to which a worker is genuinely a risk-taking entrepreneur in reality, or whether it places greater emphasis on the formal arrangements between the employer and the worker (Stewart et al., 2016). The FWA prohibits employers from misclassifying workers as independent contractors.

Precariousness of employment has been much discussed in Australia in recent years (for example Campbell and Price (2016), ACTU (2012)). Casual employment, fixed-term contracts (discussed in Section 2.4.1), employment agency work (known as labour hire) and employees misclassified as independent contractors contribute to insecure employment.

No precise data exist in Australia on the impact of work obtained through online platforms. Minifie (2016) comments that "it seems likely that fewer than 0.5% of adult Australians [80 000 people] work on peer-to-peer platforms more than once a month" (p. 33). Stewart and Stanford (2017) cite Minifie and also Deloitte Access Economics' (2017) higher estimate of 1.5% over 2015-16 in the state of New South Wales, and conclude that gig work has made little impact in Australia so far. The authors also analyse the legal uncertainty gig workers face as to their employment status.

In August 2016, there were just over 11.8 million employed people in the Australian labour force and around 720 000 unemployed people (ABS 2017a). Of the 11.8 million employed people, 9.8 million (83%) were employees, with this group comprising 7.35 million employees with paid leave entitlements and 2.46 million (25% of employees) without paid sick leave i.e. "casual workers" (Figure 2.3) (ABS, 2017a). Around 46% of the employed workforce are women. Just under a third of all workers work part time, of whom nearly 70% are women. This means that 47% of all female workers are part time, compared with 19% of men (ABS, 2017b). There is considerable underemployment in Australia. In May 2017, it stood at 9.1% (7.1% of men and 11.3% of women), which is the highest level among OECD countries (ABS, 2017c).

Second job holding affects a relatively small proportion of workers – around 7-8% (Wilkins, 2017). Among these, a growing group comprises those working part time in their main job and using multiple jobs as a means to getting enough hours of work. This group has grown in size over the last decade, rising from approximately 54% of multiple job holders in 2008 to approximately 62% in 2015. In 2014 and 2015, approximately one in four multiple-job holders were part-time in each of their jobs, but full-time in all jobs combined. This was up from approximately one in six multiple job holders in the mid-2000s (Wilkins, 2017).

In August 2016, there were just over 800 000 owner managers of incorporated enterprises (of whom 59% had employees) and 1.2 million owner managers of unincorporated enterprises (of whom 80% were without employees).[7]

Figure 2.3. One in six Australian workers is self-employed

Workers by employment type, August 2016

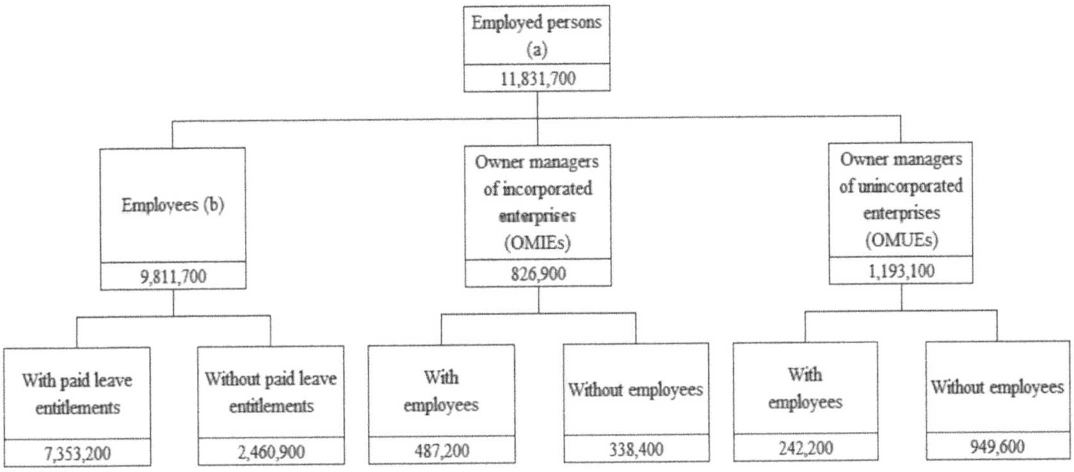

(a) Excludes persons who were contributing family workers in their main job.

(b) Prior to 2014, 'employees' comprised both Employees and OMIEs, in the Labour Force and Employee Earnings, Benefits and Trade Union Membership (EEBTUM) releases.

Source: ABS (2017a).

Independent contractors

The Australian Bureau of Statistics (ABS) (2017a) also classifies some employed people as independent contractors, which is a classification which may overlap with several categories in Figure 2.3 (employees, OMIEs and OMUEs). Independent contractors are sometimes referred to as consultants or freelancers. The term "contractors" is a broad term that is often used to describe people with a variety of forms of employment, for example, not only true independent contractors, but also employees engaged in short-term or fixed-term work, sometimes engaged through a third party (e.g. a labour hire firm/employment agency). The ABS (2017b) defines independent contractors as those who operate their own business providing services and who are not classed as employees. They have clients (possibly through an intermediary) rather than an employer and spend their time directly on client work rather than managing any employees they may have. Though in theory independent contractors should be negotiating on equal terms with their clients, in practice this is often far from the case.

Workers saying they were independent contractors may possibly in some cases be misclassified, as 42% said they could not subcontract their work and nearly two-thirds appeared not to control how their work was executed (ABS, 2017a). Concerns have been expressed about misclassification of employees as independent contractors (Productivity Commission, 2015).

There were just over 1 million people who were independent contractors in August 2016 (about 9% of all workers). Almost three-quarters (72%) of all independent contractors were men, and more than half (55%) were aged 45 years and over. Nearly one-third of all independent contractors worked in the construction industry, and a further 16% in technical services. Male independent contractors were most likely to work in construction (40%) and in technical services (14%), while female independent contractors clustered in professional, scientific and technical services (21%) as well as health care and social assistance (20%) (ABS, 2017a).

Casual employees

Casual employees are employed on a temporary "as needed" basis (though in practice many have fairly stable employment with one employer) and are not formally defined in the Fair Work Act. In awards, they are usually defined as "anyone who is engaged as a casual, or engaged and paid as such". A recent decision in the Federal Court (WorkPac Pty Ltd v Skene (2018) has provided further clarification of this.

The FWA does, however, define the employment rights to which casuals are and are not entitled. Casuals are not entitled to paid holiday and sick leave, redundancy pay and notice of termination (Stewart et al., 2016). The FWA does grant some rights to casuals, though some are restricted to those with regular and systematic employment for a qualifying period with an employer and who have an expectation of such employment continuing. An employer of a casual worker must (subject to certain exceptions) make the statutory superannuation contributions on their behalf (see below). Casual workers are also covered by workers' compensation arrangements.

A casual worker under an award should be paid 25% more for each hour than another worker doing the same job on a permanent basis. In enterprise agreements, the casual loading varies by sector, but tends to be between 15% and 25% (Healy and Nicholson, 2017). A recent study by Healy and Nicholson (2017) points out that "the practice of paying a casual loading developed for two reasons. One was to provide some compensation for workers missing out on paid leave. The other, quite different, motivation was to make casual employment more expensive and discourage excessive use of it."

There are two main areas of costs savings to employers in hiring casuals. The first is their lack of entitlement to paid leave. Despite the casual loading that is intended to compensate for less favourable conditions, a range of research has found that there are still detriments to employees – and thus benefits to employers. Lass and Wooden (2017) use the HILDA longitudinal household survey to examine the existence of wage penalties or premia for temporary workers including casuals. They summarise prior Australian research as finding "that casual employment is associated with, at most, a very modest wage premium" (pp 1-2). For example, Watson (2005) analysing an earlier version of the same survey as Lass and Wooden, found small premia for casual workers (significantly less than the nominal loading for casuals). After controlling for the loading, casual workers were actually experiencing a wage penalty.

Unlike this earlier research which "focused on the mean of the wage distribution", Lass and Wooden (2017 p2) the authors examine the penalty/premia throughout the wage distribution. Casuals in HILDA (as in ABS data[8]) appear disproportionately in the lowest-paid jobs. They conclude a wage penalty does indeed exist for those in the lowest-paid casual jobs, moving towards a premium at higher pay levels. Yet even at higher pay levels, the premia (except in a few cases) do not fully reach the level of the loading (p.16).

More difficult to calculate is the benefit to employers of the flexible way casuals' low level of job protection enables their labour to be called on to meet employers' fluctuating staffing requirements. This stems from a lack of realistic protection from unfair dismissal and their lack of notice rights or redundancy payments, together with the ease with which employers can adjust their hours at short notice (Campbell, 2017; Productivity Commission, 2015, Vol. 2, p. 801). The Productivity Commission (2015) notes the variability of hours, the possibility of dismissal and fewer prospects of workplace training "are far more difficult to quantify [than loss of specific payments]".

The share of casual workers increased in the late 1980s and 1990s(Figure 2.4). Over the period since 1988, female workers have been much more likely to be casual than men, with the share of female employees employed casually being over 30% for much of the period. After 2000, however, this proportion dropped from a high of 31%. More recently, the proportion of casual employees increased from 23.5% in August 2012 to 25.1% in August 2017, with the proportion of casual male employees increasing from 21.0% to 23.1% and the proportion of casual female employees increasing from 26.2% to 27.1%. The overall growth in casual employment has been driven by its growing prevalence among men, with the proportion nearly doubling from 11.7% in 1988 to 22.7% in 2004, but it has been roughly stable since then. Analysis by Campbell (forthcoming, using ABS data) suggests that the variability of casuals' hours and income has increased between 2012 and 2017. Casuals are much more likely to work short hours than permanent staff. Of all casuals, 19.3% worked less than ten hours per week in 2016 (ABS, 2017a). Casual employment is predominately part time (70% of casual employees) and the majority (52.6%) of it is undertaken by women (of whom 81.1% are part-time) with a large proportion of it carried out by young people (37.3% by those under 25).

Figure 2.4. Women are more likely to be casual workers than men, but the growth of casual employment is mainly due to its growing prevalence for male workers

Share of employees who are casual workers, in percent, 1988 to 2016

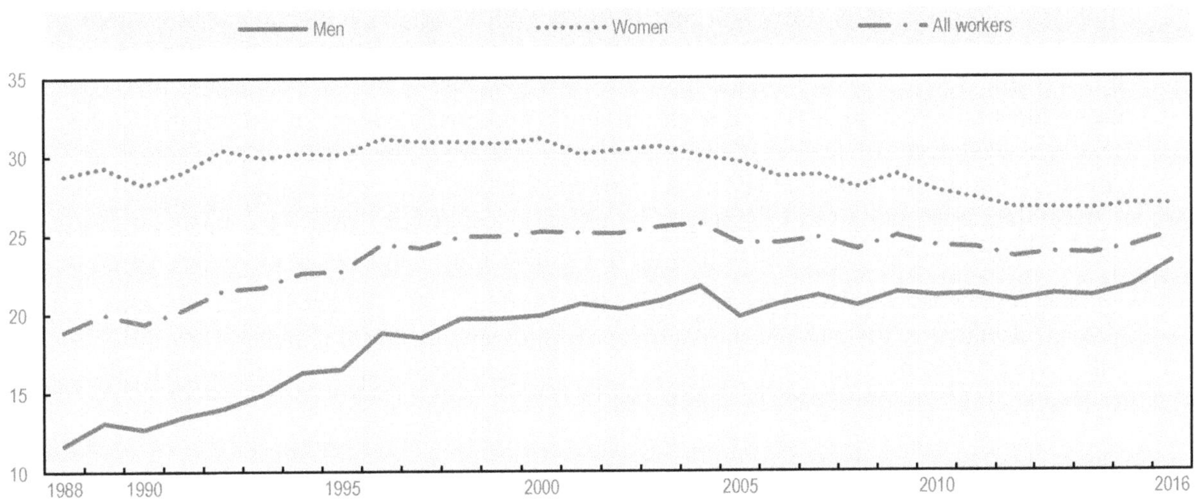

Source: Australian Bureau of Statistics (ABS), Australian labour market statistics, Cat. No. 6105.0, ABS, Canberra, July 2014.

As with independent contractors, it appears that considerable avoidance of legal minima applicable to casuals may be occurring. Lass and Wooden (2017), whilst acknowledging that permanent staff are often paid more than the minima applicable to their job, comment that their findings "suggest...a considerable degree of non-compliance on the part of employers of low-wage casual labour" (p. 16). In July 2017, the FWC decided that a clause enabling casuals to ask to become permanent employees (subject to fulfilling certain conditions) would be inserted into awards (industry-specific legal minima for wages and working conditions, see Section 2.3.1). How far this will reduce misclassification of permanent employees as casuals is debatable, but it is an indication of concerns about the undermining of employment rights.

It is unclear how extensive compliance is with labour laws (Landau et al., 2014). The Fair Work Ombudsman (FWO), Australia's labour inspectorate and employment conditions enforcement agency pursues numerous claims of underpayment of wages to largely low-paid workers[9], amongst whom will be casuals and "sham" contractors. Concerns are regularly expressed in the media about underpayment of wages, with franchisees a particular concern.[10] Following concerns expressed by the Productivity Commission (2015), legislation recently strengthened protections for vulnerable workers.

Australia's international ranking in terms of the share of temporary employees is unclear. The definition used in the OECD Labour Force Statistics is that in 2017 only 5.3% of dependent employment was temporary, giving Australia the fourth lowest share of temporary workers in the OECD (Figure 1.1 in Chapter 1).

The definition used is derived from the Australian Labour Force Survey with temporary workers defined as those employees (excluding owner-managers of incorporated enterprises) where the employment in a person's 'main job' (to which are attached a number of measurement issues) has a set completion date or event (fixed-term contract), or casuals (those without leave entitlements) where employment is expected to continue for less than 12 months with "seasonal/temporary job/fixed contract" reported as the reason.

In contrast, much of the Australian literature treats most casual workers as temporary employees. For example, Campbell and Burgess (2001) estimate that in the late 1990s around one in three employees in Australia were temporary workers. More recently, Lass and Wooden (2017, page 1) note that in Australia "the share of temporary in total employment is very high, and … it is casual work, and not fixed-term contracts that is the most prevalent form of temporary employment. Data from the Household, Income and Labour Dynamics in Australia (HILDA) Survey, for example, indicate that around 32% of Australian employees were employed on either a casual basis or a fixed-term contract in 2014, but with casual workers representing the majority of this group (72%)".

Using a somewhat similar approach with HILDA data, OECD (2015) estimate that in 2013 Australia had the third-highest share of non-standard employment in the OECD with close to 40% of total employment being "non-standard", but this included part-time permanent employees and the self-employed.

Temporary migrant workers

Among OECD countries, Australia has the third highest share of foreign-born people in its population – 27.7% in 2013 (OECD, 2017). Traditionally, Australia has been a country of permanent settlement and for most of the period after the Second World War, there was no category analogous to guest workers.

The test of 'community membership' which must be satisfied to be qualified for most Australian social security payments is Australian residence status. For working-age payments such as Newstart Allowance, migrants not covered by an 'assurance of support' must wait two years to become payable, and for Age and Disability Support Pensions they must accrue ten years of 'qualifying residence', except in the case of disabilities acquired after settling in Australia. Temporary migrants, however, are not regarded as 'community members' for Australian social security purposes (unless they can establish eligibility under one of Australia's agreements on social security with other countries).

This pattern of migration has changed significantly since the late 1990s towards greater economic and temporary migration. More than 600 000 temporary migrants with rights to work entered Australia in 2014/15 alone (Wright et al., 2016). They include international students, skilled migrants on '457' visas[11] and working holidaymakers.

At 31 December 2015, there were 328 000 student visa holders in Australia, 155 000 Working Holiday Maker visa holders, 160 000 Temporary Skilled ('457') visa holders, and more than 600 000 New Zealand visa holders (Department of Home Affairs, 2015).

Qualitative research and reports indicate employer evasion of employment standards in relation to migrants with temporary work rights, which has caused concern in Australia. The Productivity Commission (2015) in its review of the evidence concludes that migrant workers are more vulnerable to exploitation and less able to enforce their employment rights than permanent residents. Many of those affected work in casualised industries such as retail or hospitality (Wright et al., 2016; Campbell et al., 2016).

In general, temporary migrant workers will have no rights to social security benefits due to the residence requirements for payments, and in many cases will have limited entitlements to health care, unless they come from a country with which Australia has a reciprocal healthcare agreement. Temporary migrant workers have the same rights at work as permanent residents and will be covered by workers' compensation schemes; they will also be entitled to superannuation if they are earning over AUD 450 per month. Temporary workers following their departure from Australia can claim their accumulated superannuation contributions and earnings, but these are taxed at rates of between 35% and 65%.

New Zealanders are entitled to travel freely to Australia without visas. However, since 1994, when a Special Category Visa (SCV) was introduced for New Zealanders, they have no longer been treated as de facto permanent residents irrespective of their length of residency. If they wish to apply for permanent residency they must do so under skilled migration requirements, which will generally exclude those aged 45 years and over and those with limited educational qualifications. After 2001, the rights to social security of these visa holders were also significantly restricted. A new permanent residency pathway was introduced from 1 July 2017 for New Zealand citizens who arrived in Australia post 26 February 2001, but on or before, 19 February 2016.

Overall, changes in migration policies and related social security policies have meant that there has been a significant increase in the share of the immigrant population with limited access to Australian social security payments.

Labour hire, fixed-term employees and unpaid work experience

Approximately 600 800 people (about 5% of all employed persons) were placed in their job by a labour hire firm/employment agency in August 2016, of whom 133 700 were employed by the labour hire firm. Those who work for a labour hire company are usually employees of that company not of their host business who gives them work but pays the labour hire company. They are often casuals whilst some may be independent contractors to their labour hire employer (Stewart et al., 2016; Victorian Government, 2016). The latter arrangements are subject to the tests described above if the worker contests their status and alleges that they are an employee. The Labour Hire Inquiry Report (Victorian

Government, 2016) found greater economic vulnerability existed for labour hire company employees than other types of employees in many areas.

Men comprised 59% of the overall total and 64% of labour hire direct workers. Overall, the manufacturing (21%) and construction (10%) industries were where many men were hired. Women using this method to find jobs were placed primarily in the healthcare and social assistance (16%) and the public administration and safety (11%) industries (ABS, 2017a). Over half of those finding work through a labour hire firm or employment agency were aged between 25 and 44 (ABS, 2017a).

Fixed-term employees are employed for a specified length of time or until a job is completed. They comprise between 3% and 9% of employees (Stewart et al., 2016). Their rights to employer-provided conditions impacting on social security risks are similar to permanent workers. Unpaid work experience (often known as internships) is reported to be common in Australia, especially for young adults. This experience "occup[ies] an ambiguous space in employment and workplace law" (Oliver et al., 2017, p. 18) as some may be entitled to an employee's pay and conditions. Some paid interns may also be entitled to student payments.

2.4. Access to social protection

In many instances, differences in employment status between employees and the self-employed and between casual and permanent employees do not impact on their rights to social security. Indeed, because casual employees receive no coverage for sick leave as a condition of employment and can be more easily dismissed, they are conceivably more likely to claim some entitlements than regular employees. While there is no direct information on whether social security recipients who are also working are casual workers or not, it seems likely that many would be. As discussed earlier (Figure 2.2), a total of around 11% of social security recipients receive earnings, including around 20% of Newstart Allowance recipients and a similar proportion of Youth Allowance (Other) recipients. This suggests that for casual workers there are no inherent barriers to combining social security payments with part-time employment.

This section discusses what differences could nevertheless emerge between standard and non-standard workers in Australia: how the income and asset tests treat different sources of income and wealth; Paid Parental Leave as the only programme that has a work history requirement (with this used to determine eligibility as opposed to level of assistance received which is 'flat rate'); and superannuation and occupational pension plans and coverage of work accidents.

2.4.1. How the social security system treats different sources of income and wealth

Box 2.1. Definition of employment income taken into account for income tests for pensions and allowances, Australia 2017

Employment income includes

- salary
- wages
- commissions
- allowances in excess of relevant expenses
- pay for piece work
- fixed and variable price contracts
- fringe benefits related to employment
- remuneration from own private trusts, but not distributions
- remuneration from own company, but not dividends
- regular drawings of income for work performed such as directors' fees

Employment income does not include

- drawings by a principal from a sole trader business or partnership
- superannuation pensions
- personal injury compensation
- insurance payouts related to employment
- leave payments received as a lump sum on termination of employment

Source: Australian Department of Human Services, https://www.humanservices.gov.au/customer/enablers/examples-employment-income.

As discussed in Section 2.2, most benefits in Australia are subject to income and asset tests. In the income tests, deductions for self-employment expenses are more restricted than those allowed for income tax purposes.[12] In the income test, the self-employed can deduct costs needed to earn business income, depreciation of business assets and employer superannuation contributions for their employees. They cannot claim, however, past year losses, losses from another business, superannuation for themselves or business partners, and some capital costs, which can be claimed in their tax returns.

The self-employed and others obtaining 'business income' (i.e. income from profits generated by the carrying on of a business) are required to provide Centrelink, the agency tasked with the delivery of social security payments by the Department for Human Services (DHS), with their most recent taxation notice of assessment, or a profit and loss statement for a recent period (usually 13 weeks) – if a taxation notice of assessment for the most recently concluded financial year is has not yet available, or income has changed since the last statement (Australian Government, Department of Human Services, 2017).

However, the difference in employment status is significant in relation to the accumulation of savings for retirement through the superannuation system and in relation to ill-health payments particularly where ill health arises from a work-related cause. Before turning to these issues, the paper will discuss the one payment made by the national government that does require a recent employment history for eligibility and two work-related payments which provide social protection apart from paid sick leave mentioned earlier.

2.4.2. Paid Parental Leave and Dad and Partner Pay

Australia's first national scheme of Paid Parental Leave (PPL) was introduced in January 2011 and paid leave was extended to fathers as Dad and Partner Pay (DaPP) in January 2013. These payments differ from most other social security payments in that while they do not require contributions, eligibility is conditional on previous periods of employment. Currently, Parental Leave Pay in Australia is payable for up to 18 weeks at the minimum wage.

There is a work test for eligibility (as well as a range of other tests such as residency requirements). This requires a PPL recipient to have worked for 10 of the 13 months prior to a birth (or adoption) for a total of at least 330 hours; (which averages out to just over one day per week in that period). There are two important exclusions that may particularly affect casual workers, who cannot be sure of ongoing work and who are not usually entitled to paid leave. These are: (1) there must not be a period greater than eight weeks between any two days of qualifying work; (2) paid leave (e.g. due to ill health or holidays) counts as work whilst unpaid leave does not.

The work test however is wide and can encompass casuals even where they have worked for several employers (and this is true of anyone otherwise satisfying the work test e.g. seasonal workers) and also includes independent contractors and the self-employed. Dad and Partner Pay has very similar eligibility rules.

There is also a cap on earnings. This means that individuals with an adjusted taxable income above AUD 150 000 a year (or about 2.7 times the median wage in July 2017) from employment or business income or from a wide range of taxable government pensions and benefits, receive no PPL. There is no taper, but entitlement is lost as soon as one earns above this threshold.

In addition, because these payments are made at a flat rate and at the full-time minimum wage, they are more advantageous (in terms of their replacement rate) to low-income and part-time workers earning below the full-time minimum wage than to higher-paid, full-time workers. The official evaluation of these schemes (Martin et al., 2014) shows stronger effects for low-paid, casual and self-employed workers than for full-time workers on permanent contracts. This was based on comparing outcomes for different categories of workers after the scheme was introduced, compared to a sample of workers before the scheme was introduced. The main result of interest was whether parents spent more time with their infants before returning to work. For mothers, the evaluation estimated that for low-income workers, the proportion surveyed who had not returned to work by 13 weeks increased from 80% to 90%, for casual workers from 79% to 90% (compared to 85% to 92% for those not on casual contracts), and for previously self-employed mothers from 43% to 66% (compared to 86% to 94% for those not self-employed). Prior to DaPP, 13% of all fathers in an online survey reported they had not been eligible for any type of leave, but this ranged from 3% of those with permanent contracts, to 41-54% of the self-employed and 65% of fathers in casual employment. After the introduction of DaPP, 36% of all surveyed fathers used the provision in the first six months after the birth of their baby, but roughly half of casual and self-employed fathers (Martin et al., 2014).

In summary, while PLP/DaPP are the only government social security provisions in Australia to explicitly require previous employment as a condition of eligibility, it appears that it was designed in a way – a flat-rate payment replacing full-time minimum wages – that had a greater impact on outcomes for irregular workers than to those with a permanent contract.

2.4.3. Superannuation

The Superannuation Guarantee Act 1992 (SG Act) requires employers to pay a proportion of ordinary time earnings (which includes the loading for casuals) into a superannuation fund. This is a defined-contribution scheme and there is no requirement that it be converted into an annuity on retirement. This contribution is now 9.5% of wages (up to a cap of AUD 51 620 per quarter in 2016-17), and is legislated to rise to 12% beginning in 2021-22. Individual contracts, enterprise agreements and modern awards may make provision for higher contributions, or 'defined benefit' superannuation (so long as the employer contribution is at least 9.5%).

Superannuation covers employees and contractors with a contract "wholly or principally" for their labour, effectively employees.[13] There are exemptions for those who earn under AUD 450 per calendar month in a particular job, those doing private or domestic work up to 30 hours per week, and part-time workers under 18. The AUD 450 threshold (which is not uprated for wage or consumer price inflation) is equivalent to around six hours per week at current minimum wage rates. This has implications for those working in multiple small part-time jobs as they potentially will not be covered even if their total hours of work put them over this level.[14] In 2013/14, 66% of women and 73% of men over the age of 15 were having superannuation paid into a fund on their behalf.

Individuals may contribute to their own superannuation fund before tax (subject to financial year limits) at a 15% tax rate, whilst contributions from after tax income sources are not subject to a contributions tax (Australian Tax Office, 2017b). The higher an individual's marginal tax rate the more advantageous it is to do this – the top marginal tax rate is 45%. The self-employed are generally regarded as being less likely to make these contributions – despite the tax advantages (including tax deductibility of 'notified' personal super contributions) – because they are more likely to retain earnings as cash in their businesses (which boosts the eventual sale price of the business, with income from the sale of the business treated as a 'capital gain' which is taxed at half the taxpayer's top marginal income tax rate). However, recent changes introduced in the 2016-17 Budget have made it easier to make such contributions. There is also a Low-Income Superannuation Tax Offset under which the government pays up to AUD 500 a year into a superannuation account on a 'low-income' earner's behalf (Australian Tax Office, 2017d).

The SG Act requires employers to pay superannuation quarterly into the superannuation funds of their eligible workers. An employer who fails to do this faces financial penalties on top of repaying the superannuation guarantee amount. The penalty is 10% of the shortfall (the nominal interest component) and AUD 20 per employee affected per quarter (the administration fee). The Tax Office also has discretion to levy an additional penalty of up to 200% of the outstanding amount, including shortfall, interest component and administration fee. Company directors are also personally liable for the whole amount owing to each employee.

Despite these penalties for non-compliance, approximately 20 000 employees and ex-employees (largely of small businesses) report a suspected underpayment or non-payment to the Australian Tax Office annually (ATO, 2017c). An employee often cannot claim their unpaid superannuation directly from their (ex) employer and their fund cannot do it on their behalf as it is for the ATO to initiate compliance (Stewart et al., 2016).

Conflicting estimates of the superannuation compliance gap have been made recently. A report from a Senate committee (Senate of Australia 2017) states that Industry Super Australia (ISA), an organisation managing research, policy development and advocacy projects for industry superannuation funds (which jointly manage about 5 million accounts), estimated that "Australian employers failed to pay at least AUD 3.6 billion in SG contributions in 2013/14" (revised now to AUD 5.6 billion in 2013-14) (pp. 13-14). This is roughly equivalent to 10% of total employer superannuation contributions for the 2013/14 financial year. A more modest sum has been subsequently estimated by the ATO of AUD 2.85 billion (5.5% of the amount of AUD 51.51 billion collected) in 2014/15 (ATO, 2017c). This is net of AUD 414 million which it reports as recovered by ATO compliance activities in that year (ATO, 2017c).

Two main causes were identified: underpayment of SG for employees and those contractors who are in effect disguised employees, and contributions not being paid in the cash economy. Projected accumulated losses over the next ten years were estimated as having an effect on a large number of individuals. The ATO and the Senate of Australia (2017) note that employees of small businesses and in the hospitality, construction, manufacturing and retail industries (noted by the Senate report to be areas of insecure and low-waged jobs) suffer from non-payment disproportionately. The Government has recently introduced a suite of targeted reforms to introduce stronger penalties for non-compliance, ensure more reliable collection of liabilities and improve the visibility of superannuation payments to the ATO.

There are significant concerns about the adequacy of superannuation particularly for women with interrupted work histories due to caring responsibilities. Women on PPL payments and those receiving social security benefits while caring are not eligible for superannuation contributions. Interruptions to work will thus reduce the total amount of superannuation in retirement. Data compiled by the Workplace Gender Equality Agency show the superannuation gap is 46.6% on average. This means the average Australian man currently retires with AUD 197 054 while the average woman retires with just AUD 104 734 (Commonwealth of Australia, 2016).

There are also concerns about the generosity of tax expenditures for superannuation. Unlike most other countries, superannuation in Australia has operated on a "ttE" basis[15]; in broad terms, this means that contributions into superannuation are taxed at a flat rate of 15% and earnings within superannuation funds are also taxed at a flat rate of 15%, rather than at the marginal rate of the individual.

Because existing taxes on contributions and earnings are at a flat rate, they are more valuable for higher-income earners, who would otherwise pay higher marginal rates on these incomes. It is estimated that close to a third of the value of the tax concessions in

Australia accrue to the top 10% of taxpayers (Ingles and Stewart, 2015), however changes introduced in the 2016-17 Budget will address this equity issue going forward.

2.4.4. Accidents at work

The principal method of compensating workers for workplace-related injuries and illness is through the (eleven different) workers' compensation schemes provided in states and territories for most workers, and by the federal government for its own and a limited number of other employees (Stewart et al., 2016). The workers' compensation schemes[16] require most employers to insure against occurrences of workplace related injuries by paying a standardised average premium rate. The rate applied to the employer varies by industry classification. In 2015-16[17] the rates applied ranged from 0.26% to 3.43% of payroll.

Rules about the amount and nature of earnings compensated vary as do the periods of incapacity covered and the lump sums for permanent incapacity and death. For example, in New South Wales – the most populous Australian state – injured workers receive up to 95% of their pre-injury average weekly earnings up to a ceiling of roughly twice median earnings for up to 13 weeks. Between 14 and 130 weeks they can receive up to 80% of their pre-injury earnings up to the same ceiling, and after this they can still receive 80% of previous earnings if they are assessed as unable to work. Those who are able to return to work on a program of reduced hours are eligible for the same levels of support, less their actual earnings. Special provisions are made where employees are uninsured. However, many jurisdictions do not require insurance to include any or all superannuation contributions, so during the period of an injury, workers may not have contributions to their superannuation savings maintained.

According to data in the OECD Social Expenditure Database for Australia, in 2014 payments made by workers' compensation schemes amounted to AUD 8.5 billion or roughly 50% of the government's level of spending on the public Disability Support Pension (costing AUD 16.5 billion in that year).[18]

Independent contractors are not always covered by workplace accident schemes. The summary of coverage compiled by Safe Work Australia (2016) suggests variation across jurisdictions in the coverage of independent contractors, with many not covered at all, though labour hire workers must usually be covered by their labour hire employers (i.e. not the employer with whom they are placed). In general terms, the federal government guidance advises independent contractors: "You may not necessarily be entitled to workers' compensation unless you have arranged your own accident protection insurance. Some independent contractors are covered for workers' compensation in some states and in specific circumstances" (Department of Innovation, Industry and Science, 2016, p.18).

Claims for workers' compensation and/or civil damages actions may take some time to be settled, and individuals may claim an income support payment while waiting for settlement. In these cases the social security system makes provision to recover a proportion of income support (i) already paid from a lump sum or (ii) otherwise payable from ongoing instalments of compensation if a workers' compensation claim and/or civil damages action succeeds (Stewart et al., 2016).

2.5. The incomes and assets of the self-employed

The share of households whose principal source of income is from self-employment (unincorporated business income) was 4.1% in 2013/14. There are a further 0.5% of households with zero or negative income – most of whom are likely to be self-employed (ABS, 2015). Households with an incorporated business providing their main income source are largely found among a group that the ABS classifies as "other", who in total make up about 10% of households. However, the "other" group also includes people with property and investment income, and it is not possible to definitively say what share are only reliant on incorporated business income.

Figure 2.5 shows the distribution of income by main source of gross household income, comparing the self-employed, employees and all households. The self-employed have mean equivalised disposable incomes that are around 94% of those with employee income. Their relative median income is much lower at a little over 80%, reflecting the much higher inequality among self-employed households – the Gini coefficient for employee households is 0.269 while that for the self-employed is 0.389. This in turn reflects the fact that incomes at the 10th percentile of the respective distributions are much lower for the self-employed (by more than 25%) while incomes at the 90th percentile are about 9% higher.

Figure 2.5. The self-employed have lower incomes, but more assets than employees

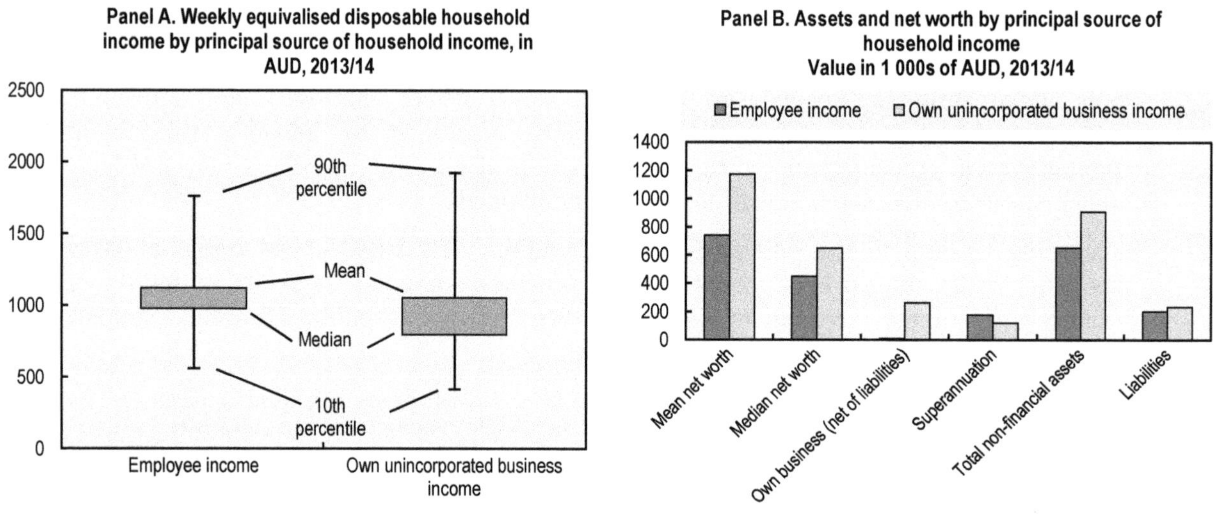

Source: ABS, 2015.

Figure 2.5 shows, however, that self-employed households have considerably higher net worth than employee households, with mean net worth being 60% higher and median net worth 44% higher – again implying higher inequality in the distribution of wealth among the self-employed. The main explanation for their higher net worth is that the average value of their own unincorporated business exceeds AUD 250 000. In addition, however the value of their non-financial assets is considerably higher than that of employees, including the value of their family home and other property. Their superannuation wealth, however, is lower than that of employee households and considerably lower than that of the "other" group. They also have the highest level of liabilities, mainly due to higher property debts.

The self-employed have slightly more one-earner households and they are more likely to be home owners, both with and without a mortgage, relative to employee households. They are also more likely to be couples with and without dependent children, and their average age is somewhat higher.

Figure 2.6 shows receipt of government benefits by source of income. While the self-employed receive the lowest level of cash benefits on average of any of the household groups, it is notable that the average value of family support benefits received (Family Tax Benefits A and B) is about the same as for employee households. In absolute terms, they have the highest level of benefits received from education programmes, but the lowest from health benefits. Again, in absolute terms they pay the highest average income taxes, about 20% or AUD 100 a week more than employee households even though their gross income is lower than employee households. This may reflect the fact that the self-employed have more unequal incomes than employees, with higher incomes at the top of the distribution range.

Figure 2.6. The self-employed benefit slightly less from social spending

Average weekly benefit receipt, by principal source of household income, in AUD, 2013/14

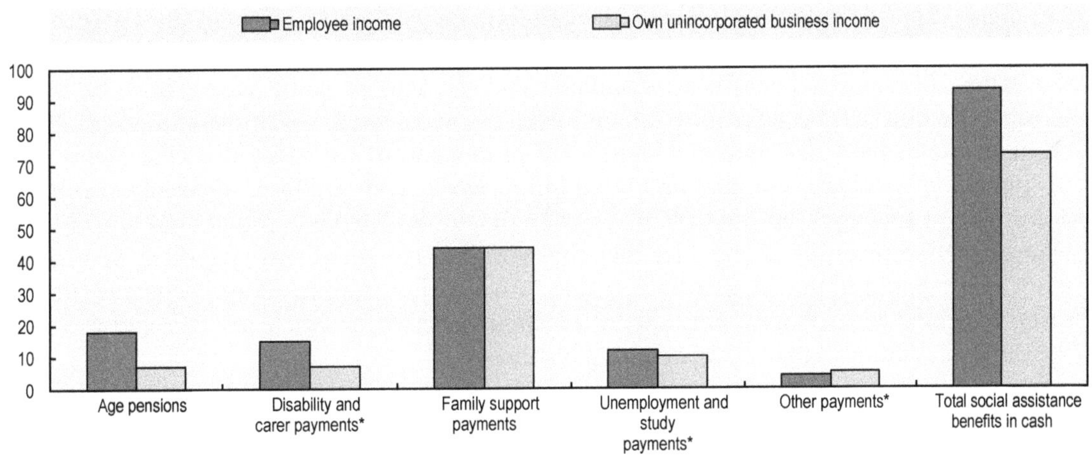

Note: For categories marked with *, the estimate for households with own unincorporated business income have a relative standard error of 25% to 50% and should be used with caution
Source: ABS, 2015.

2.6. Discussion and conclusions

The Australian system of public social security differs significantly from those in most other OECD countries (apart from New Zealand), in not being based on social insurance principles and therefore not requiring previous contributions as a condition of eligibility. Over the last 50 years or so, the Australian social security system has also evolved from a tightly targeted scheme of social assistance designed around the assumption that work is full-time, to a system that recognises that part-time work and other non-standard arrangements exist and may be either a stepping stone to full-time work or sufficient in and of itself sufficient to meet participation requirements. The system is now something more like a set of categorical negative income taxes that encourage part-time work, but which place higher effective marginal tax rates on those who move from part-time to full-time work (OECD Benefits and Wages database).

The Australian story is complicated, however, by its interaction with a system of workplace entitlements that privilege full-time permanent employees. As discussed in Section 2.2, as well as having less access to generous entitlements to paid leave, temporary workers are much more vulnerable to dismissal with little or no notice, their work shifts can be changed at short notice, and they have less control over their patterns and hours of work. The scope and enforcement of this system of workplace-based entitlements that are not directly provided by the government would appear to have diminished over time, due to declining unionisation and growing casual and part-time work. Additionally, independent contractors are outside these workplace protections though a number should in fact be classified as employees, or depend significantly on one or two employers even where they are genuinely independent.

Australia has relatively low levels of self-employment compared with other countries in the OECD (OECD, 2015a). There are other forms of non-standard employment including independent contractors as well as the emerging "gig economy" but data on these trends are less definitive. The last 20 years has also seen a very large increase in temporary migrant workers, who because of residence requirements for social benefits and health services will not be eligible for most forms of government social protection, and are also at higher risk of exploitation at work.

For many categories of non-standard workers, the design features of the Australian system do not exclude them from social protection. Non-standard workers are entitled to the same government benefits as standard workers, and in some cases, may be more likely to be eligible, because they are on lower incomes, work part-time and do not have entitlements to paid sick leave. A significant proportion of social security recipients and of part-time workers are already combining work and welfare. Overall, the non-contributory nature of the Australian system appears to achieve broad coverage and high take-up. Offsetting this is the fact that for working-age recipients, payment levels are modest compared to the levels of assistance provided in insurance-based schemes (this is to be expected from 'safety net' social assistance transfers, which are directed towards 'poverty alleviation' rather than wage replacement).

Analysis of the economic circumstances of the self-employed in unincorporated businesses finds that they have lower average and median incomes than employees, but with a more unequal distribution of income. This means that lower-income self-employed people are worse off than comparable groups of employees, but the higher-income self-employed are better off. The self-employed generally have significantly higher levels of wealth than employee households, although less of this is in superannuation. It is not possible to say, however, whether the self-employed – who are not covered by compulsory superannuation – are disadvantaged by this, as income data do not identify the previous work status of those currently retired.

Having said this, non-standard workers appear to be, and likely to continue to be, disadvantaged in relation to occupational superannuation, which has become much more significant since the 1990s, a trend that is expected to continue over the next two decades. This may have a stronger negative impact on part-time workers and women than the self-employed, who, while they are less likely to contribute to superannuation, have other forms of savings through their own business and the family home and other real property.

Of particular interest are the Parental Leave Payment arrangements, which advantage workers with incomes below the full-time minimum wage and encompass the self-employed. These have a broad coverage with eligibility based on prior employment and are funded by government and not employers. Overall, while the Australian government social security system does not exclude non-standard workers, many of the features of the systems of work-based support are exposed to the same sorts of challenges from the changing nature of work.

In considering the lessons of Australia's experience, it should be noted that income-testing potentially raises complications that are not necessarily as salient in non-targeted systems. An income-tested benefit is inherently vulnerable to problems of overpayments and underpayments. To some degree, there may be similar issues with receipt of social insurance benefits where overpayments are possible if recipients do not accurately report their status, e.g. people receiving unemployment payments but who are doing undeclared work in the underground economy. But in a system like Australia's, correct payments are regarded as more central to the objective of targeting benefits. Accurate targeting will necessarily become more problematic as patterns of work vary in terms of hours per week and weeks per year.

Getting payments "right" in any means-tested system is a complex process necessarily involving trade-offs between responsiveness and simplicity. If the aim is to precisely match income and benefits in real time, then there must be updating and checking of income and adjustments of benefits. But such a system is potentially intrusive and administratively complex.

There are specific examples of these problems arising in the early 2000s in relation to overpayments of family tax benefits in Australia as well as tax credits in the United Kingdom (Whiteford, Millar and Mendelson, 2003), as also more recently in Australia in relation to presumed overpayments of income support benefits (Whiteford and Millar, 2017).

The increasing trends towards more insecure and variable employment patterns – and hence irregular pay packets – will make balancing accuracy and timeliness in means-tested welfare benefits more difficult. This new reality requires both a policy solution and a technical response aimed at harnessing real-time information on earnings and income in a timely way. These complexities need to be borne in mind in assessing the lessons of Australia's approach to social security.

Notes

[1] For example, many single parent 'pensioners' were in employment during this period, and durations of unemployment benefit receipt beyond 12 months became more commonplace.

[2] Resulting in 'Parenting Payment (single)' which, although defined as a 'social security pension' under the *Social Security Act 1991* (Cth), has design features of both pensions and benefits, and has become an 'intermediate' category of income support.

[3] Cash spending includes social security and other payments made in cash to individuals and excludes services or subsidies. The main non-income-tested spending relates to state government schemes of workers' compensation and pensions for retired public servants.

[4] For social security benefits income free areas largely recognise the costs of taking up work, with 'credit' or 'banking' mechanisms providing an added incentive to take-up intermittent casual work.

[5] In effect student assistance rates expect recipients to have additional income from part-time work (or another income source) so as to achieve a similar living standard to that achieved by an unemployed adult.

[6] We describe the federal industrial relations system which now covers most Australian employees (Productivity Commission, 2015).

[7] "[An] owner manager of an incorporated enterprise (OMIE)...[is] a person who operates his or her own incorporated enterprise, that is, a business entity which is registered as a separate legal entity to its members or owners (also known as a limited liability company). ... [An] owner manager of unincorporated enterprise (OMUE)... [is] a person who operates his or her own unincorporated enterprise or engages independently in a profession or trade." These workers may employ others, or they may not.(ABS 2014).

[8] Lass and Wooden note that "45% of casual (non-managerial) employees are paid exactly the award rate, which compares with just 18% of permanent (non-managerial) employees" (ABS, Data Cube 5, Table 2, Australian Bureau of Statistics (ABS). Employee Earnings and Hours, Australia, May 2016. ABS cat. no. 6306.0. Canberra: ABS.). (p7)

[9] In 2016/17 the Fair Work Ombudsman (2017) states it obtained AUD 30.6 million for over 17 000 Workers, https://www.fairwork.gov.au/annual-reports/annual-report-2015-16, downloaded 11 March 2018

[10] See for example, the 7 Eleven grocery franchise, Ferguson and Danckert (2015), http://www.smh.com.au/interactive/2015/7-eleven-revealed/, downloaded 10 September 2017

[11] Replaced by new Temporary Skill Shortage (TSS) visa with effect from March 2018. See Department of Home Affairs (2017) https://www.border.gov.au/Trav/Work/457-abolition-replacement.

[12] For income tax purposes, expenses are broken down into direct expenses, those that are directly linked to the generation of the income and sometimes called cost of sales, and indirect or overhead expenses. Direct expenses are those that increase or decrease depending on the level of income being generated. For a manufacturer, direct expenses include materials and direct labour costs, while for a retailer it is the net cost of stock purchases. Overhead expenses are those that do not depend on the amount of revenue produced, but must be paid just because the business is operating. Overhead expenses include rent, interest on loans taken out to purchase the business, insurance and vehicle costs. Generally, income tax allows the deduction of direct expenses (Australian Tax Office, 2017a).

[13] The tests which the Australian Tax Office (ATO) applies appear similar to those for deciding if a worker is an employee, https://www.ato.gov.au/individuals/super/getting-started/contractors/ https://www.ato.gov.au/business/employee-or-contractor/difference-between-employees-and-contractors/ Senate of Australia (2017) comments on "the complexity of classifying workers correctly for superannuation purposes" (p. 42). It also reports one lawyer providing evidence that "individuals suffer a serious injury or health event and seek access to a disability or income protection insurance payment, only to find that due to SG non-payment, they are in fact ineligible for assistance under their superannuation fund policy's benefit" (pp 24-5).

[14] Workers working multiple part-time jobs can pay into their superannuation fund voluntarily, but will not receive employer contributions.

[15] The abbreviation "ttE" means that contributions to pension schemes are taxed as concessional rates (t), their earnings in funds are also taxed at concessional rates (t), and pension payments are exempt from taxation (E).

[16] The Australian Insurance Brokers (2013) Summary of Workers' Compensation Australia, states 'Private sector insurers provide workers compensation in the risk states (being West Australia, ACT, Tasmania and Northern Territory) while state monopolies operate in New South Wales, Victoria, South Australia and Queensland': http://www.aisinsurance.com.au/wp-content/uploads/2013/04/Summary-of-the-Australian-Workers-Compensation-System.pdf Downloaded 24 July 2017

[17] https://www.safeworkaustralia.gov.au/system/files/documents/1806/comparative-performance-monitoring-report-19th-edition-part-3_0.pdf.

[18] It is worth noting that workers' compensation schemes in Australia are not 'exhaustive' (i.e. it is possible to get workers' compensation for a work-related illness or injury, and also pursue a civil damages award in relation to the same compensable event).

References

Australian Bureau of Statistics (ABS) (2014), *Standards for Labour Force Statistics, Issue For Dec 2014*, Cat. No. 1288.0, ABS, Canberra, http://www.abs.gov.au/ausstats/abs@.nsf/Lookup/by%20Subject/1288.0~Issue%20For%20Dec%202014~Main%20Features~Underlying%20Concepts~20, Downloaded 18 December 2017.

ABS (2015), *Household Income and Wealth, Australia, 2013–14,* Cat. No. 6523.0, http://www.abs.gov.au/AUSSTATS/abs@.nsf/DetailsPage/6523.02013-14?OpenDocument

ABS (2016) *Employee Earnings and Hours, Australia, May 2016*, Cat No. 6306.0, http://www.abs.gov.au/AUSSTATS/abs@.nsf/Lookup/6306.0Main+Features1May%202016?OpenDocument, downloaded 24 July 2017.

ABS (2017a), Characteristics of Employment, Australia, August 2016, Cat. No. 6333.0, ABS, Canberra http://www.abs.gov.au/ausstats/abs@.nsf/Latestproducts/6333.0Main%20Features6August%202016?opendocument&tabname=Summary&prodno=6333.0&issue=August%202016&num=&view,downloaded 10 August, 2017.

ABS (2017b) Labour Force, Australia, Nov 2017, Cat. No. 6202.0 (Trend data), ABS, Canberra, http://www.abs.gov.au/AUSSTATS/abs@.nsf/allprimarymainfeatures/3D6FA35FFE7566BACA258162001958A8?opendocument, downloaded 18 Dec 2017.

ABS (2017c), Labour Force, Australia, Detailed, Quarterly, Aug 2017, ABS, Canberra, http://www.abs.gov.au/AUSSTATS/abs@.nsf/DetailsPage/6291.0.55.003Aug%202017?OpenDocument, downloaded 18 Dec 2017

Australian Insurance Brokers (2013) *Workers' Compensation Australia*, http://www.aisinsurance.com.au/wp-content/uploads/2013/04/Summary-of-the-Australian-Workers-Compensation-System.pdf, downloaded 24 July 2017

Australian Government, Department of Human Services (2017), https://www.humanservices.gov.au/individuals/forms/su580.

Australian Super Funds Association (ASFA), 'Superannuation Statistics' August 2017, https://www.superannuation.asn.au/resources/superannuation-statistics

Australian Tax Office (2017a), Income and deductions for business, https://www.ato.gov.au/Business/Income-and-deductions-for-business/Assessable-income/

Australian Tax Office (2017, b) Tax on contributions, https://www.ato.gov.au/individuals/super/super-and-tax/tax-on-contributions/#Beforetaxsupercontributions, downloaded on 15 Dec 2017

Australian Tax Office (2017c), Super Guarantee Gap, https://www.ato.gov.au/About-ATO/Research-and-statistics/In-detail/Tax-gap/Superannuation-guarantee-gap/, downloaded 15 Dec 2017.

Australian Tax Office (2017d), New low income super tax offset, https://www.ato.gov.au/Individuals/Super/Super-changes/New-low-income-super-tax-offset-contribution/, downloaded 15 Dec 2017.

Campbell I (forthcoming), *On-call and related forms of casual work in New Zealand and Australia*, ILO Geneva.

Campbell, I., & Price, R. (2016). Precarious work and precarious workers: Towards an improved conceptualisation. *The Economic and Labour Relations Review*, *27*(3), 314-332.

Campbell I, Tham J-C and Boese M (2016/7) 'Inhospitable workplaces? International students and paid work in food services', *Australian Journal of Social Issues*. 51: 279–298.

Castles F. G. (1986), *The Working Class and Welfare: Reflections on the Political Development of the Welfare State in Australia and New Zealand, 1890-1980*, Sydney, Allen and Unwin

Charlesworth, S. and A. Heron (2012), New Australian working time minimum standards: Reproducing the same old gendered architecture? *Journal of Industrial Relations*, 54, 2, pp 164-181.

Commonwealth of Australia (2016), 'A husband is not a retirement plan': Achieving economic security for women in retirement, Report of Senate Standing Committees on Economics, 29 April 2016, Canberra.

Davidson, P. et al. (2018), Poverty in Australia, 2018, ACOSS/UNSW Poverty and Inequality Partnership Report No. 2, ACOSS, Sydney.

Deloitte Access Economics (2017) *Developments in the Collaborative Economy in NSW*. NSW Department of Finance, Services & Innovation Sydney, NSW, Australia: Deloitte Touche Tohmatsu.

Deeming, C. (2013), "The Working Class and Welfare: Francis G. Castles on the Political Development of the Welfare State in Australia and New Zealand Thirty Years On", *Social Policy & Administration*, 47, 6, pp. 668 – 691.

Department of the Treasury (2017), *2016 Tax Expenditures Statement*, Canberra.

Department of Employment (2017) Trends in Enterprise Bargaining, June quarter, p 11, from Australian Bureau of Statistics Employee Earnings and Hours, Cat. No. 6306.0 (May 2010, May 2012, May 2014, May 2016), unpublished data – all employees.

Department of Human Services (2017), *Definition of Income*, https://www.humanservices.gov.au/individuals/enablers/income

Department of Home Affairs (2015) T*emporary entrants in Australia (stock data) statistics, 31 December 2015*, Canberra. https://www.homeaffairs.gov.au/about/reports-publications/research-statistics/statistics/live-in-australia/temporary-entrants-in-australia

Department of Home Affairs (2017), Abolition and replacement of the 457 visa – Government reforms to employer sponsored skilled migration visas, https://www.homeaffairs.gov.au/Trav/Work/457-abolition-replacement.

Department of Innovation, Industry and Science (2016) *Independent Contractors: The essential Handbook,* Commonwealth of Australia.

Department of Social Services (2016) *Payment Demographic data*, https://data.gov.au/dataset/dss-payment-demographic-data.

Edelman Betrand for Upwork, August 2015 https://www.slideshare.net/upwork/freelancing-in-australia-2015, downloaded 22 July 2017.

Fair Work Ombudsman (2017), Fair Work Ombudsman and Registered Organisations Commission Entity Annual Report 2016 - 2017 (PDF 2MB).

Ferguson, A. and S. Danckert (2015), "Revealed: How 7-Eleven is Ripping of its Workers", Sydney Morning Herald, http://www.smh.com.au/interactive/2015/7-eleven-revealed/.

Healy J and Nicholson (2017), "The costs of a casual job are now outweighing any pay benefits", *The Conversation*, September 4, https://theconversation.com/the-costs-of-a-casual-job-are-now-outweighing-any-pay-benefits-82207.

Hernananz, V., F. Malherbet and M. Pellizzari, (2004), *Take-up of welfare benefits in OECD countries: a review of the evidence*, Organisation for Economic Co-operation and Development, Paris, March 2004.

Howe B, Munro P, Biddington J and Charlesworth S (2012) *Lives on Hold: Unlocking the Potential of Australia's Workforce*. The Report of the Independent Inquiry into Insecure Work in Australia. Melbourne: Studio Alto.

Ingles D and Stewart M (2015), *Superannuation tax concessions and the age pension: a principled approach to savings taxation,* Tax and Transfer Policy Institute, Australian National University, Canberra. https://taxpolicy.crawford.anu.edu.au/publication/ttpi-working-papers/7561/superannuation-tax-concessions-and-age-pension-principled.

Landau I, Cooney S, Hardy T and Howe J (2014) *Trade Unions and the Enforcement of Minimum Employment Standards in Australia,* Research Report, Centre for Employment and labour Relations Law, University of Melbourne

Lass, Inga; Wooden, Mark (2017) : The Structure of the Wage Gap for Temporary Workers: Evidence from Australian Panel Data, IZA Discussion Papers, No. 10670

Martin B., Baird M., Brady M., Broadway B., Hewitt B., Kalb G., Strazdins L., Tomaszewski W., Zadoroznyj M., Baxter J., Chen R., Foley M., McVicar D., Whitehouse G., and Xiang N. (2014) *Paid Parental Leave Evaluation: Final Report*, the University of Queensland commissioned by the Department of Social Services, Brisbane. https://www.dss.gov.au/sites/default/files/documents/03_2015/finalphase4_report_6_march_2015_0.pdf

McClure. P., Sinclair, S. and Aird, W. (2015), *A New System for Better Employment and Social Outcomes – Full version of the Final Report*, Department of Social Services, Canberra. https://www.dss.gov.au/review-of-australias-welfare-system

Minifie J (2016) *Peer-to-peer pressure: policy for the sharing economy*, The Grattan Institute, Melbourne.

OECD (2008), *Growing Unequal?: Income Distribution and Poverty in OECD Countries*, OECD Publishing, Paris, https://doi.org/10.1787/9789264044197-en.

OECD (2009), "Is Work the Best Antidote to Poverty?", in *OECD Employment Outlook 2009: Tackling the Jobs Crisis*, OECD Publishing, Paris, https://doi.org/10.1787/empl_outlook-2009-4-en.

OECD (2013), *How's Life? 2013: Measuring Well-being*, OECD Publishing, Paris, https://doi.org/10.1787/9789264201392-en.

OECD (2015a), *In It Together: Why Less Inequality Benefits All,* OECD Publishing, Paris, https://doi.org/10.1787/9789264235120-en.

OECD (2015b), *Focus on Minimum Wages after the Crisis*, http://www.oecd.org/social/Focus-on-Minimum-Wages-after-the-crisis-2015.pdf

OECD (2017a) *Real Minimum Wages*, https://stats.oecd.org/Index.aspx?DataSetCode=RMW, downloaded 24/08/2017

OECD (2017b), "Evolution of the tax burden (2000-16)" in *Taxing Wages 2017,* OECD, Paris, http://dx.doi.org/10.1787/tax_wages-2017-8-en, downloaded 24/08/2017.

OECD (2017c), *Foreign-born population*, http://dx.doi.org/10.1787/5a368e1b-en (Accessed on 11 September 2017).

OECD (2018), OECD Benefits and Wages: Statistics (database), http://www.oecd.org/els/benefits-and-wages-statistics.htm.

Oliver D, Stewart A, MacDonald P and Hewitt A (2016) Unpaid Work Experience: Prevalence nature and impact, commissioned by the Australian Department of Employment, Canberra.

https://docs.employment.gov.au/system/files/doc/other/unpaid_work_experience_report_-_december_2016.pdf.

Owens, R., Riley, J., & Murray, J. (2011). *The law of work.* Oxford University Press.

Productivity Commission (PC) (2015), *Workplace Relations Framework, Final Report*, Canberra.

Safe Work Australia (2016) *Comparison of workers' compensation arrangements in Australia and New Zealand,* Commonwealth of Australia.

Senate of Australia Economic References Committee (2017) 'Superbad – Wage theft and non-compliance of the Superannuation Guarantee: Report', Canberra.

Stewart, A., Forsyth, A., Irving, M., Johnstone, R., & McCrystal, S. (2016). *Creighton and Stewart's Labour Law*. The Federation Press.

Stewart, A., & Stanford, J. (2017). Regulating work in the gig economy: What are the options? *The Economic and Labour Relations Review, 28*(3), 420-437.

Stewart, M. and P. Whiteford, (2018), "Balancing Equity and Efficiency in the Tax and Transfer System" in R. Breunig and M. Fabian (Eds) *Hybrid Public Policy Innovations: Contemporary Policy Beyond Ideology,* Routledge.

Victorian Government (2016), Report of the *Victorian Inquiry into the Labour Hire Industry and Insecure Work*, Industrial Relations, Melbourne.

Watson, I. (2005). Contented Workers in Inferior Jobs? Re- Assessing Casual Employment in Australia. *The Journal of Industrial Relations*, *47*(4), 371-392.

Whiteford, P. (2010), 'The Australian tax-transfer system: architecture and outcomes', *Economic Record,* 86 (275), 528-544. Online ISSN: 1475-4932.

Whiteford P, (2017), Social Security and welfare spending in Australia: Assessing long-term trends Policy Brief no: 1/2017, Tax and Transfer Policy Institute, Crawford School of Public Policy, Australian National University, Canberra.

Whiteford, P. and W. Adema (2007), "What Works Best in Reducing Child Poverty: A Benefit or Work Strategy?", *OECD Social, Employment and Migration Working Papers*, No. 51, OECD Publishing, Paris. DOI: http://dx.doi.org/10.1787/233310267230.

Whiteford, P. and and G. Angenent (2002), *The Australian System of Social Protection: An Overview, 2nd Edition.* Department of Family and Community Services, Canberra, Occasional Paper No. 7, Canberra.

Whiteford, P. Millar J. and Mendelson M. (2003), Timing it right? Tax credits and how to respond to income changes, Joseph Rowntree Foundation, London.

Wilkins R (2017) 'Three charts on: Who holds more than one job to make ends meet?' The Conversation 18 September 2017, https://theconversation.com/three-charts-on-who-holds-more-than-one-job-to-make-ends-meet-83299 (downloaded on 14 Dec 2017)

Wooden, M. (2017), Has the level of casual employment in Australia stayed steady for the past 18 years? The Conversation, downloaded 23 July 2017.

Wright C.F. and Lansbury R. (2016) 'Employment Relations in Australia' in Bamber G.J., Lansbury R.D., Wailes N. and Wright C.F. (eds) (2016) *International and Comparative Employment Relations: National Regulation and Global Changes* (6th edition) Allen & Unwin/Sage: London

Wright C.F., Clibborn S., Piper N. and Cini N. (2016) *Economic Migration and Australia in the 21st Century*. Sydney: Lowy Institute for International Policy.

Chapter 3. Austria: How social protection rules affect self-employed and independent contractors

Marcel Fink and Wolfgang Nagl

The social protection of people in non-standard forms of employment has been a political issue in Austria since the mid-1990s. Non-standard workers have been integrated into the general social insurance system through a series of reforms, with the declared goal of preventing evasion from compulsory insurance and integrating all types of earned income from employment into social security. These reforms are likely to have contributed to a substantial reduction in the number of independent contractors. However, the number of self-employed tradespeople and of so-called "new self-employed" continued to rise and there are some indications that this to some degree compensated for the reduction in the number of independent contractors. Tradespeople and the new self-employed in most cases benefit from lower statutory insurance contributions than for those in standard dependent employment, which may imply a financial incentive to opt for these forms of employment. Furthermore, the lack of unemployment insurance coverage, in the case of self-employed people, and comparatively low employment stability and often low incomes, in the case of self-employed people and independent contractors, increase the likelihood that people in these types of employment later become (partly) dependent on tax-financed basic financial security.

3.1. Introduction

Over the past few decades new forms of work or types of non-standard employment have evolved in many developed countries (see Eurofound, 2015; ILO, 2016; OECD, 2015; Spasova et al., 2017). Among other things, this includes employment located between or on the borders between self-employment and dependent employment. The key objectives of this chapter are: 1) to show how such forms of work are embedded in the Austrian social protection system; 2) to analyse the characteristics and spread of these forms of employment over the past decade; and 3) to give some insights on incentives to take up such forms of employment and their likely consequences for public budgets.

The analysis concentrates on single-person businesses and independent or freelance contractors (*Freie Dienstnehmer*) and the inter-relation of the development of these new forms of work with the Austrian social protection system.

The chapter is structured as follows. Section 3.2 presents a brief overview on the legal definition of dependent employment, self-employment and independent or freelance contractors in Austria. Section 3.3 describes the institutional integration of the self-employed and independent contractors into social protection schemes in Austria. To examine the efficiency and effectiveness of the system, Section 3.4 analyses trends in the numbers of single-person businesses and independent contractors, the financial incentives to choose such contractual arrangements instead of dependent employment, the take-up of voluntary insurance schemes and possible additional costs for public budgets resulting from the growth of these forms of employment.

3.2. Definitions of self-employment and independent contractors/freelance contractors

The distinction between dependent employment and self-employment in Austria primarily derives from jurisdiction, with a number of different criteria defining the characteristics of a given activity. According to decisions[1] by the Austrian Supreme Administrative Court (Verwaltungsgerichtshof), the following characteristics are typical for a dependent employment relationship: restrictions on the employee's freedom of choice on how to implement the activity (a subordinate relationship between the employer and worker), an obligation to carry out the activity in person, reporting requirements, work equipment provided by the employer, performance of the activity at the premises of the customer, only one or a small number of clients/principals, being paid in exchange for time and endeavour (rather than for completion of a specific task) and restrictions on working for other customers (non-competition clauses). For an employment relationship to be defined as dependent employment not all of these criteria have to be met. The most important factor is the subordinate relationship between employer and worker, which is concerned with whether the employer/customer determines the working time, workplace, workflow etc.

In Austria the person performing the work and their customer or employer do not have a free choice as to whether they define their relationship as dependent or independent employment. It is the different social insurance providers and other public bodies up to the Supreme Administrative Court who can decide whether an employment relationship is classified as dependent or independent employment. The social insurance providers can examine the type of an employment relationship either on their own initiative or at the request of one or both of the contracting parties. Furthermore, since 2017 the assessment is carried out automatically when people register themselves as so-called "new self-employed" or as self-employed in specific fields of so-called "free crafts and trades" (*freie Gewerbe*), where there is no requirement for a training or specific authorisation.[2]

The largest number of self-employed people in Austria (outside farming) are so-called tradespeople (*Gewerbetreibende*). They fall under the Trade Regulation Act (*Gewerbeordnung*), hold a trade certificate (*Gewerbeschein*) and are – on a mandatory basis – registered with the Austrian Economic Chamber (*Wirtschaftskammer Österreich*), the association of Austrian businesses. Some of these self-employed have to prove that they have completed specific training in order to get licensed to perform so-called "qualified crafts and trades"[3] (*gebundene Gewerbe*), whereas for other activities – free crafts and trades[4] (*freie Gewerbe*) – no obligation exists for specific training or authorisation.

Other types of self-employed include the liberal professions professions[5], who are subject to their own specific regulations and mandatory membership of professional bodies, and the so-called "new self-employed" (*Neue Selbständige*). The latter perform self-employed tasks not mentioned in the Trade Regulation Act and without specific professional registration or regulation, for example as lecturers, artists, trainers, scientists and experts, journalists, writers and people who work independently in specific jobs in health care (nurses, midwives etc.). Overall, it appears that "new self-employment" is practised in a large variety of different tasks, offering a "low-threshold" opportunity to perform work on the margins of dependent employment and self-employment.

Independent or freelance contractors (*Freie Dienstnehmer*) represent a specific form of employment on the border between self-employment and dependent employment. Unlike the self-employed, independent contractors normally are not required to achieve a specific task; instead, like employees, they contribute their working time and effort. Yet, unlike normal employees, independent contractors face fewer restrictions in terms of their freedom of choice on how to perform the activity, e.g. in terms of working time, workplace, workflow etc. In other words, the subordinate relationship being typical of regular employment does not apply to independent contractors. Independent contractors are – as with the self-employed – not covered by most labour law regulations, and they have to arrange their own income tax payments (employers are obliged to withhold income taxes for their standard employees).[6]

3.3. Institutional setting: social protection schemes and self-employment / independent contractors

The Austrian welfare state provides highly developed social protection schemes for all major types of social risks. The system is characterised by a mix of social insurance benefits, universal benefits and services available to the entire resident population and some means-tested benefits granted based on documented financial need (see Table 3.1). The Federal Republic is responsible for most areas of social policy, including social insurance benefits und universal benefits. The regional entities, i.e. the federal provinces (*Bundesländer*) and local and municipal governments, have responsibilities for specific parts of health care, housing, different kinds of social services (childcare facilities, long-term care services etc.) and means-tested minimum income (MMI) schemes.[7]

The social protection of people in non-standard forms of employment has been a political issue in Austria since the mid-1990s (Tálos, 1999). Non-standard workers have been integrated into the general social insurance system through a series of reforms. Self-employed tradespeople registered according to the Trade Regulation Act have been covered by statutory pension insurance (including old-age pensions, invalidity and survivors' pensions) since the 1950s and by statutory health insurance and accident insurance since the 1960s. For new self-employed and independent contractors, statutory pension insurance, health-care and accident insurance was introduced in 1996. The declared goal of these reforms was to prevent people from evading compulsory insurance and to integrate all types of earned income from employment into social security (Tálos, 1999: 276).

In 2008, independent contractors were furthermore integrated into unemployment insurance and the severance pay scheme (so-called *Abfertigung neu*; see BMASK, 2016: 50). Since then, they have also had the right to receive sick pay.[8] And from January 2009, different types of self-employed people, including the new self-employed, have been able to opt in to unemployment insurance on a voluntary basis.

Table 3.1. Social protection coverage of self-employed and independent contractors by benefit type

Social risk/benefit scheme	Type of system	Coverage	
		Self-employed[1]	Independent contractors
Health: payment of medical costs	insurance based	yes	yes
Health: cash benefits	insurance based	partly/voluntary	yes
Old-age & survivors' pensions	insurance based plus means-tested minimum	yes	yes
Invalidity	insurance based plus means-tested minimum	yes	yes
Unemployment	insurance based	voluntary	yes
Maternity: non-cash & cash benefits	insurance based	yes	yes
Family benefits: family allowance	different types: universal & insurance based	yes	yes
Childcare services	universal (partly private co-payments and means-tested exemption from co-payments)	yes	yes
Long-term care: cash benefits	universal	yes	yes
Long-term care: payment of care costs	means tested	yes	yes
Minimum income[2]	means tested	yes	yes

1. Crafts- and tradespeople (*Gewerbetreibende*) and new self-employed.
2. Means-tested minimum income (*Bedarfsorientierte Mindestsicherung*) replaced benefits of earlier social assistance schemes from 2010 (see Fink, 2015).

Table 3.2. Compulsory social insurance contribution rates by employment type

2017

	Standard employees	Freelance/independent contractors	Self-employed: crafts-and tradespeople[1]	New self-employed[2]
Marginal earnings threshold[3]/Minimum contribution basis[4] EUR/month	425.70	425.70	Health insurance: 425.70[8] Pension insurance: 723.52	425.70
Maximum contribution basis EUR/month	4 980[5]	no special payments[6] agreed: 5 810 special payments agreed: 4 980	5 810	5 810
Contribution rate				
Health insurance	7.65% (Employer: 3.78%; Jobholder: 3.87%)	7.65% (Employer: 3.78%; Jobholder: 3.87%)	7.65%[7]	7.65%
Accident insurance	Employer: 1.3%	Employer: 1.3%	Flat rate EUR 9.33/month	Flat rate EUR 9.33/month
Pension insurance	22.8% (Employer: 12.55%; Jobholder: 10.25%)	22.8% (Employer: 12.55%; Jobholder: 10.25%)	18.5%	18.5%
Unemployment insurance	6.0% (Employer: 3.0%; Jobholder: 3.0%)	6.0% (Employer: 3.0%; Jobholder: 3.0%)	no compulsory insurance	no compulsory insurance
Insolvency Remuneration Fund[8]	Employer: 0.35%	Employer: 0.35%	-	-
Chamber of Labour Levy[9]	Jobholder: 0.5%	Jobholder: 0.5%	-	-
Economic Chamber Levy	-	-	Depending on turnover, the wage bill and social insurance contributions; often ca. EUR 200-400 min. per year[10]	-
Occupational pension fund[7]	Employer: 1.53%	Employer: 1.53%	1.53%	1.53%

1. Tradespeople registered with the Economic Chamber.
2. New self-employed not registered with the Economic Chamber.
3. The marginal earnings threshold (gross earnings/month) applies to standard workers and independent contractors. See text in this section for more details.
4. The minimum contribution basis applies to self-employed tradespeople and new self-employed. Tradespeople have to pay insurance contributions according to the minimum contribution basis even if actual earnings turn out to be lower than the minimum contribution basis. For new self-employed the minimum contribution basis also serves as a yearly marginal earnings threshold (EUR 425.70 x 12 = EUR 5 108.40), with no compulsory insurance in case of income from this type of employment below this level.
5, 6. Standard workers get two months of special payment per year. These special payments are also subject to social insurance contributions, up to the normal maximum monthly contribution basis (*Höchtbeitragsgrundlage*). Independent contractors may or may not be granted special payments, depending on agreement with their employer. In case of no special payment agreed, a higher maximum monthly contribution basis of EUR 5 810 applies (EUR 4 980 x 14/12 = EUR 5 810). The same maximum contribution basis also applies for tradespeople and for new self-employed.
7. For tradespeople newly registered with the Economic Chamber and starting a new business a flat-rate insurance contribution applies for health insurance during the first two years. It amounts to 7.65% of the minimum contribution basis (EUR 425.70), i.e. EUR 32.50 per month.
8. The Insolvency Remuneration Fund pays displaced workers any owed wages and other claims not covered by the insolvent firm's assets.

9. The Chamber of Labour represents the interests of Austrian Employees in the Austrian system of Social Partnership, including in collective bargaining. Membership is compulsory for all employees in Austria (membership in labour unions, in contrast, is voluntary).
10. The Economic Chamber Levy is calculated according to complex rules and differs according to turnover, wage bill, social insurance contributions and the actual profession performed. For single-person businesses only the so-called basic levy (*Grundumlage*) is relevant, calculated according to a flat-rate contribution and the social insurance contributions paid. The numbers given only provide a very rough estimate for single-person businesses.
Source: Main Association of Austrian Social Insurance Providers.

Both (standard) dependent employees and independent contractors are enrolled in the pension insurance, health insurance, accident insurance and unemployment insurance systems (Table 3.1). In contrast to standard employees, independent contractors have no right to the payment of wages when on sick leave but may receive a sickness benefit (*Krankengeld*) from the health insurance system from the fourth day of sickness.

Standard employment contracts and independent contracts with a gross monthly income below the marginal earnings threshold (*Geringfügigkeitsgrenze*) of EUR 425.70 in 2017[9] are – with the exception of accident insurance – not subject to statutory social insurance. This is called *marginal part-time employment*. However, workers reaching the marginal earnings threshold of compulsory health or pension insurance through a combination of several marginal part-time contracts or a combination with other insured income from gainful employment are liable for the same (employee) social insurance contributions as standard employees for health and pension insurance (14.12%, see Table 3.2).[10]

Companies employing several people on marginal part-time employment contracts have to pay a general social insurance contribution to health and pension insurance if the total wage bill for those people in marginal part-time employment exceeds 1.5 times the marginal earnings threshold.[11] This general social insurance contribution paid by the employer amounts to 16.4% of the contribution base. These rules were introduced in the late 1990s to reduce fiscal incentives for marginal part-time employment. Yet, insurance contributions for marginal part-time employment remain lower than for contracts with income above the marginal earnings threshold, as no unemployment insurance applies.

Both self-employed tradespeople and the new self-employed are covered by pension insurance, health insurance and accident insurance under the Act on the Social Security of Self-Employed Workers in Industry and Craft Trades (GSVG).[12] Furthermore, since January 2009 both types of self-employed have been able to opt in to unemployment insurance.

New self-employed and tradespeople pay the same health insurance contribution as dependent employees, and a flat-rate contribution for accident insurance (Table 3.2). Their pension contribution rate is 18.5% of earned gross income, substantially lower than that of dependent employees (22.8%). But since their pension benefits are calculated according to the same principles[13], their lower contribution rate does not imply lower pension benefits compared with dependent employment.

All active registered tradespeople have to pay insurance contributions for a contribution base of at least EUR 425.70 per month in health insurance, and of at least EUR 723.52 per month in pension insurance, regardless of their actual income. This means that for tradespeople, rules on marginal part-time employment do not apply. Their maximum contribution base is the same as the maximum contribution base of employees and independent contractors (see Table 3.2).

For the new self-employed, compulsory insurance begins once annual income from this type of self-employment exceeds the marginal earnings threshold of currently EUR 5 108.40.[14] This may only become evident when the income declaration is made for the preceding year. The compulsory insurance then starts on the date on which self-employment activities commenced – or, if that cannot be clearly determined, on 1 January of the year concerned. In other words, compulsory insurance may come into force retroactively. New self-employed may also declare that their income will exceed the marginal earnings threshold, and insurance then starts with this declaration. As a general principle, once they are insured, new self-employed remain insured even if their yearly income from self-employment later turns out to be lower than the marginal earnings threshold. To terminate the insurance, the (previously) self-employed person has to cease their activities or inform the social insurance provider that their income will be below the yearly marginal earnings threshold. Overall, this means that new self-employment may take the form of marginal self-employment not subject to compulsory insurance, an option not available to self-employed tradespeople.

Regarding health insurance, insured tradespeople and new self-employed generally have access to the same medical services as insured employees. However, unlike most types of employees, the self-employed normally have to pay a patient's contribution amounting to 20% of the cost of the health services obtained.

Regarding cash benefits from health insurance, the self-employed normally can only receive limited cash benefits in case of prolonged illness, payable from the 43rd day of work incapacity due to sickness. However, a voluntary supplementary insurance for sickness benefit is available to self-employed tradespeople and new self-employed (see Section 3.4.3 for more details). It provides an additional cash benefit to replace earned income during a short-term illness. This voluntary insurance can partly compensate for the fact that they are not entitled to the payment of wages when on sick leave, unlike normal employees.

Since 1 January 2009 self-employed tradespeople as well as new self-employed with health and pension insurance under the GSVG have been able to unemployment insurance (see also Section 3.4.3 below). However, the decision to do so has to be taken within six months of starting the business[15] and is then binding for eight years. Within this timeframe, the self-employed person cannot leave or join the public unemployment insurance system.

Contributions for this voluntary unemployment insurance are not explicitly tied to earnings but are chosen by those enrolling. There are three different options for levels of insurance contributions, corresponding to three different levels of benefits: the self-employed can choose a contribution base of 25%, 50% or 75% of the maximum contribution base.[16] The contribution rate is 6%, which is equal to that of employees and independent contractors (see Table 3.2). Rules on minimum insurance records for benefit access and maximum benefit duration are similar to those that apply to normal employees, and the income replacement rate is similar to that of dependent employees.

If someone combines labour income from several sources subject to compulsory insurance – e.g. insured dependent employment is combined with insured self-employment – then insurance contributions have to be paid on the sum of the income from different sources, but only up to the yearly maximum contribution base. If people are insured with more than one provider for health insurance, they can choose one of these as their provider of health services. In old-age insurance, different types of earned income (i.e. salaries, income from independent contracts and from self-employment as tradespeople or new self-employed) are registered in one common pension account, and insured periods spent in different types of employment are aggregated in one combined insurance history. This pension account (*Pensionskonto*) applies to most groups of people covered by statutory pension insurance, including farmers. The only major exceptions are civil servants and some liberal professions.

Regarding other social risks and social protection schemes (family benefits, maternity, long-term care) tradespeople, new self-employed and independent contractors have access to monetary benefits and/or social services according to largely similar rules as standard employees (see Table 3.1 and Fink, 2017 for more details).

This also applies to benefits from the means-tested minimum income (MMI) schemes, which are the responsibility of the nine federal provinces (see Fink 2015 for more details). MMI is granted on a means-tested basis, taking into account both earned income and assets, which largely have to be liquidated before MMI is granted. MMI can be granted if no earned income exists or can act as a top-up for low earned income. In fact, the latter is the case for the majority of benefit recipients of working age who do not have severe health issues. In principle, MMI may be granted as a top-up to income earned from any employment type. However, self-employed individuals reportedly often face problems in claiming MMI as a top-up, among other factors because their actual income situation is often difficult to assess or rather volatile. Empirical evidence on this issue is limited, but results by Bergmann et al. (2012: 109) on the socio-demographic composition of recipients of MMI indicate that only 0.2% of all recipients of MMI in 2012were self-employed at the same time. This is probably related to the fact that the means test generally requires business assets to be liquidated.

3.4. Quantitative development and assessment of effectiveness and efficiency

To provide insights about the efficiency and effectiveness of the social protection schemes for independent contractors and single-person businesses it is essential to discuss the quantitative development of these forms of employment over time. This section therefore describes how the numbers of independent contractors and one-person businesses have developed in Austria and what their socio-demographic characteristics and employment intensities are.[17] In this context, it also addresses the financial incentives to take up such forms of employment. In a second step, the section examines the integration of self-employed people into voluntary unemployment insurance and health insurance (the latter concerning cash sickness benefit), with a special focus on one-person business owners. Third, it elaborates on the (likely) consequences for public budgets.

3.4.1. Independent contractors

Numbers and characteristics of independent contractors

In 2016 there were 32 000 independent contractors in Austria (Figure 3.1). Their number steadily increased until 2007 but then started to drop and is currently at an all-time low. This pattern can partly be explained by new regulations that came into force on 1 January 2008.

Before 2008 independent contractors were only covered by the statutory health insurance, accident insurance and pension insurance. From 2008 they were integrated into the unemployment insurance scheme and became liable for contributions to the Chamber of Labour as well as the Insolvency Remuneration Fund, on the same basis as dependent employees (Table 3.2). They were also integrated into the statutory severance pay scheme (*Abfertigung neu*), implying an employer contribution of 1.53 % of gross income. This reform appears to have contributed to reducing the number of independent contractors.

Compared with dependent employees, independent contractors are more likely to be female (62% of independent contractors vs. 48% of dependent employees, Figure 3.2), young (51% of independent contractors are aged 34 and under, compared with 38% of dependent employees) and to be foreign citizens (19% of independent contractors are not Austrian citizens, compared with 15% of dependent employees, not shown). They are also more likely to work in the service sector (95% vs. 81% of standard employees, not shown).

Independent contractors have a relatively high level of formal education. The majority have completed a tertiary education (53% compared with 33% of all dependent employees) and very few completed only lower secondary education (8% compared with 13% among all employees, Figure 3.2). Also, a large share of independent contractors works in the occupational group of professionals[18] (40%), compared with only 16% of independent employees.

The vast majority of independent contractors work part time, a tendency that has been increasing over the past decade. In 2004 nearly 30 % of independent contractors worked full time whereas in 2016 fewer than 20 % did so (see Figure 3.1). The prevalence of part-time work also increased among all dependent employees, but remains much smaller.

Figure 3.1. The number of independent contractors is at its all-time low

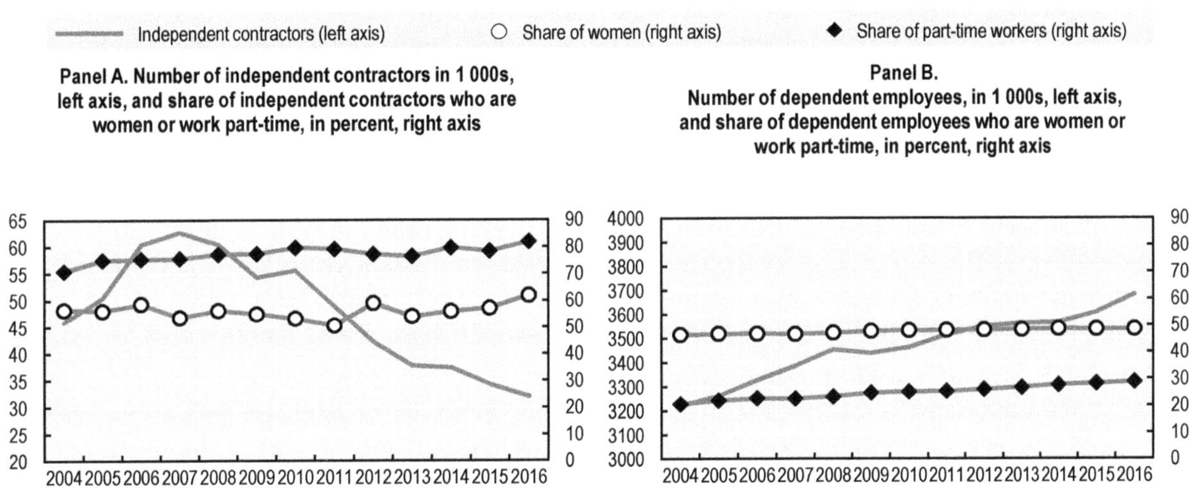

Source: Austrian Component of the European Labour Force Survey.

Figure 3.2: Independent contractors are on average better educated than dependent employees

Independent contractors and dependent employees by educational attainment, 2016, in percent

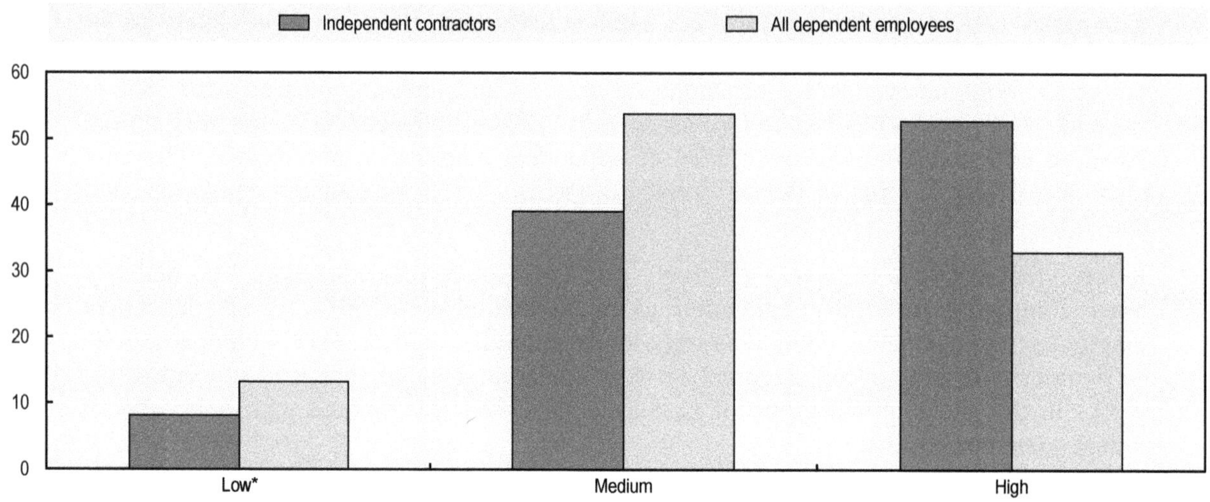

Notes: * The share of the low-skilled independent contractors cannot be statistically interpreted because it results from a sample with fewer than 3 000 projected individuals. Low education refers to ISCED levels 0-2, medium to ISCED 3-4 and high to ISCED 5-8. The Austrian Component of the European Labour Force Survey is collected as part of the Austrian Micro Census survey.
Source: Austrian Component of the European Labour Force Survey.

Independent contractors' length of service within a firm is rather short, indicating high turnover. Nearly half of all independent contractors in 2016 had a length of service of less than two years within their firm, compared with 27% of dependent employees. About 35% had been with their firm for under a year, compared with 16% among dependent employees (LFS, not shown).

According to registry data, about two-thirds of independent contractors have a contract with income below the social insurance marginal earnings threshold of EUR 425.70 per month in 2017 – that is, they are in marginal part-time employment, which does not provide statutory insurance (see Section 3.3). This share remained largely stable over the last decade. In contrast, only 9 % of all dependent employees are marginal part-timers.[19]

In 2015, around one-third of all marginally employed independent contractors also had a fully insured main job, 17 % were retirees and about 7 % received unemployment benefit (it is possible to combine most benefits with marginal part-time work). The remaining 40 % were not covered by an individual[20] social insurance through a main job or benefit receipt (Figure 3.3).[21]

Overall the situation appears to be more problematic for women than men. For women, marginal employment in the form of an independent contract is much more often their sole employment status than is the case for men. In 2015 about 45 % of all women with a marginal independent contract have no other form of employment other than independent contracts, whereas this is the case for only about one-third of men with marginal independent contracts (Haydn, 2016).

Figure 3.3: The majority of *marginal* independent contractors are otherwise insured

Breakdown of independent contractors earning less than the lower earnings limit by insurance status, as of 1 July 2015, in percent

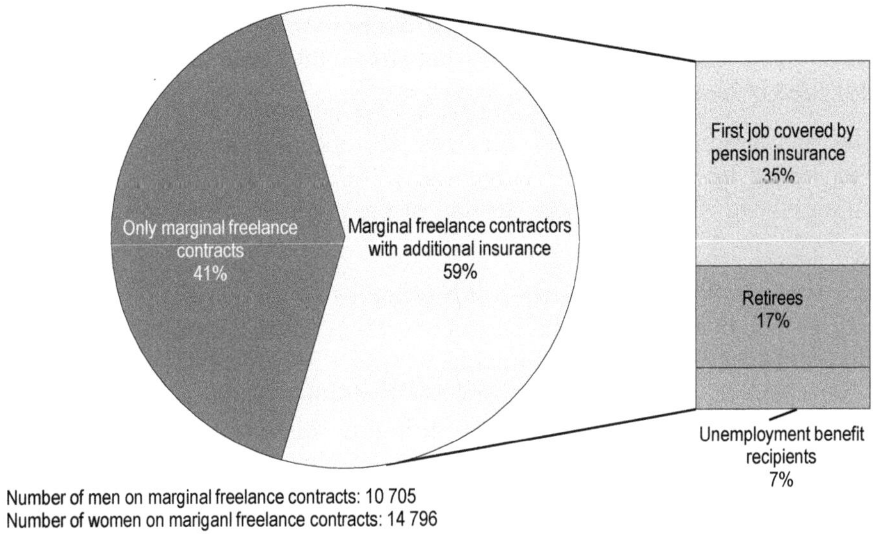

Note: The marginal earnings threshold was EUR 425.7 per month in 2017. Earnings below this limit are not subject to statutory social insurance.
Source: Austrian Main Association of the Social Insurance Providers, Haydn (2016).

Assessment of financial incentives

Since 2008 independent contracts have been treated in the same way as standard employment contracts in terms of social insurance. Since 2008 independent contracts no longer offer any possibilities to avoid social insurance contributions and other levies (see above Table 3.2).

However, by using independent contracts, employers can still reduce or even completely avoid many direct and indirect costs deriving from labour law regulations., In contrast to regular employees, independent contractors are not subject to collective agreements (including regulations on minimum wages), not entitled to holiday pay and continued payment of wages during sick leave and also not covered by standard-working time regulations. Furthermore, regulations on dismissal protection do not apply. Hence, defining an employment relationship as an independent contract seems to be more beneficial for the employer than the employee.

More rigorous checks by the social insurance providers on whether independent contractors are de facto regular employees are also likely to have contributed to the fall in the number of independent contracts. Social insurance providers are interested in correctly identifying dependent employees, partly because independent contractors are entitled to cash benefits from the fourth day of illness, while employers have to continue wage payments for sick employees for 10 to 16 weeks, depending on length of service with the employer.

The 2008 reform, making independent contracts costlier for employers, may have led to a reduction in the number of freelance contracts, but at the same time contributed to a rise in the number of both single-person businesses of tradespeople and new self-employed. These forms of employment are analysed in the following section.

3.4.2. Single-person businesses

Numbers and characteristics of single-person businesses

In 2016, 280 000 people ran a single-person business in Austria. These include all self-employed people without employees, as well as the new self-employed (see Section 3.2). While this number increased by about 8% between 2004 and 2016, the increase was uneven and lagged behind overall employment growth.

However, in the manufacturing and services sectors, the number of single-person businesses increased by 27 800 or 17% between 2007 and 2010 alone. This substantial increase coincides with the start of the decline in the number of independent contractors (Figure 3.1).

Overall, there was a shift in the sectoral composition of single-person businesses towards services: the share of single-person businesses operating in the agricultural sector dropped from 40% in 2004 to 27% in 2016 (compared with just 3% of total employment). At the same time, the share of single-person businesses operating in the service sector steadily increased from 50% in 2004 to 64% in 2016, bringing this more in line with the overall share of workers in services (71%).

About 60% of all single-person business owners are men, but the number of female single-business owners has been rising in recent years (Figure 3.4). Single-person business owners are somewhat better educated than other workers: over 40% have a university degree, compared with around 34% of all workers. They are also older: in 2016, 60% were over the age of 45 (total employment: 42%) and only 17% were younger than 35 (total employment: 35%).

Foreign citizens are somewhat less likely to run a single-person business than Austrian citizens (12% of single-business owners do not have Austrian citizenship, compared with 15% of all workers).

Most single-person business owners work full time (see Figure 3.4). The overall share of single-person business owners who worked part time was 31% in 2016 but there was a marked difference between the genders, with 48% of female business owners working part time compared with only 19% of male business owners. The part-time employment rate among all workers is very similar for women (47%) but considerably lower for men (11%). For both genders the share of part-time single-person business owners has increased over time. In 2004 it was 8% for men and 26% for females. A similar trend is also evident for total employment, where the part-time share in 2004 stood at 5% for men and 28% for women.

Figure 3.4: The number of single-person business is growing tentatively

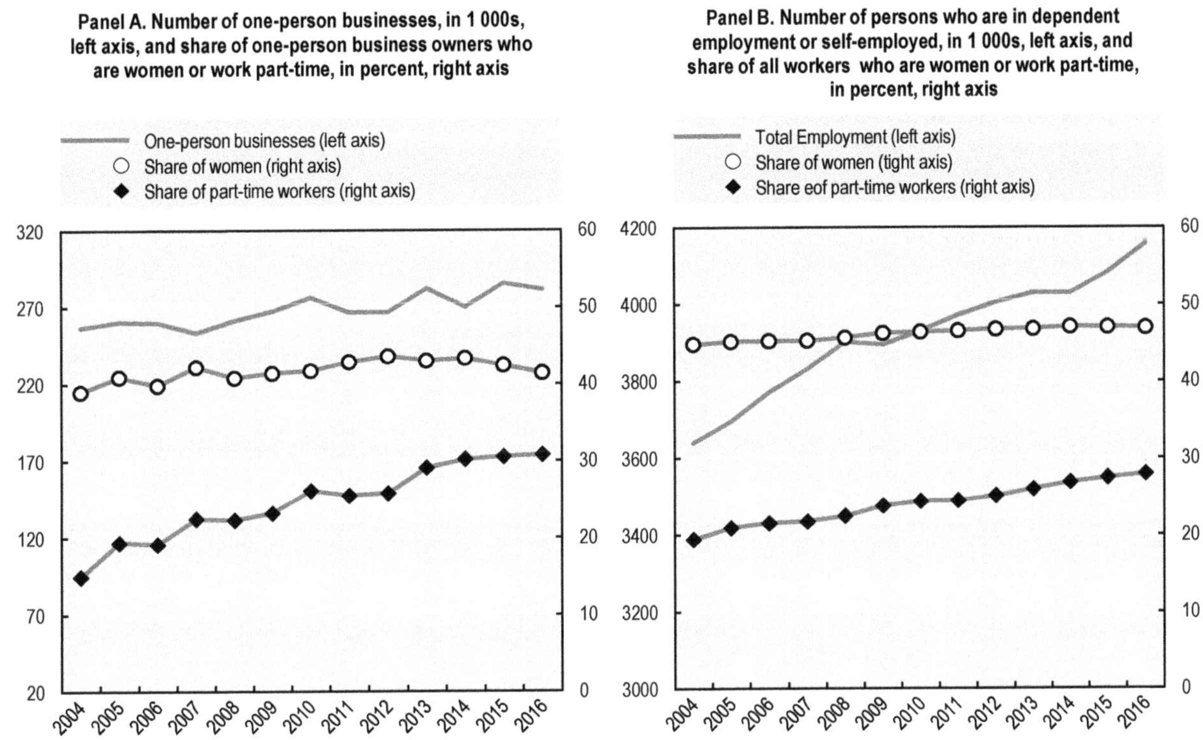

Source: Austrian Component of the European Labour Force Survey.

The survey data on one-person business owners presented above includes different types of self-employed people registered according to the Trade Regulation Act (i.e. single-person businesses of trades- and craftspeople), farmers, self-employed people in the liberal professions and the new self-employed (see Section 3.2).

According to the membership statistics of the Economic Chamber, the number of one-person businesses of trades- and craftspeople increased from about 183 000 in 2006 to about 305 000 in 2016 (see Figure 3.5) These data relate to the number of companies rather than people, and one person can run several single-person businesses. In 2016, around 52.1 % of all registered single-person businesses of trades- and craftspeople were owned by women.

In 2008 and 2009 there was a particularly pronounced increase in the number of one-person businesses of trades- and craftspeople was especially pronounced, with their numbers rising by around 19 100 (about 10%) in 2008 and around 20 300 (a further 10%) in 2009. This coincided with the period of decline in the number of independent contractors after the social security reform described above.

Results from a recent survey of registered tradespeople indicate that 58% of single-person businesses were exclusively self-employed and owned only one business (Dörflinger et al., 2017: 33), 10% owned more than one business and 24% were also dependent employees, while 6% were simultaneously receiving a pension and 5% combined business ownership with other situations. This is largely in line with earlier analyses of tax registry data, showing that around 25% of all single-person business owners (for whom data were available) were at the same time in dependent employment or receiving a pension (Lukawetz et al., 2015: 14).

Some more specific data are also available on the new self-employed. According to calculations by the Federal Ministry of Labour, Social Affairs and Consumer Protection their number increased from around 36 500 in 2006 to 49 500 in 2016 (see Figure 3.5). The growth in their numbers of around 3% per year in 2008 and 2009 was less pronounced than for single-person businesses of trades- and craftspeople (Figure 3.5).

The majority of the new self-employed are men, but the share of women increased from 39.3 % in 2004 to 45.5 % in 2016.

Figure 3.5. The number of single-person business of trades- and craftspeople and of "new self-employed" increases progressively

Number of single-person businesses of registered trades- and craftspeople, in 1 000s, left axis, and number of "new self-employed", in 1 000s, right axis, 2006-2016

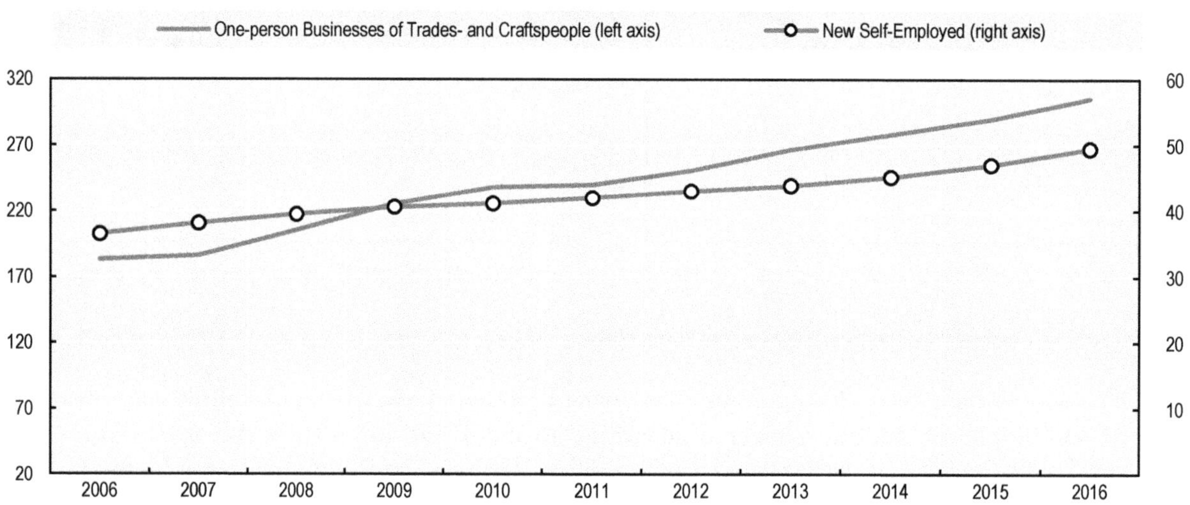

Source: Member statistics of the Austrian Economic Chamber (*Wirtschaftskammer Österreich*) and Austrian Ministry of Labour, Social Affairs and Consumer Protection (2017)

Unfortunately, there are no data on how long one-person businesses survive but data on years of activity are available (see Figure 3.6). About half of one-person business owners have been in business for over ten years but a relatively large number of business owners have been in operation for only one or two years, while only 15.8 % have been in activity for between two and five years. This suggests that many owners halt operations in the early years of business.

Figure 3.6. Many single businesses do not survive the first years of business

Breakdown of single person businesses by the number of years the business has existed, in percent, 2016

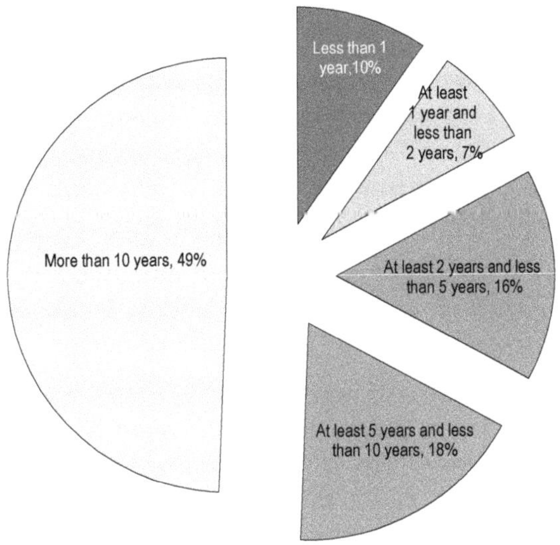

Source: Austrian Component of the European Labour Force Survey.

The earned income of single-person businesses has not been extensively analysed in Austria (see Lukawetz et al., 2015). However, tax and social insurance registry data indicate that comparatively low earned income is a more common phenomenon in self-employment than in dependent employment. The yearly pre-tax median income of people who are exclusively self-employed amounted to EUR 11 388 in 2013. Some 25% had an income below EUR 4 197 and 25% an income exceeding EUR 27 137. The average yearly income amounted to EUR 24 597 (Rechnungshof, 2016: 319). When compared with people with earned income exclusively from dependent employment, self-employment shows a substantially lower median income and a higher incidence of very low earned income. The median "adjusted"[22] earned income of people exclusively engaged in dependent employment (including apprenticeships) amounted to EUR 20 116 in 2013, with 25% having an income below EUR 8 616 and 25% an income of over EUR 31 599. The average yearly income was EUR 23 684 (ibid., 320).

Results by Lukawetz et al. (2015: 89), derived from pooled data from EU-SILC 2011-2014, show that the yearly median equivalised per head net household income of people running a single-person business of EUR 22 716 is substantially lower than of people in dependent employment (EUR 25 372). Furthermore, 13.8% of single-person business owners are regarded as being at risk of poverty, compared with 7.4% for dependent employees.[23]

Assessment of financial incentives

When compared with standard dependent employment and also with freelance contracts, some initial financial incentives exist in Austria to take up self-employment as a registered tradesperson and especially in the form of new self-employment. For standard dependent employment with income above the minimum earnings threshold, social insurance contributions and other relevant levies (excluding income tax) amount to slightly over 40% of gross income, compared with 28% for new self-employed and a starting rate of around 29% for crafts- and tradespersons, although this may be somewhat higher, depending on the Economic Chamber Levy (see Section 3.3, Table 3.2).

On the other hand – and in contrast to standard dependent employment, independent contracts and new self-employment – for tradespeople there is no marginal income threshold for statutory social insurance. That is, they have to pay social insurance contributions on the minimum contribution basis, even if actual earnings are lower (see Section 3.3, Table 3.2). This reduces financial incentives to choose this form of employment. Moreover, if the self-employed opt in to voluntary unemployment insurance and the short-term sick-pay scheme, they face largely similar overall social security contribution rates as dependent employees (see Section 3.4.3).

But for employers, opting for a contract with a self-employed worker instead of hiring an employee means that standard labour law regulations do not apply and that costs for social insurance can be transferred to the self-employed person.

If and to what degree the increase of registered single-person businesses and of new self-employed is caused by a rise in bogus self-employment is a contested issue in Austria, with limited empirical evidence. Yet, a study by Danzer et al. (2014) on single-person businesses in different sectors came to the conclusion that for up to 40% of those interviewed, there were several indications that self-employed status could be called into question. And according to estimates by the Trade Union of Private Sector Employees (GPA), about two-thirds of all new self-employed and freelance contractors would be classified as standard employees, if the legal definitions were implemented properly.[24] In contrast, the Economic Chamber rejects such interpretations and argues that the increasing number of single-person businesses is a result of the shift towards a more knowledge-based economy, with single-person businesses playing a key role as innovators (see e.g. WKÖ, 2017a; WKÖ, 2017b).

3.4.3. Integration of the self-employed into voluntary insurance

Unemployment insurance

Since January 2009 self-employed tradespeople and the new self-employed insured in health and pension insurance under the GSVG have the opportunity to opt in to unemployment insurance within six months of starting their self-employment.[25] Once a decision is made, it is binding for eight years. Self-employed people are not allowed to leave or join the public unemployment insurance scheme during this period.

The number of self-employed people entitled to opt in to the public unemployment insurance scheme has been limited. In 2015 around 43 500 self-employed, most of them single-person businesses, would have had the opportunity to join voluntary unemployment insurance[26], equivalent to around 11% of active self-employed people insured under the GSVG.[27] But out of these 43 500, only 117 (or 0.3 %) opted in to voluntary unemployment insurance. Take-up rates for multiple-person business owners are slightly higher than average, but still extremely low (2015: 0.7%). The take-up rate of one-person business owners was just 0.2 % in the same year. The extremely low take-up rates have been largely constant over time, resulting in only 867 self-employed people being covered by voluntary unemployment insurance in 2015 (yearly average), only 0.22% of the total number (yearly average) of active self-employed insured under the GSVG. Furthermore, two thirds of the few people who opt in to the unemployment insurance scheme choose the lowest possible level of insurance contributions (see Section 3.3).

Health insurance

Within the statutory public health insurance for self-employed, sick pay is only paid from the 43rd day of sickness. To cover the possible substantial period of sickness without income there is the possibility of a voluntary supplementary insurance granting sick pay from the fourth day of sickness. The contribution rate is 2.5 % of the individual assessment base (i.e. the earned income), up to the maximum contribution base, with a minimum contribution of EUR 30.77 per month. The daily sick-pay payment is generally 60% of actual daily income. Earlier, a minimum daily benefit of EUR 29.23 was granted, which was then reduced to EUR 8.51 a day in January 2017. For all insured self-employed people with an income below EUR 1 461.50 per month this reform involves a reduction in benefit levels. And for self-employed people with an income below EUR 1 230.80 the new regulation involves an increase in the contribution rate. The contributions paid are unchanged at EUR 30.77 a month, but for this group the daily benefits in case of sickness now vary between EUR 8.51 and EUR 24.62.

Out of around 407 700[28] active self-employed insured under the GSVG (tradespeople and new self-employed) in 2016, only about 30 850 or 7.6% were insured within the supplementary health insurance scheme. The majority of voluntarily insured people are women with low incomes. Of the 20 743 insured females, 90% were paying the minimum contribution, indicating a monthly income below EUR 1 230.80. The share of minimum contributors is much smaller for males, at 48% of the 10 105 insured, but it is still very significant. Due to the legal situation prevailing until 2017, these high shares are not unexpected. Accordingly, one might presume that the total numbers of voluntary supplementary insured people and the number of minimum contributors will decline in the future due to the now significantly reduced benefits for low-income earners, who still have to pay the same contributions as before the reform.

The share of voluntarily insured self-employed people who receive sick-pay benefits is quite substantial. About 45% of the voluntarily insured in 2016 received benefits from supplementary health insurance at least once a year. There is also a gender gap in the take-up of benefits: 53% of voluntarily insured women received sick-pay benefits at least once a year, whereas only 30% of voluntarily insured men did.

On average 21.5 days of sick pay were granted in 2016 per self-employed person covered by voluntary health insurance. The number is substantially higher in the case of women (26 days) than in case of men (14.5 days). Statistics for people in dependent employment indicate a lower average number of annual days of sick leave per employed person of 12.5 days in 2016 (men: 12.1 days; women: 13 days) (Statistik Austria, 2018).

Consequences for the public budget

The public budget might face an additional burden from the growth of new forms of work if it is more likely for people working in these new forms to become dependent on tax-financed basic financial security. What is relevant in this context is the issue of coverage by social insurance, the level of social insurance contributions, stability of employment and the level of (earlier) earned income.

As previously mentioned, independent contractors in Austria are integrated into the unemployment, health and pension insurance schemes according to similar rules as regular employees. However, in contrast to regular employees, most of the independent contractors work part time in the form of marginal part-time employment, with income below the marginal earnings threshold for statutory social insurance and are for this reason not fully integrated into social insurance in relation to their work as independent contractors.

Furthermore, they are still missing out on other benefits, such as paid holiday and advantageously taxed 13th and 14th monthly wage payments, have less labour law protection and are not covered by collective agreements. This, together with widespread marginal part-time employment, is likely to translate into lower incomes for independent contractors, compared with regular employees.

Comparatively low earned incomes, discontinuous employment and gaps in social insurance coverage are likely to cause subsequent problems in accessing social insurance benefits or comparatively low benefit levels. Thus, in times of unemployment and in old age (previously) independent contractors might face a higher risk of having to rely on other sources of household income or needing top-up benefits from tax-financed basic financial assistance schemes. Yet, there are currently no empirical studies on this topic specifically addressing independent contractors.

When compared with regular employees, a higher financial burden for public insurance providers for independent contractors derives from the fact that they receive short-term sick pay from social insurance, as independent contractors are not entitled to the payment of wages during sick leave. However, more detailed data on this issue are not available.

Access to social insurance schemes for self-employed people appears to be rather high in Austria in comparison with some other countries (Spasova et al., 2017). They are, in principle, covered by health and pension insurance, and can opt in to public insurance against the risk of unemployment and for (short-term) cash benefits in case of illness.

Regarding pension insurance, the contribution rate paid by the self-employed is lower than for regular employees and freelance contractors. However, pension benefits are calculated according to the same formula as for these groups, which might create incentives to opt for self-employment, and which implies higher co-financing of the pensions of the former self-employed from the state budget.

Income from self-employment is often relatively low in Austria, compared with standard dependent employment. This is likely to translate in to low old-age pensions. Very low old-age pensions derived from a person's insurance record are topped up to a quasi-minimum pension in Austria via the so-called equalisation supplement (*Ausgleichszulage*). The latter is financed from taxation and therefore involves additional spending from the federal public budget.

Furthermore, as sketched out above, only a very small minority of the self-employed opt in to unemployment insurance. Data on the years of activity of single-person businesses indicate that many of them halt operations in the first years of business. This might lead to reliance on benefits from tax-financed minimum income schemes if a person becomes unemployed after their period of self-employment. However, no clear empirical evidence exists on whether this is actually the case.

The new self-employed are treated as a distinct group by the social insurance system, as this form of employment may be performed as marginal employment with no social insurance contributions being paid up to a yearly income of EUR 5 108.40, even if it is combined with dependent employment, which is not the case for marginal part-time employment as an employee or independent contractor. However, no clear evidence exists on the budgetary effect of this exemption from compulsory social insurance.

3.5. Conclusions

Over the past few decades substantial attempts have been made in Austria to increase coverage and close social insurance gaps for different types of self-employed people and independent contractors.

This is likely to have contributed to a substantial reduction in the number of people employed as independent contractors. However, the number of self-employed tradespeople and new self-employed continued to rise and there are some indications that this to some degree compensated for the reduction in the number of independent contractors.

Those working as tradespeople and new self-employed in most cases benefit from lower insurance contributions for statutory insurance than for those in standard dependent employment. This is caused by lower contribution rates for pension insurance and exemption from statutory unemployment insurance, which may imply a financial incentive to opt for these forms of employment.

Voluntary unemployment insurance, available for active self-employed people insured under the GSVG, shows extremely low rates of coverage. The same applies to voluntary insurance for short-term sick-pay benefits, which could partly compensate for the fact that they are not entitled to the payment of wages when on sick leave, unlike normal employees. Overall, this indicates that voluntary insurance does not appear to be an effective measure in Austria, which may be caused by often volatile and low income from newly established small businesses and the aim to avoid additional fixed costs.

The lack of unemployment insurance coverage, in the case of self-employed people, and comparatively low employment stability and often low incomes, in the case of self-employed people and independent contractors, increase the likelihood that people in these types of employment later become (partly) dependent on tax-financed basic financial security. However, there is little concrete evidence on this problem at the time of writing and this would have to be examined in more detail by further research.

Notes

1 See, for example, the decision by the Supreme Administrative Court of 22 February 2006, Zl. 2005/09/0012, https://www.ris.bka.gv.at/Dokument.wxe?Abfrage=Vwgh&Dokumentnummer=JWT_2005090012_20060222X00

2 For details see: Sozialversicherungs-Zuordnungsgesetz – SV-ZG 2017, https://www.parlament.gv.at/PAKT/VHG/XXV/I/I_01613/index.shtml#tab-Uebersicht

3 The Trade Regulation Act (§94) lists 75 qualified crafts and trades. See https://www.ris.bka.gv.at/GeltendeFassung.wxe?Abfrage=Bundesnormen&Gesetzesnummer=10007517

4 Tasks not reserved to the qualified crafts and trades may be performed as free crafts and trades. The Federal Ministry of Economic Affairs publishes a (non-exhaustive) list of free crafts and trades (see: BMFWF 2017). Applicants, registering a business, may however "invent" new free crafts and trades, if they do not offer tasks reserved for qualified crafts and trades.

5 Lawyers, notaries, architects, civil engineers, accountants, pharmacists and physicians.

6 In tax law, income from freelance contracts is treated as income from self-employment.

7 For a more detailed overview see BMASK (2016).

8 This reform increased health insurance contributions 0.55 percentage points, harmonising their contribution rate with that of standard employees.

9 The figure is subject to annual indexation.

10 Since the late 1990s, persons in marginal part-time employment may also opt in to health insurance and pension insurance if no compulsory insurance applies. The monthly costs of opting in to health and pension insurance is currently (2017) EUR 60.09 per month. In effect, this option creates a very low-cost opportunity to obtain health insurance and contribution periods for pension insurance.

11 The threshold is 1.5 x EUR 425.70 = EUR 638.55.

12 See https://www.ris.bka.gv.at/GeltendeFassung.wxe?Abfrage=Bundesnormen&Gesetzesnummer=10008422.

13 For both groups the level earnings for which insurance contributions have been paid (the so-called assessment base) is constitutive for the level of pension benefit, but not the actual contribution rate.

14 This income limit is equal to the monthly marginal earnings threshold for standard workers and independent contractors (EUR 425.70) multiplied by 12 (months); see above on marginal part-time employment and Table 3.2.

15 Active self-employed people who had started their business before 1 January 2009 had the opportunity to opt in to unemployment insurance during the whole of 2009.

16 A monthly contribution of EUR 87.15 corresponds to a daily unemployment benefit of EUR 23.36 (option 1); a monthly contribution of EUR 174.30 equates to a daily unemployment benefit of EUR 37.42 (option 2); and a monthly contribution of EUR 261.45 yields a daily unemployment benefit of EUR 51.74 (option 3) in 2017.

[17] If not indicated otherwise all presented data in this subsection are calculated using the Austrian component of the European Labour Force Survey.

[18] According to the ISCO 08 classification the occupational group of professionals consists of: science and engineering professionals; health professionals; teaching professionals; business and administration professionals; information and communications technology professionals; legal, social and cultural professionals.

[19] Source: Main Association of Austrian Social Insurance Providers; http://www.dnet.at/elis/Arbeitsmarkt.aspx

[20] Regarding health insurance, these people may be co-insured with family members covered by statutory insurance. It is estimated that about 98% of the people living in Austria are covered by public health insurance (see Fuchs 2009 and https://www.gesundheit.gv.at/gesundheitssystem/gesundheitswesen/gesundheitssystem).

[21] This to a large degree resembles the situation of marginal employment of normal employees. However, a somewhat lower share (24%) of this group also had a fully insured first job and a higher share (11%) received unemployment benefit (see Haydn, 2016: 68).

[22] To make gross income of people in dependent employment comparable with that of the self-employed, the figures for those in dependent employment are adjusted by deducting social insurance contributions from gross income (see Rechnungshof 2016, 171).

[23] At-risk-of poverty threshold: 60% of the median of the national equivalised per head net household income.

[24] See: https://www.watchlist-prekaer.at/

[25] People who were self-employed before 2009 had the possibility to opt in until the end of 2009.

[26] The data on self-employed people entering voluntary unemployment insurance is collected from various parliamentary inquiries with answers from the Federal Minister of Labour, Social Affairs and Consumer Protection. Data source: registry data by the Hauptverband der Österreichischen Sozialversicherungsträger.

[27] In 2015, 397 504 active self-employed people were insured for health insurance under the GSVG (yearly average); Source: Hauptverband der Österreichischen Sozialversicherungträger (2017, Table 2.08).

[28] Yearly average. Source: Hauptverband der Österreichischen Sozialversicherungsträger (2017, Table 2.08).

References

Austrian Ministry of Labour, Social Affairs and Consumer Protection (2017). Entwicklung der atypisch Erwerbstätigen http://www.dnet.at/elis/Arbeitsmarkt.aspx retrieved 24/10/2017

Bergmann, Nadja/Andreas Riesenfelder/Claudia Sorger (2012). Auswirkung der Einführung der Bedarfsorientierten Mindestsicherung auf die Wiedereingliederung der LeistungsbezieherInnen ins Erwerbsleben [*Impact of the introduction of needs-based minimum income support on the reintegration of benefit recipients into working life*], Vienna, http://www.lrsocialresearch.at/files/EB_Evaluierung_BMS_(23).pdf.

BMASK (Federal Ministry of Labour, Social Affairs and Consumer Protection) (2016). The Austrian Welfare State. Benefits, expenditure and financing 2016, Vienna, https://www.sozialministerium.at/cms/site/attachments/2/8/0/CH3434/CMS1485938122480/the-austrian-welfare-state2016.pdf.

BMFWF (2017). Bundeseinheitliche Liste der Freien Gewerbe [*Nationwide list of free trades and crafs*], Vienna, https://www.bmdw.gv.at/Unternehmen/Gewerbe/Documents/Bundeseinheitliche_Liste_der_freien_Gewerbe.pdf

Dörflinger, Céline/Karin Gavac/Kerstin Hölzl/Sascha Ruhland/Doris Schmoller (2017). Ein-Personen-Unternehmen (EPU) in Österreich. Monitoringbericht 2016/17 [One-person-companies in Austria. Monitoring Report 2016/17], Vienna.

Eurofound (2015), New forms of employment, Luxembourg, Publication Office of the European Union, https://www.eurofound.europa.eu/sites/default/files/ef_publication/field_ef_document/ef1461en.pdf

Fink, Marcel (2015). ESPN Thematic Report on minimum income schemes, Austria, 2015, European Commission, Brussels, http://ec.europa.eu/social/BlobServlet?docId=15098&langId=en

Fink, Marcel (2017). ESPN Thematic Report on Access to social protection of people working as self-employed or on non-standard contracts, Austria, European Commission, Brussels, http://ec.europa.eu/social/BlobServlet?docId=17684&langId=en

Hauptverband der Österreichischen Sozialversicherungsträger (Main Association of Austrian Social Insurance Providers) (2017). Statistisches Handbuch der österreichischen Sozialversicherung 2017 [Statistical Manual of Austrian Social Security 2017], Vienna, http://www.sozialversicherung.at/cdscontent/load?contentid=10008.555191&version=1507639741

Haydn, Reinhard (2016). Personenbezogene Statistiken 2015 [Person-related Statistics 2015], in: Soziale Sicherheit, 2/2016, 65-74.

ILO (International Labour Organization) (2016). Non-standard employment around the world, Understanding challenges, shaping prospects, Geneva, http://www.ilo.org/wcmsp5/groups/public/---dgreports/---dcomm/---publ/documents/publication/wcms_534326.pdf

Lukawetz, Gerhard/Andreas Riesenfelder/Lisa Danzer (2015). Demographie und Sozialstatistik von EPU/Solo-Selbstständigen [*Demographics and Social Statistics of One-Person-Businesses / Solo Self-employed*], Vienna, https://www.sozialministerium.at/cms/site/attachments/1/2/9/CH3434/CMS1453735536682/focus_1_epu-grundlagenforschung_endbericht_final.pdf.

OECD (2015), *In It Together: Why Less Inequality Benefits All*, OECD Publishing, Paris, http://dx.doi.org/10.1787/9789264235120-en.

Rechnungshof (Austrian Court of Audit) (2016). Allgemeiner Einkommensbericht 2016 [*General Income Report 2016*], Vienna, http://www.rechnungshof.gv.at/fileadmin/downloads/_jahre/2016/berichte/einkommensberichte/Einkommensbericht_2016.pdf

Spasova, Slavina/Denis Bouget/Dalila Ghailani/Bart Vanhercke (2017). Access to social protection for people working on non-standard contracts and as self-employed in Europe. A study of national policies, European Social Policy Network (ESPN), European Commission, Brussels, http://ec.europa.eu/social/BlobServlet?docId=17683&langId=en

Tálos, Emmerich (1999). Atypische Beschäftigung in Österreich [*Atypical employment in Austria*], in: Emmerich Tálos (ed.): Atypische Beschäftigung. Internationale Trends und sozialstaatliche Regelungen [*Atypical employment. International trends and welfare state regulations*], Vienna, 252-284.

WKÖ (Austrian Economic Chamber) (2017a). Fact Sheet EPU 2017, Vienna, https://www.wko.at/service/netzwerke/epu_fact_sheet_2017.pdf.

WKÖ (Austrian Economic Chamber) (2017b). 14 EPU-Mythen [*14 single-person business myths*], Vienna, https://www.wko.at/service/netzwerke/epu-mythen.pdf.

Chapter 4. France: Social protection for the self-employed

Pierre Cahuc

This chapter discusses the ongoing efforts to integrate the social protection of self-employed workers into the general social protection system in France. Several autonomous schemes and a complex system of contribution rates and entitlements obscure the relationship between gross and net wages and hinder the mobility of workers across jobs and occupations. While there have been efforts to harmonise the social protection of self-employed workers and employees, differences in coverage and contribution rates remain. The social protection of employees and self-employed workers is also managed by diverse institutions which are imperfectly coordinated. This paper describes the contribution rates and the social protection of various forms of employment in France. It provides information about the different components of the social protection of self-employed people (the organisation of schemes and their financial architecture, membership of the schemes, contributions and benefits) and compares the situation of different kinds of self-employed workers with that of employees. The chapter also discusses a special unemployment scheme for performing artists and related occupations, the Intermittents du spectacle.

4.1. Introduction

In France, the social protection of employees is provided by the general social security system and by the public unemployment insurance scheme. Self-employed workers are covered by separate schemes. These schemes have been progressively integrated into the general social security system, but this convergence remains partial: self-employed workers pay lower contributions and have lower coverage than employees. This situation, which creates complexities, is a source of problems for the overall management of the social protection system. It also creates inequalities between self-employed workers and employees, and barriers to mobility between paid employment and self-employment. And this situation is becoming more problematic because current changes in forms of work and employment call into question the boundaries between employment and self-employment.

In order to shed light on this issue, this paper describes the contributions rates and the social protection of various forms of employment in France. It provides information about the different components of the social protection of self-employed people (the organisation of schemes and their financial architecture, membership of the schemes, contributions and benefits). It compares the situation of different kinds of self-employed workers with that of employees.

The paper shows that there have been various efforts to harmonise the social protection of self-employed workers and employees during the last three decades, starting from a situation in which the self-employed had significantly less social insurance coverage than employees. However, the systems are not fully harmonised. The social protection of employees and self-employed workers is managed by diverse institutions which are imperfectly coordinated. This is a source of complexity and a lack of transparency.

In particular, contribution rates for employees change according to the level of the wage, with different thresholds for different types of contributions. There are also different rates for self-employed workers, with thresholds depending on income, but these rates and thresholds are different from those of employees. The complexity of contribution rates, and the lack of clear distinction between contributory and non-contributory schemes make it difficult to compare the contributions and the social benefits of employees and self-employed workers at present. This situation represents a barrier to mobility between self-employment and dependent employment as it is difficult to figure out the relationship between gross income and net income, including social benefits, in each situation. This is also an obstacle to the convergence of the social protection of employees and self-employed workers.

This paper is organised as follows. Section 4.2 briefly presents the general architecture of the French social protection system, including the situation of self-employed workers within this system. Section 4.3 outlines the characteristics of self-employed workers. Section 4.4 highlights the social contributions paid by self-employed workers and compares them with those paid by wage earners. Section 4.5 outlines the social benefits available to self-employed workers, while the financial situation and the administrative organisation of the social protection schemes for self-employed workers are described in Section 4.6. Section 4.7 focuses on the situation of workers of the entertainment industry, who benefit from a special system called *intermittents du spectacle.* Section 4.8 summarises the main findings and makes proposals to improve the French social protection system.

4.2. An overview of the French social protection system

4.2.1. The general architecture of the social protection system

In France, social protection is provided by the general social security system, established in 1945, and by the public unemployment insurance scheme, created in 1958.

The general social security system aims to unify all forms of social insurance in France within a single fund, which is financed by a single-rate contribution and managed by the government with the participation of social partners. Functionally, social security assists people when they are confronted throughout their lives with different events or situations that can have a costly financial impact. Four branches are defined by the Social Security Code, each of which is intended to cover a type of risk, with their own methods of coverage and benefits:

1. The health branch (sickness, maternity, incapacity, death)
2. The occupational accidents and diseases branch
3. The old-age and retirement branch
4. The family branch (including disability, housing)

The unemployment insurance scheme was created by the social partners. This scheme is not linked to the general social security scheme but is run by an independent association (Unédic), which is managed by employer bodies and trade union organisations. It is compulsory for the majority of employers and employees in the private sector. The self-employed are not eligible for unemployment insurance.

4.2.2. A brief overview of the social protection situation of the self-employed

A short history

At the time of the creation of the general social security system in 1945, the self-employed opposed their integration into the main system. This was followed by a period of piecemeal integration of some professions and some risks, but not others.

Compulsory, but occupation-based and independently organised pension systems were established, and in the 1960s, the self-employed acquired health and accident insurance protection. However, because these schemes were not fully integrated with the general scheme and had lower contribution rates, the self-employed still received lower benefits, which led to concerns that the status would become less attractive. Demographic shifts within professions – such as the increase in the average age in the farming industry – led to infusions of government money into individual occupational schemes.

Since the late 1970s, the social protection treatment of the self-employed has been gradually aligned with the general system: Family benefits for the self-employed were incorporated into the general scheme in 1978; in-kind benefits from the health insurance were aligned to the general system in 2000, followed by sickness benefit payments in 2016. Also, the pension system has converged with the general system to some extent, especially for craftsmen and retail traders, but to a lesser degree for the liberal professions.

The current situation

The organisation of basic social protection for self-employed workers remains characterised by a plurality of schemes, the scope of which varies across professions.

Self-employed workers are covered by six basic compulsory schemes:

1. the system for farmers (managed by the social mutual agricultural – MSA);
2. the sickness insurance scheme for non-agricultural non-salaried workers, managed by the Régime Social des Indépendants (RSI), the social security agency for the self-employed;
3. the two pension schemes for craftsmen on the one hand and managers and traders on the other hand (managed by the RSI);
4. the basic pension scheme for the liberal professions, managed by the CNAVPL fund (Caisse nationale d'assurance vieillesse des professions libérales);
5. the basic pension scheme for lawyers, managed by the CNBF fund (Caisse nationale des barreaux français);
6. certain self-employed people are also covered by the general scheme for all or part of their social protection (for instance, doctors charging authorized fees and other liberal health care professionals).

Comparing the benefits available to employees in the general social security scheme with those available to self-employed workers, three main types of benefits can be distinguished:

1. Universal benefits that are not contingent on professional status by design, but which might still be less accessible to the self-employed in practice (family and housing benefits, basic health insurance, minimum retirement pension);
2. benefits provided by occupation-specific schemes, some of which are relatively harmonised between the self-employed and dependent workers, such as retirement benefits, while others differ quite substantially, as with replacement income in the event of sickness, maternity, paternity or disability;
3. coverage for risks that are uninsured or only insured on an optional basis for the self-employed (occupational accidents, complementary health and welfare benefits, unemployment or loss of income).

Individuals are assigned to a scheme once it is determined that they exercise an activity professionally and are not salaried employees. The nature of this activity – commercial, artisanal, industrial, liberal profession or agricultural – determines which scheme manages their contributions and entitlements. In case of disagreement between the social security agency and the worker, the civil courts decide.

This process raises several issues: first, the distinction between dependent employees and the self-employed is not simple in practice. The concept of *legal subordination*, derived from case law, is central in this respect: it describes a work relationship in which the employer has the power to issue orders and directives, to supervise their execution and to punish any infractions. A person who performs work on behalf of an employer in return for remuneration in a permanent legal subordination relationship is considered to be an employee. While self-employment is determined on the basis of material evidence – e.g. absence of an employment contract, registration in the Trade and Companies Register (Registre du Commerce et des Sociétés) – if there is found to be a relationship of permanent legal subordination, the person is treated as a dependent employee. In this case, a reclassification of the employment relationship leads to a change in its affiliation scheme and penalties for the employer.

Second, whether the activity is salaried or not, affiliation to a scheme presupposes that the activity is of a professional nature. A voluntary activity that does not offer remuneration in kind or in cash does not give rise to affiliation. The professional nature of the activity is established in a variety of ways. For the commercial, craft or liberal professions, affiliation is triggered by registration in professional registers and registers of firms via a *centre de formalité des entreprises* (CFE).

Third, the recognition of a self-employed activity results in affiliation to a scheme for self-employed people, which will receive the contributions paid and provide the associated benefits. However, there are numerous exceptions that may lead to independent workers (in particular, non-salaried managers of co-operatives or companies) being affiliated to the general scheme for wage earners. These exceptions make the social protection system more complicated.

4.3. The characteristics of self-employed workers

Self-employed workers are all affiliated to the social protection scheme for self-employed people, the Régime Social des Indépendants (RSI) for non-agricultural workers. A distinction can be made between traditional self-employed workers and *micro-entrepreneurs*. The *micro-entrepreneur*[1] scheme, introduced in 2009, simplifies the process of setting up a business, as well as the payment of social contributions if business revenue remains below set thresholds (see Section 4.3). These are essentially individual contractors or managers of limited liability companies. In 2015, economically active[2] *micro-entrepreneurs* accounted for 28% of self-employed workers.

4.3.1. The share of self-employment in total employment

Self-employed workers accounted for about 10.3% of total employment in 2015. Their share of total employment decreased until the early 2000s, falling from 12.8% in 1990 to 8.8% in 2002 (Figure 4.1). It began to increase from 2003 onwards, with an acceleration following the introduction of the *micro-entrepreneur* scheme in 2009, and reached a plateau of about 10.4% in 2013. Over the long term, it is the decline in agricultural employment, driven by strong productivity gains, but also by a greater propensity to work under the status of dependent employee, which explains the decline in self-employment.

From 1990 to the mid-2000s, a significant number of self-employed jobs were lost in the tertiary sector, particularly as a result of the shift in the retail sector and the accelerated development of large stores (Panel A, Figure 4.2). In the more recent period, it has been the relative dynamism of the creation of self-employed jobs in services, but also in the construction sector, which has led to a revival of non-wage employment. It has been driven by the creation of the *micro-entrepreneur* scheme in 2009, although some of the jobs created in this context have simply replaced traditional non-salaried jobs.

Panel B in Figure 4.2 shows that self-employment has accounted for a large share of job creation since the beginning of the 2000s, in contrast to the previous period. From 2001 to 2015, self-employment accounts for 34% of net job creation in all non-agricultural sectors. From 2009 to 2015, the creation of self-employed jobs was (nearly) twice as great as growth in paid employment. This important contribution of self-employment to job creation has also been observed in the United States since 2005.[3]

Figure 4.1. *Micro-entrepreneurs* are driving the recent increase in self-employment

Micro-entrepreneurs and other self-employed as a share of total employment 1989-2015, in percent

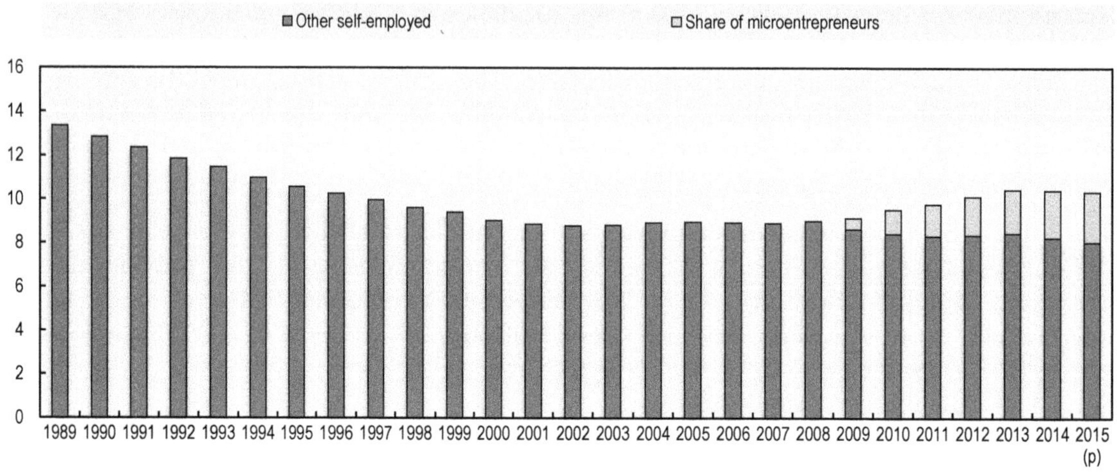

Source: Estimation d'emploi, https://www.insee.fr/fr/statistiques/2424696; and Acoss Stat n° 227 – July 2017

Figure 4.2. Self-employment was the main driver of job creation during the recovery

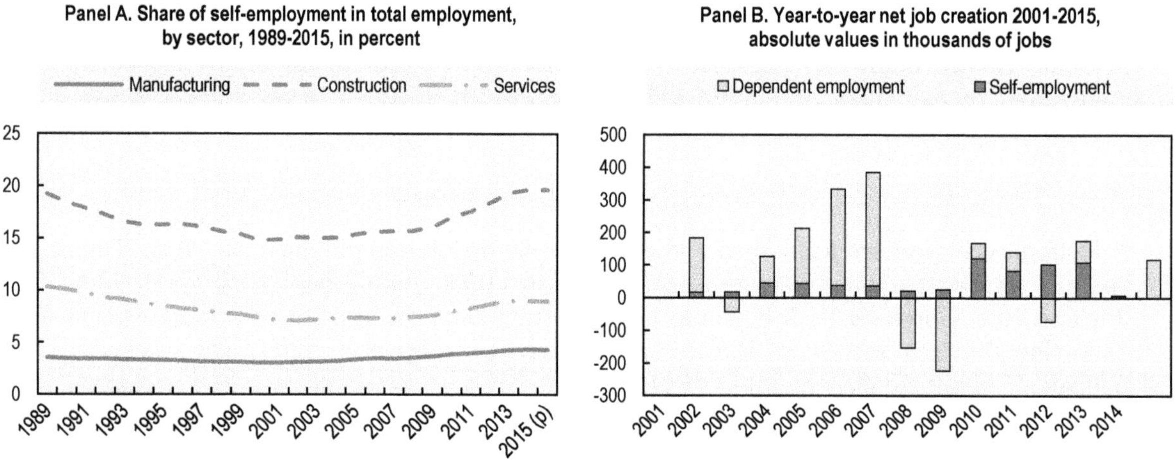

Source: Source: Estimation d'emploi, Insee; https://www.insee.fr/fr/statistiques/2424696.

4.3.2. Sectors of activity of self-employed workers

For 89% of self-employed workers, self-employment is their main activity, with the rest deriving most of their earned income from paid employment.[4] Half of the self-employed are concentrated in commerce and commercial crafts (21%), health care (17%) and construction (14%), whereas these sectors account for only one-third of private employees. There are also many self-employed workers in services: 13% work in specialised scientific and technical activities (legal professions, accounting, management consulting, architecture, engineering, advertising, design etc.) and 21% in services for individuals: catering, accommodation, artistic and recreational activities, teaching, hairdressing, beauty care or other personal care services. On the other hand, less than 5%

of the self-employed work in industry (excluding commercial crafts), whereas the share of wage earners in industry is three times that level.

4.3.3. The strong income disparities among self-employed workers

Income disparities among the self-employed are much more pronounced than among dependent employees. In 2014, 10% of non-salaried workers (excluding *micro-entrepreneurs*) reported a zero income because they did not receive any benefits or professional income (ranging from 2% for health professionals to more than 20% for those working in real estate or arts and entertainment). Excluding those who had no income, one in ten received less than EUR 480 per month. This share is 2.5 times higher than that of private sector employees. One self-employed worker in four receives less than EUR 1 080 per month and half less than EUR 2 230. At the top of the remuneration scale, one in four self-employed workers receives more than EUR 4 320 per month and one in ten more than EUR 7 880. This amount is more than twice as high as that of paid employees. Non-store[5] retailing generates the lowest revenues (EUR 1 040 per month on average), behind hairdressing and beauty care, artistic and recreational activities, taxis and other personal care services (EUR 1 330 to 1 410 monthly). Doctors and dentists receive the highest incomes (EUR 8 310), followed by the legal and accounting professions (EUR 7 630) and the pharmaceutical trade (EUR 7 480).

4.3.4. The number of micro-entrepreneurs

Since the creation of the *micro-entrepreneur* scheme in 2009, the presence of *micro-entrepreneurs* has expanded in many sectors of activity. They represent 65% of self-employed workers in the non-store retail trade, design, photography, translation and certain personal care services such as cosmetics. On the contrary, there are hardly any of them in sectors composed mainly of regulated professions which do not qualify for this status.

Economically active *micro-entrepreneurs* earned an average of EUR 410 per month in 2014, one-eighth of the average income of other self-employed. More than one in four earned less than EUR 70 per month, half less than EUR 240 and one in ten more than EUR 1 110. The low income of *micro-entrepreneurs* is partly due to the ceilings imposed on revenue to be eligible for the scheme, but also to the fact that it is often a supplementary activity: at the end of 2014, nearly one in three *micro-entrepreneurs* combined self-employment and dependent employment, compared with one in ten of other self-employed workers. The total earnings of those who combine self-employment and dependent employment reached EUR 2 100 per month in 2014, of which only 14% came from self-employment. *Micro-entrepreneurs* who did not engage in paid employment earned an average of EUR 460 per month. Among the regular self-employed, the total earned income of those who combined self-employment and dependent employment amounted to EUR 5 820 per month, of which almost half came from their self-employment. The parallel exercise of a wage-earning activity is very common for non-salaried workers in education, health care, and artistic and recreational activities.

4.4. The social contributions paid by self-employed workers

Any analysis of the social contributions of the self-employed and their comparison with that of wage earners is complicated by the fact that the self-employed can carry out their activities under different company structures. While craftsmen and retail traders can choose from a wide range of company legal forms, this is not the case for certain liberal professions: the legal and judicial professions, as well as most health professionals, cannot practice within the scope of a limited liability company (SARL in France). Only those who operate alone, who are not among the so-called "regulated" liberal professions or farmers, and whose income does not exceed a certain threshold can be *micro-entrepreneurs*.

Hence, the social security treatment of different types of self-employed people can vary considerably, and depends both on the sector and the profession that the self-employed person is active in, as well as their chosen form of self-employment. This section first describes the social contributions paid by craftsmen, traders and *micro-entrepreneurs*, leaving aside the liberal professions and the farmers.[6] The social contributions of self-employed workers are then compared with those of dependent employees.

4.4.1. Contributions paid by craftsmen, traders and micro-entrepreneurs

Craftsmen and traders

Tax base

The contributions of self-employed workers are calculated on the basis of the professional income taken into account for the calculation of income tax, i.e. the profits of the firm or the remuneration of the head of the company. This calculation excludes any tax exemptions and includes dividends received if more than 10% of the share capital is held. It also incorporates the 10% flat-rate tax allowance for professional expenses.

For the first and second year of activity, the contributions are determined provisionally on a flat-rate basis. They are recalculated the following year, after the first tax declaration.

Contribution rates

Contributions are proportional to self-employment income. Each type of contribution is subject to a specific rate. Initially, contributions are calculated on a provisional basis. Then they are recalculated on the basis of the real income declared at the time of the self-employed person's income declaration. At the beginning of the year, the first contributions are based on the income of two years earlier. In the course of the year, contributions are adjusted to take account of the previous year's income and contributions adjustment.

If the entrepreneur makes a loss or their income is below the minimum income threshold, some of their contributions are set at a fixed minimum amount (Table 4.1). One annual minimum pension contribution counts as three contribution quarters for basic pension entitlement (160-172 contribution quarters are required to receive a basic pension, depending on the year of birth).

The compulsory contribution rates of artisans and traders whose income exceeds these thresholds are displayed in Table 4.2. The CSG social security contribution (*contribution sociale généralisée*) and the CRDS contribution to repayment of debt of the social security system (*contribution au remboursement de la dette sociale*) do not give entitlement to specific benefits but have been introduced to contribute to the financing and reduction of the debt of the social security system. They are levied on all earnings, including pensions. The contribution for vocational training gives the self-employed person a right to vocational training.

Table 4.1. Minimum contributions for craftsmen/traders with annual income below the minimum income threshold, 2017 (EUR)

Type of contribution	Minimum income threshold	Minimum contribution
Daily sickness benefit	15 691	110
Basic pension	4 511	801
Incapacity and death	4 511	59
Vocational training	38 616	97

Source: https://www.rsi.fr.

Table 4.2. Social security contributions rates for craftsmen/traders with annual income below the minimum income threshold, 2017

Type of contribution	Contribution base (EUR)	Rate
Health	Professional income < 27 459.60	3.5% to 6.5%
	Professional income > 27 459.60	6.5%
Sickness benefit	Income up to 196 140	0.7%
Basic pension	Income up to 39 228	17.75%
	Income above 39 228	0.6%
Complementary pension	Income up to 37 546	7.0%
	Income between 37 546 and 156 912	8.0%
Incapacity and death	Income up to 39 228	1.3%
Family allowances	Income up to 43 150.80	2.15%
	Income between 43 150.80 and 54 919.20	2.15% to 5.25%
	Income above 54 919.20	5.25%
CSG-CRDS	Professional income + compulsory social security contributions	8.0%
	Replacement income	6.2%
Vocational training	39 228	0.25%

Note: The CSG and CRDS are compulsory flat-rate taxes which contribute to the financing of social security.
Source: https://www.rsi.fr.

Unlike wage earners, the self-employed do not make contributions and are not covered for accidents at work, occupational diseases and unemployment risks. However, it is possible to take out voluntary insurance for these risks. The contributions are tax deductible, within a certain limit, as explained below, in Section 4.5.

Micro-entrepreneurs

The social contributions of *micro-entrepreneurs* are determined so as to ensure an equivalent level between the effective rate of social contributions paid and income tax for *micro-entrepreneurs* and artisans and traders. But *micro-entrepreneurs* benefit from a simplified system for calculating and paying compulsory contributions and social contributions. To be able to file as *micro-entrepreneurs*, their 2017 revenue was not allowed to exceed:

- EUR 82 800 for the sale of goods, or for accommodation services, except for rental of furnished accommodation, which had a threshold of EUR 33 200.

- EUR 33 200 for services in the industrial/commercial and non-commercial categories. The company is not subject to VAT (no billing of VAT or recovery of VAT on purchases). *The micro-entrepreneur* cannot deduct any costs (telephone, travel etc.).

Each month or each quarter, the *micro-entrepreneurs* must calculate and pay their social contributions based on their actual gross revenue. They pay a flat rate that includes all contributions related to compulsory social protection: health care, daily sickness benefit (for artisans and traders only), CSG, CRDS, family allowances, basic pension, complementary pension, incapacity and death.

There are three different rates depending on the field of activity of the *micro-entrepreneur*: 13.1% for purchase/resale of goods, sale of foodstuffs for consumption on site and accommodation services; 22.7% for commercial or craft services; 22.5% for liberal professions. In contrast to artisans and traders, *micro-entrepreneurs* do not have to pay minimum contributions.

Micro-entrepreneurs pay a contribution for vocational training, calculated as a percentage of revenue, which amounts to 0.10% for traders, 0.20% for professionals and service providers, and 0.30% for craftsmen.

4.4.2. Comparison of the total amount of contributions due for self-employed workers and employees

This section analyses the social charges levied on identical income profiles of regular self-employed workers (craftsmen and traders) and dependent employees. The amount paid by *micro-entrepreneurs* is in principle identical to that of artisans and traders, even though *micro-entrepreneurs* pay social contributions at a flat rate.[7] The following therefore compares the situation of regular self-employed workers with that of employees, on the assumption that that the situations of *micro-entrepreneurs* and regular self-employed workers are similar.

Table 4.3 details the contributions charged for employees, making a distinction between employees' and employers' contributions. This table shows that the different contributions change depending on the wage level and also the status (executive versus non-executive) of the employee. Therefore, comparing the contributions paid by employees and by self-employed workers is not an easy task.

Another source of complexity arises from the fact that the tax base for income tax is not calculated in the same way for these two categories of workers. Moreover, there are significant reductions in contribution rates for employees whose hourly wage is less than 1.6 times the French minimum wage (known as the Smic). For this reason, Figure 4.3 presents several examples illustrating the situation of single full-time workers at five different income levels relative to the monthly French minimum wage.[8] The following types of charges (including reductions for those on low wages) are taken into account when they apply: family allowances, health care, pensions, unemployment, occupational accident, training, transport, apprenticeship contributions, and income tax (including the flat-rate tax CSG and CRDS taxes).

Table 4.3. Social security contribution for dependent employees

In percent, 2017

Type of contribution		Employee contribution	Employer contribution
Health, maternity, incapacity, death		0.75%	12.89%
Autonomy solidarity contribution (*contribution solidarité autonomie*)		-	0.3%
Basic pension		6.94%	9.45%
Accidents at work		-	Variable based on company size and risks
Basic arduous work contribution		-	0.01%
Family benefits		-	5.25% or 3.45%
CSG		7.5% of 98.5% of gross salary	-
CRDS		0.5% of 98.25% of gross salary	-
Unemployment		2.4%	4.05%
AGS*			0.15%
Supplementary pensions			
Non-executive employees (ARRCO)			
	up to EUR 3 269	3.9%	5.85%
	from EUR 3 269 to 9 807	9%	13.45%
Executive employees (AGIRC)			
	up to EUR 3 269	3.1%	4.65%
	from EUR 3 269 to 26 152	8.70%	14.05%

Note: The upper limit of the tax base for the unemployment contribution is equal to four monthly social security ceilings (4 x EUR 3 269). Thresholds refer to monthly incomes.
*AGS: wage guarantee insurance association which guarantees the payment of employees' wages, notice period and compensation if a company goes into a court-ordered liquidation.
Source: www.cleiss.fr/docs/regimes/regime_france/an_a2.html.

The total tax wedge is almost identical for self-employed workers and dependent employees up to the minimum wage (see Figure 4.3). Up to this level, the share of gross income taken up by social contributions and income taxes is almost identical for these two categories of workers. Theoretically, the social contributions paid by employees are higher than for the self-employed, but this is cancelled out by deductions at low levels. These deductions become smaller as the wage rises and come to an end once income reaches 1.6 times the minimum wage. This means that employees pay more social contributions than self-employed workers when income is above the monthly minimum wage. The lower social contributions paid by self-employed workers above the minimum wage are partly offset by higher income tax. Nevertheless, the total tax wedge is about 10 percentage points higher for employees than for self-employed workers when the income is above the minimum wage.

Figure 4.3. Above the minimum wage, the tax wedge is lower for the self-employed

Income tax rates and social security contributions for crafts- and tradespeople and dependent employees, in percent of total gross income, 2016

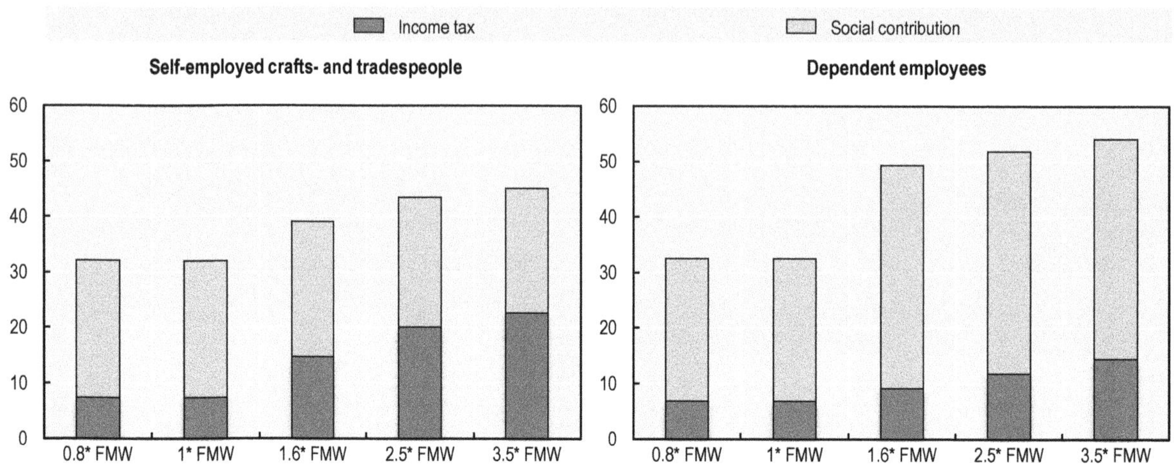

Note: Gross income for dependent employees is equal to the labour cost, including employers' social security contributions. Gross income for self-employed workers is equal to the income added to total contributions paid. FMW is the French Minimum Wage. In 2017, the full-time monthly minimum was EUR 1480; 64% of the median wage.
Source: *Haut conseil de la sécurité sociale* (2016), vol 1, page 240.

4.5. Social benefits for self-employed workers

As mentioned in Section 4.2, three main types of coverage are available for self-employed workers: 1) universal coverage that is not connected to status; 2) coverage based on occupation-specific schemes; 3) coverage which is not insured or is only insured on a voluntary basis. This section covers these three types of coverage.

4.5.1. Universal coverage: family and housing benefits, basic health insurance

Family and housing benefits

For family benefits and basic health insurance, the coverage proposed by the social security system is now not linked to professional status: the rights are identical, regardless of the schemes that people are affiliated to. The amount of family and housing benefits is also not dependent on a person's professional situation. It depends on the family configuration, the income level and whether the person owns or rents their home.

Basic health insurance

The payment of health care costs is guaranteed for everyone, either by virtue of their professional activity or their regular and stable residence in the country. The professional regimes only manage the provision of health care – entitlements do not vary across professional schemes. That is, the system is designed such that individuals transitioning between professions do not have to worry about a change in their or their dependents' health care coverage.

Moreover, like the rest of the population, self-employed workers are eligible for aid for the acquisition of supplementary health coverage (ACS) and complementary universal health insurance (CMU-C).[9]

4.5.2. Specific benefits: old-age pensions, sickness, maternity, paternity or disability[10]

Old-age pensions

In France, all old-age pension regimes have two compulsory components: basic and supplementary pensions. All regimes know this duality. The pensions of craftsmen and traders are managed by the RSI.

The pension scheme for craftsmen and traders is now equivalent to that of private sector employees with respect to parameters such as the retirement age and the annual revaluation of pensions. However, the contribution bases and rates continue to differ because the nature of self-employed income necessarily means that contribution bases are calculated differently and there are no employer contributions.

Sickness

Traders and craftsmen can be entitled to cash sickness benefits if they have been affiliated for more than a year and are up to date with their contributions for health insurance and daily sickness benefit.

The self-employed are entitled to a cash sickness benefit that provides the same basic replacement rate as employees, equal to 50% of their daily income, but:

- their period for averaging earnings is longer (three years rather than three months);
- they do not benefit from a higher replacement rate if they have dependent children, while dependent employees do;
- they have a longer waiting period (seven rather than three days).

Self-employed workers (except *micro-entrepreneurs*) also have the option of paying a specific contribution to benefit from a minimum daily allowance of EUR 21 (in 2017).

Maternity and paternity

In-kind medical services related to pregnancy and childbirth are fully covered for all women, regardless of employment status.

Self-employed women are entitled to maternity benefits if their contributions were paid on time by the end of the previous year. A daily allowance is payable for up to 74 days, and 30 additional days may be added in the case of complications. The period for averaging earnings is the past three years. The daily allowance is EUR 54 if the annual income is above EUR 3 608 and just EUR 5 otherwise.

The situation is more favourable for dependent employees: if they have worked for at least 150 hours during the three months preceding the maternity leave, they receive their full salary payment up to a ceiling. Collective agreements however may stipulate continued payment of the full salary by the employer during the entire maternity leave.

The leave period is 112 days for the first and second birth, and 182 days for subsequent births.

Employees and self-employed workers are granted 11 days' paternity leave when a child is born. The daily allowance amounts to 79% of the daily wage for employees, with a minimum of EUR 9.30 and a maximum of EUR 85. The daily allowance for self-employed workers is EUR 50.

Disability

Like employees, self-employed workers can benefit from pensions for either total or partial disability. The pension for total disability is paid if the insured person is assessed by a doctor to be in a state of total and definitive disability and if access to employment is severely and permanently restricted. Similar rules and allowances apply to wage earners.

4.5.3. Optional coverage: occupational accidents, complementary health and welfare benefits, unemployment or loss of income

Occupational accidents and occupational diseases

Occupational accident and occupational disease coverage is restricted to employees or people working on behalf of an employer. This principle is founded on the idea of the subordination of the employee to the employer who has obligations and the means to reduce occupational risks. As a result, craftsmen and traders, as well as the liberal professions, are not subject to compulsory insurance for the risk of occupational accidents and occupational diseases.

The RSI does not cover its members for industrial accidents and occupational illnesses. However, it offers a health promotion and risk prevention programme (*RSI Prévention Pro*) that includes specially tailored and personalised medical support (a free medical appointment entirely dedicated to the avoidance of occupational hazards) as well as comprehensive information on the risks connected with different jobs and how to protect oneself. However, self-employed workers can apply for voluntary membership in the work accident and occupational illness insurance programme of the general scheme. The contribution rates are determined by the regional social insurance agencies, and are aligned, in principle, with those of employees belonging to similar professions.

The lack of compulsory coverage may pose a problem for self-employed workers who are exposed to occupational risks, for example in subcontracting or activities in construction or the delivery business In fact, the lack of occupational accident and occupational illness coverage is one of the most important reasons why self-employed workers appeal to courts to requalify their work relationships as employment relationships..[11]

Complementary health insurance

Since 1 January 2016 all private sector companies have to offer complementary health insurance which covers part of the expenditure on medical care and equipment (especially dental and glasses) not reimbursed by basic health insurance. The self-employed can take out such additional health insurance on a voluntary basis. In order to encourage the development of social protection for the self-employed, contributions to certain group insurance contracts, known as Madelin contracts, and certain optional supplementary pension schemes were made tax deductible. The Madelin Law (11 February 1994), allows business and traders (except *micro-entrepreneurs*) to deduct contributions for voluntary insurance for incapacity to work, disability and death, unemployment and health insurance from their taxes, up to a ceiling. The subsidy is similar to that for dependent employees. [12] In 2012, 94% of the self-employed were covered by a complementary health insurance, provided by private insurers, compared with 96.6% for private sector wage earners.[13]

Unemployment

For unemployment risks, coverage for self-employed workers is optional. However, they can deduct contributions to a loss-of-employment contract subscribed under the Madelin scheme from their taxable income.[14] This insurance is supplied by private insurers, who define when a self-employed worker is "unemployed" for the purpose of their insurance plan in their contracts.[15]

The public unemployment insurance for private sector dependent employees provides two schemes for entrepreneurs who paid contributions when they were wage earners. Entrepreneurs have the choice between the two schemes and may benefit from both schemes in succession.

1. The aid for starting or taking over a business (ARCE) allows unemployed people starting a business to opt for the payment of a capital amount corresponding to 45% of the remaining entitlement to unemployment insurance benefits, which is in two instalments. To access this, applicants already have to have been granted another aid called ACCRE, which provides relief from social security contributions for unemployed people starting or taking over a business. ACCRE is only awarded after the authorities have examined the validity of the entrepreneur's plan. The first half of the ARCE capital payment is made on the date on which all the required conditions are met. The second half is paid six months after the establishment of the company, provided that the beneficiary is still carrying on the activity. If the beneficiary ceases the activity for reasons beyond their control (for example, a natural disaster requiring them to close their business or abandon their project due to the impossibility of meeting their social and/or tax obligations), they may get monthly unemployment insurance benefits, up to the level of their remaining entitlement minus the amount of aid received. Some 40 900 people benefited from the ARCE in 2016 (out of a total of about 3.2 million recipients of unemployment insurance).[16]
2. Rather than a capital endowment, the person starting or taking over a company can choose to receive monthly unemployment benefits, minus 70% of the remuneration from their activity. The combination of unemployment insurance benefits and remuneration cannot exceed the former monthly reference salary (salary of the former activity on which the unemployment benefit rights are opened). According to Unédic, in the second quarter of 2015, there were on average 44 760 unemployment benefit recipients who simultaneously had a self-employed activity.

The two previous sections have shown that for the rights of a universal nature, such as health care costs or family benefits, the self-employed regimes have been integrated into the general social security scheme. For rights of a more contributory nature (pensions, cash benefits), acquired rights are generally slightly lower for the self-employed, due to (overall) lower contributions. For certain other aspects of social protection, self-employed workers have chosen not to put in place a collective protective system (unemployment, work accident, incapacity and death). In these areas, employees benefit from better social protection than the self-employed, with higher compulsory contributions. Beyond these differences, the main weakness of the system is its complexity due to the diversity of rules for contributions and benefits. This diversity points to a lack of transparency. Moreover, the lack of distinction between contributory and non-contributory schemes make it very difficult to establish the relation between the contributions and the benefits, both for employees and self-employed workers.

4.6. The financial situation and management of the social security regime for self-employed workers

4.6.1. The governance and financial situation of the RSI

The social security scheme for artisans, traders and *micro-entrepreneurs* is managed by the RSI (Régime Social des Indépendants) created in 2006. It is a financially autonomous, French private-law body whose mission is to provide compulsory social protection for self-employed people. It is administered by representatives of self-employed workers.

In an effort to simplify the administration of social protection for the self-employed, the RSI gained sole responsibility for the social protection of craftsmen and traders in 2008. The RSI does not collect social security contributions, but relies on the URSSAF (Unions de recouvrement des cotisations de sécurité sociale et d'allocations familiales),[17] a network of private bodies which also collects the social security contributions of dependent employees for the general social security system.

The RSI is organised in 30 funds: a national fund and 29 regional funds. The boards of directors of the national fund (50 directors) and the regional funds (24 to 36 members) are managed by elected representatives of the self-employed.

In 2016,[18] the RSI managed the social insurance of 6.5 million active and retired self-employed workers and their dependents, 2.8 million contributors (37% traders, 35% artisans and 28% professionals), 4.6 million beneficiaries of health benefits and 2 million retirees.

RSI contribution rates and benefits are set by the general social insurance system rather than by the RSI itself. The demographic structure and income distribution of the RSI members create a structural deficit of around EUR 6 billion per year. This deficit is financed by a specific tax (the C3S tax)[19] and by transfers from other funds based on compensation mechanisms that take account of differences in their demographic structures.

The creation of the RSI in 2006 was intended to unify the management of specific schemes. The aim was to limit management costs and improve the quality of benefits for self-employed workers. However, since its inception, the RSI has suffered serious malfunctions, documented by several reports.[20]

The first stage of the reform establishing the RSI was to merge the national sickness insurance fund for self-employed workers (Canam) and the separate fund for the old-age pensions of traders and artisans (Cancava). This merger made it possible to significantly reduce the number of administrative procedures and declarations of contributions for affiliates. The number of funds decreased from 90 to 30, and the number of directors was reduced by two-thirds. This first aspect of the reform did not raise any particular difficulties.

The second stage of the reform was to entrust the URSSAF network, which already handled the self-employed's contributions for family allowances and CSG and CRDS payments, with the collection of all their social security contributions. The RSI did not have the capacity, particularly in terms of IT resources, to ensure the collection of these contributions, but the RSI administrators nevertheless endeavoured to partly hold on to this role. However, the management of contributions and benefits for the self-employed requires permanent information flows between the RSI and the URSSAF. This integration has resulted in major malfunctions, including insufficient collection of contributions, erroneous recoveries and unpaid benefits to insured workers.

The latest report on the RSI, released in 2015,[21] proposed a package of measures to improve the coverage of self-employed workers, by bringing it closer to that of employees, and to make the management of the RSI more effective, while maintaining its autonomy. However, the programme of the president of the French republic elected in 2017 does not follow the conclusions of this report: it schedules a merger of the RSI with the general social security scheme. But the managers of the RSI are opposed to this development, arguing that the URSSAF will not be able to deal with the specific situation of the self-employed.

All in all, this section has shown that the system of social protection lacks transparency and homogeneity. Its main weaknesses are the absence of a unified governance of the different schemes for all workers, whether employed or self-employed, the complexity and heterogeneity of rules for contributions and benefits, and the lack of distinction between the contributory and the non-contributory schemes.

4.7. The specific situation of the "intermittents du spectacle"

The productions of entertainment companies are often by nature of limited duration, which leads them to contract with artists, technicians and workers for defined periods. They may hire an artist or a technician, as part of a production, for a contract of one day or more. France has created an original system for artists and technicians in the entertainment industry, called *intermittents du spectacle* (intermittent performers). They are employees and benefit as such from the social security system for employees. But they are eligible for a specific unemployment insurance scheme that takes account of their particular situation, which involves a succession of fixed-term contracts and alternating periods of employment and unemployment.

This type of system was instituted in 1936 for technicians and filmmakers. It was integrated into the general unemployment insurance system (Unédic) in 1965 and progressively extended to audio technicians, the audio-visual sector and to performers and performing arts technicians.

This section presents the unemployment insurance system of the *intermittents du spectacle* and discusses the issues raised by this system.

4.7.1. The eligibility rules

Intermittent performers must belong to one of the following two categories:

1. Performing artists on a fixed-term contract;
2. Blue-collar workers or technicians working on a fixed-term contract, with both their occupations and their hiring firm's activities listed in a collective agreement.

Fixed-term contracts under the *intermittents* scheme are more flexible than under standard French labour law.[22] While standard temporary contracts may only be extended twice, there is no limit on the number of extensions under the *intermittents* scheme. There is also no waiting period between two fixed-term contracts, while labour law stipulates a waiting period of at least one-third of the contract duration.

To benefit from unemployment benefit the *intermittent* employee must have worked a certain number of hours in a given period. The minimum period is 507 hours (or 43 days if the contract stipulates days of work instead of hours, in which case one day is calculated as 12 hours) during the last 319 days for artists or the last 304 days for blue-collar workers or technicians.

The level of benefits is calculated at the time of registration on the basis of reported hours and reported earnings during the 12-month base period. The net replacement rate, calculated on the basis of the daily wage, is about 85% at the level of the minimum wage and 70% at twice the minimum wage. If claimants are totally unemployed throughout the period of their claim and receive unemployment benefits each month, the potential duration of benefits is 243 days (eight months). *Intermittent* workers claiming unemployment benefit are allowed to work, including with their previous employers. In this case, the level of unemployment benefit is reduced, and depends on the hours of work reported each month during the period of the claim. However, the benefits foregone in one month are not lost – they can be paid in a later month. The corresponding benefit transfers delay the potential benefit exhaustion date. At the exhaustion date, the eligibility condition is reassessed. If claimants have worked 507 hours over the 12-month period preceding the exhaustion date, they remain eligible for unemployment benefits.

By way of comparison, the general scheme for unemployment benefit requires 122 days of work or 610 hours of work in the last 28 months for those under 50 or 36 months for those aged 50 and over. The replacement ratio is similar to that of *intermittent* workers. One day of work provides entitlement for one day of unemployment benefit coverage with a maximum limit of 24 months for those under 50 or 36 months for those aged 50 and over. Like *intermittent* workers, workers claiming unemployment benefit in the general scheme are allowed to work, including with their previous employers.[23] The level of unemployment benefit is reduced in the same way as for *intermittent* workers and the reduction in benefits similarly delays the potential benefit exhaustion date. At the exhaustion date, the eligibility condition is reassessed. If claimants fulfil the eligibility conditions described above, they remain eligible for unemployment benefit.

4.7.2. The issues raised by the "intermittents du spectacle" scheme

All in all, the *intermittent* scheme is very generous and provides little incentive to work beyond the minimum number of hours required to gain entitlement to unemployment benefit. It allows arts workers to combine earned income with unemployment benefits indefinitely, if they work at least two months over a ten-month period, so this scheme is very attractive for them.

The number of arts workers increased fivefold between 1980 and 2015 while the number of arts workers claiming unemployment benefit jumped from 7 000 to 113 000 (Figure 4.4). In 2015, about 40% of arts workers claimed unemployment benefit thanks to the *intermittent* scheme. Moreover, the Cour des comptes (2012a) stresses that a significant number of *intermittent* arts workers leave their work situation once they have acquired sufficient rights to be eligible for unemployment benefit, and only resume their activity once these rights are exhausted. This phenomenon is also fuelled by employers' practices. A large proportion of compensated unemployment spells are attributable to comings and goings within the same company. This recurrence suggests that many companies have adapted their workforce management to take advantage of the benefits provided by the unemployment insurance system.

Figure 4.4. More and more people are using the *intermittent du spectacle* scheme

Number of persons working under an intermittents contract, and number of claimants under its unemployment scheme, 1980-2015

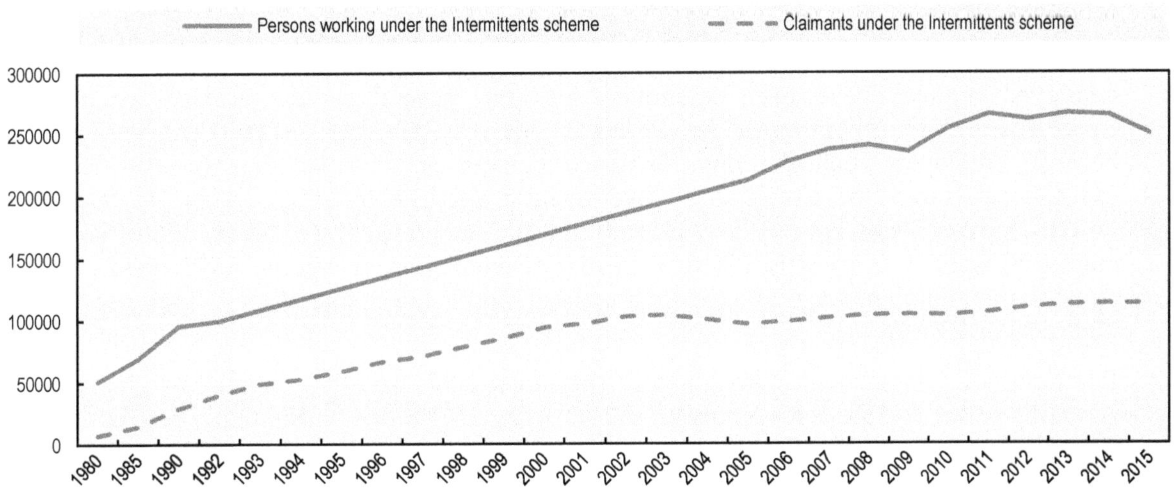

Note: linear extrapolation for the number of arts workers from 1993 to 2004.
Source: Data on claimants and non-claimants over the 1980-1992 period from Menger and Gurgand (2011). Data on the total number of arts workers over the 2005-2015 period are computed from an administrative database on arts workers' contracts (*Attestation Employeur Mensuelle*). Data on claiming arts workers over the 1993-2015 period are computed from an administrative database on unemployment spells (*Fichier National des Allocataires*).

Accordingly, arts workers cost more to the unemployment insurance system than other workers employed in unstable jobs who do not benefit from the *intermittent* scheme. In all unemployment insurance systems, the amount of unemployment benefit provided to unemployed workers previously on fixed-term contracts is larger than their unemployment insurance contributions. Nevertheless, according to the Cour des comptes (2012a), temporary agency workers receive 2.5 times more in allowances than they pay in contributions. This ratio increases to 3.6 for employees on fixed-term contracts and reaches 5.2 for *intermittent* arts workers. Financial transfers are clearly higher for *intermittent* arts workers than for other types of fixed-term contracts. The difference between the expenditure on benefits and contributions paid by arts workers amounted to about EUR 1 billion per year between 2007 and 2012.

The high cost of the *intermittent* schemes has led to many attempts at reforms by the social partners, who manage the unemployment insurance system. But the strong opposition of arts workers, who organise many demonstrations when their benefits are threatened, has prevented significant changes so far.

In order to reduce the financial cost of the scheme to the unemployment insurance system, in 2014 the government created a fund endowed with EUR 90 million every year (the FONPEPS, *Fonds national pour l'emploi pérenne dans le spectacle*), which provides bonuses to companies hiring arts workers. The bonus increases with the duration of the contract and reaches a maximum of EUR 28 000 for an open-ended contract.[24] However, it is clear that this reform is not sufficient to significantly improve the financial situation of the *intermittent* scheme.

4.8. Conclusion

The previous sections show that various paths have been taken to foster the convergence of social protection of employees and self-employed workers. Nevertheless, social protection for self-employed workers remains different to that of employees in the following ways:

For rights of a universal nature, such as health care costs or family benefits, the self-employed regimes have been integrated into the general social security scheme. Contributions for self-employed people are higher than for those in paid employment because employers' contributions for wage earners on low incomes benefit from exemptions financed from the central government budget, i.e. by all taxpayers. However, as self-employed workers pay less income tax than employees, the tax wedge of self-employed workers is roughly identical to that of employees at income levels below or equal to the minimum wage of a full-time worker, and is lower than that of employees at higher income levels.

For rights of a more contributory nature (pensions, cash benefits), acquired rights are generally lower for the self-employed, due to (overall) lower contributions, despite the financial integration of the branch pensions of craftsmen and traders and an effort to bring their contribution rates to the basic pension system closer to those of employees.

For certain other aspects of social protection, self-employed workers have chosen not to put in place a collective protective system (unemployment, work accident, incapacity and death). In these areas, employees benefit from better social protection than the self-employed, but also have higher compulsory contribution rates than the self-employed.

The *intermittents du spectacle* scheme provides generous unemployment insurance for workers in the entertainment industry, whose jobs are naturally unstable. But the cost of this system raises serious doubts about its sustainability and the possibility of extending it to other professions.

All in all, the social protection system lacks transparency and homogeneity, and these weaknesses make the system difficult to reform. On the one hand, the wide range of situations of the self-employed relative to that of employees is a real obstacle to merging the management of the social protection systems of the two groups. On the other hand, the convergence of the rules for contributions and benefits for employees and self-employed workers is difficult, in particular because the contributions of the self-employed are lower. A way to ensure this convergence could be to implement identical compulsory and optional contributions, with associated benefits, for employees and self-employed workers. But this would mean either increasing the compulsory contributions of the self-employed, who would be opposed to such a development, or lowering the compulsory contributions and associated benefits of employees. It is likely that the managers of the regimes receiving less income because of the drop in employees' mandatory contributions would strongly oppose this.

But these difficulties have to be overcome. The core of the French social protection system is designed for the archetype of a full-time, permanent worker with a single employer. This means that it is not equipped to provide adequate insurance for the growing number of workers with non-standard forms of employment (temporary jobs, part-time jobs, self-employment). The rise in non-standard forms of employment, largely resulting from globalisation and technological progress, is a fundamental trend that is likely to continue and spread in the future. It is therefore essential to adapt social protection to this new environment. In particular, social protection should pool risks and facilitate the mobility of workers across all types of jobs to ensure the adaptability of the labour force. Past experience shows that this is not an easy task: the creation of the scheme providing unemployment insurance to artists and technicians in the entertainment industry, who alternate between frequent periods of employment and unemployment, has been very costly. Its generosity has attracted a large number of people in the entertainment industry. Once created, it has been difficult to reform due to the resistance of those enjoying its generous benefits. This failure indicates that the social protection system has to be adapted cautiously, by competent bodies, avoiding the creation of significant advantages to specific categories of workers or sectors. It is also important to avoid designing a system in which some categories of workers are subject to higher social contributions, because firms then have incentives to shift work to other workers, subject to lower social contributions but with less protection.

In these circumstances, the French social protection system should be improved by unifying the governance of the different schemes for all workers, whether employed or self-employed, and by making a clearer distinction between the contributory and the non-contributory schemes.

From a practical perspective,[25] it is important to merge the schemes that cover the same risks for all workers by unifying the governance and accrual of entitlements in compulsory pension schemes and defining the set of health risks covered by universal social health care and refocusing optional insurance on health care that falls outside of this set.

Moreover, the architecture of social protection should be reorganized with a non-contributory section (family benefits, health insurance, fight against poverty, etc.) incorporated into the state budget and financed by taxation, and a contributory section (retirement pensions, unemployment insurance, daily sickness benefit allowances etc.) financed by social security contributions. The non-contributory and the contributory schemes should be homogeneous for employed and self-employed workers while some contributory schemes could be optional for both statuses.

Notes

[1] The *auto-entrepreneur* scheme allows an individual entrepreneur to declare the creation of his business in a simplified way, and to benefit from a specific system for determining social contributions (a flat rate as a percentage of turnover) and the *micro-entreprise* tax regime (exclusion from VAT and the calculation of taxable profit as turnover minus a flat-rate allowance for professional expenses, which varies depending on the type of activity). Since 19 December 2014, *auto-entrepreneurs* have been referred to as *micro-entrepreneurs*. Certain activities are excluded from the *micro-entrepreneur* regime, particularly activities relating to real estate VAT (transactions involving property dealers, developers or real estate agents, and transactions in the shares of real estate companies), and the leasing of commercial buildings, equipment and consumer durables.

[2] A *micro-entrepreneur* is economically active if he/she has reported positive turnover in the year. Some 61.2% of *micro-entrepreneurs* were economically active in 2015 (Acoss, 2016).

[3] Katz and Krueger (2016).

[4] Insee (2016)

[5] Retail sales via mail order, the Internet, direct sellers and vending machines.

[6] This part relies mainly on the report of the Haut conseil de la sécurité sociale (2016) which presents the work of a special commission composed of representatives of the different administrations and stakeholders, and in particular the Direction de la sécurité sociale and the Direction de la législation fiscale.

[7] This has been the case since 2013. Before 2013, *micro-entrepreneurs* benefited from lower social contributions, but the Finance Law of 2013, laid down the principle of such rates being determined in a way that ensured equivalence in the effective rates of social contributions paid and income tax for *micro-entrepreneurs* and artisans and traders (IGF-IGAS, 2013).

[8] In 2017, the hourly minimum wage was set at EUR 9.76, which corresponds to a full-time monthly wage of EUR 1 480. It represents 64% of the median wage.

[9] http://www.aide-complementaire-sante.info/comparatif-cmu-acs/

[10] The information provided in this section has been retrieved from the web site https://www.rsi.fr for self-employed workers and from https://www.ameli.fr for employees. More details can be found on these sites.

[11] Chauchard (2009).

[12] Haut conseil pour l'avenir de l'assurance maladie, (2013), p 60.

[13] DREES (2016), p 52.

[14] *Micro-entrepreneurs are not eligible for this deduction.*

[15] *Haut conseil de la sécurité sociale* (2016), p 289.

[16] Unedic (2017).

[17] The URSSAF (Unions de recouvrement des cotisations de sécurité sociale et d'allocations familiales) are private bodies entrusted with a public service mission, which consists of collecting employees' and employers' contributions to the general social security system as well as other bodies and institutions (the unemployment insurance scheme, the national housing fund, the old age solidarity fund, the supplementary pension schemes etc.).

[18] RSI (2017).

[19] Established in 1970, C3S (*contribution sociale de solidarité des sociétés*) is a turnover tax. The basis of the C3S is turnover minus EUR 19 million. The normal tax rate is 0.16% of turnover. The C3S contributes to the financing of pension schemes for artisans, traders and *micro-entrepreneurs*.

[20] Bulteau and Verdier (2015), Cardoux and Godefroy (2014), Cour des Comptes (2012).

[21] Bulteau and Verdier (2015).

[22] More flexible, fixed-term contracts, called *contrats d'usage,* can also be used for some other activities, the list of which is set by decree, including hotels and restaurants, education, removals, leisure centres.

[23] Cahuc and Prost (2015).

[24] EUR 10 000 the first year, EUR 8 000 the second year, EUR 6 000 the third year and EUR 4 000 the fourth year if the wage is lower than three times the minimum wage.

[25] See Bozio and Dormont (2016).

References

Acoss, 2016, Les auto-entrepreneurs fin 2015, Acoss Stat n°235 - Juillet 2016.

Archambault, H. Combrexelle, J.D. Jean-Patrick Gille, J.P., (2015) , Batir un cadre stabilisé et sécurisé pour les intermittents du spectacle. Rapport au Premier Ministre.

Blandin, M.C and Blondin, M. (2013), Régime des intermittents : réformer pour pérenniser, , Sénat, Rapport d'Information, 23 December 2013.

Bozio, A. and Dormont, B. (2016), Governance of Social Protection: Transparency and Effectiveness, Les notes du conseil d'analyse économique, no 28, January 2016

Bulteau, S. and Verdier, F., (2015), Rapport de la Mission parlementaire sur le Régime Social des Indépendants (RSI), Rapport au Premier Ministre.

Cahuc, P. and Prost, C. (2015), Improving the Unemployment Insurance System in Order to Contain Employment Instability, Les notes du conseil d'analyse économique, n° 24, September 2015.

Cardoux, J.N and Godefroy, J.P. (2014), Rapport d'information fait au nom de la mission d'évaluation et de contrôle de la sécurité sociale et de la commission des affaires sociales sur le régime social des indépendants, Sénat.

Chauchard J.-P (2009), Les avatars du travail indépendant , Droit social, n°11.

Cour des Comptes, (2012), Rapport annuel sur le financement de la sécurité sociale en septembre 2012,

Cour des Comptes (2012a), Le régime des intermittents du spectacle : la persistance d'une dérive massive, Cour des comptes, Rapport public annuel 2012 – février 2012, pp. 369-393.

Cour des Comptes, (2016), Rapport annuel sur le financement de la sécurité sociale en septembre 2016.

DREES, (2016), La complémentaire santé : acteurs, bénéficiaires, garanties - édition 2016.

Haut Conseil du financement de la protection sociale, (2016), Rapport sur la protection sociale des non salariés et son financement.

Haut conseil pour l'avenir de l'assurance maladie, (2013), La généralisation de la couverture complémentaire en santé.

IGAS, (2016), Contribution au rapport au Parlement sur les aides fiscales et sociales à l'acquisition d'une complémentaire santé, rapport 2015-143R, avril 2016.

IGF-IGAS, (2013), Evaluation du régime de l'auto-entrepreneur, Rapport, avril 2013.

Insee, (2015), Emploi et revenus des indépendants Insee Références Édition 2015.

Insee (2016), Revenus d'activité des non-salariés en 2014, Hausse pour les indépendants « classiques », baisse pour les auto-entrepreneurs, Insee Première, n°1627, December.

Katz, L., Krueger, A., 2016, The Rise and Nature of Alternative Work Arrangements in the United States, 1995-2015, NBER Working Paper No. 22667.

Menger, P.M. (2005), Les intermittents du spectacle. Sociologie d'une exception, Éditions de l'école des hautes études en sciences sociales, 2005.

Pole Emploi (2016) Intermittents du spectacle, Décret du 13 juillet 2016, September 2016.

RSI (2017), Rapport annuel 2016.

Unedic, (2017), Rapport d'activité 2016 : L'Assurance chômage en actions.

Chapter 5. Germany: Social insurance for artists and writers

Verena Tobsch and Werner Eichhorst

This chapter discusses the German Artists' Social Security Fund, a special social security scheme for self-employed artists and writers within the German Statutory Insurance Scheme. It starts with a brief overview of the general German Social Security System. It then goes on to discuss why the Artists' Social Insurance Fund was established and how it works, including descriptive statistics on its members, their earnings and the scheme's coverage rates. Among other relevant aspects, it highlights how financial contributions are shared between the artists, users and state subsidies. The chapter concludes with a short discussion of the efficiency and the effectiveness of the Artists' Social Security Fund compared to the standard pension scheme.

We thank Larissa Nenning for comprehensive research regarding data on the Artists' Social Security Fund and related literature reviews.

5.1. Overview of the German social security system

The German social security system is comprised of five statutory social insurance funds: Pension, health, long-term care, unemployment and occupational accidents. The vast majority of employees are required to be enrolled in all of these funds. The insurance funds follow the pay-as-you-go principle – those in employment pay contributions, while those in old age, ill health or unemployment as well as surviving dependents and pregnant women receive payouts. Health risks of non-working spouses and the dependent children of those enrolled in the statutory health insurance system are covered without any surcharges. Maternity allowance (*Mutterschaftsgeld*) is conditional on being in the statutory health insurance scheme, while maternity leave benefits (*Elterngeld*) are financed from taxation and paid to all working parents including self-employed people and those receiving unemployment benefits (*Arbeitslosengeld I*).

Regular employees and their employers contribute equally to the pension and unemployment insurance funds. This is also the case for long-term care insurance, except for childless employees, who have to pay an added premium, and in the federal state of Saxony where the share paid by employees is higher. Employees pay higher contribution rates than employers for health insurance, while there are no employee contributions to the occupational accident insurance fund. Special regulations apply for marginal part-time jobs with earnings up to EUR 450 per month (*Minijobs)* and part-time jobs with monthly earnings between EUR 450 and EUR 850 *(Midijobs*) where the employers' contributions are higher than those paid by employees (Table 5.1).

The foundations for the social security system in Germany were laid in the 19th century under Bismarck to insure male, dependent full-time workers with low wages. Whilst dependent employment is still the norm in the German labour market, changing labour market characteristics and compositions led to various reforms in the 20th and 21st century.

The German Statutory Pension Insurance Scheme is obligatory for all dependent employees and certain self-employed occupations (listed below). Since 2013 all employees in marginal part-time employment have been automatically enrolled in the scheme, but can opt out. Pension insurance remains optional for other self-employed workers.

Table 5.1. Artists and writers only pay half of their total contributions for pension, health and long-term care insurance, in line with the system for regular dependent employees

Contribution rates to the statutory German social security system by employment form, 2017

	Compulsorily insured				Voluntarily insured
	Dependent full- and part-time employees*	Marginal part-time employees (*Minijobs*: <EUR 450 /month)	Self-employed artists and writers	Other self-employed (insured statutorily and upon request)	(non-compulsorily insured self-employed, freelancers, homemakers, ...)
Statutory Pension Insurance Scheme (**18.7%**)					
Employee	9.35%	3.70%**	9.35%	18.70%***+	arbitrary within limits +
Employer	9.35%	15.00%**	app. 9.35% (employers' levy and state contribution)	---	---
Health (**14.6%+surcharge of 0.6%-1.7% depending on insurance company)**					
Employee	7.30%+surcharge	---	7.30%+surcharge	(14.60%+surcharge)	(14.60%+surcharge)
Employer	7.30%	13.00%**	app. 7.30% (employers' levy and state contribution)	---	---
Long-term care (**2.55%)**					
Employee****	1.275%++	Not eligible	1.275%	(2.55%)	(2.55%)
Employer	1.275%++	---	app. 1.275% (employers' levy and state contribution)	---	---
Unemployment (**3.0%**)					
Employee	1.50%	Not eligible	Eligible upon request and prerequisites	Eligible upon request and prerequisites	Eligible upon request and prerequisites
Employer	1.50%	---	---	---	---
Occupational accidents					
Employee	---	---	Not eligible	Not eligible	
Employers	depending on occupational risks	depending on occupational risks	---	---	Not eligible ---

Notes: Contribution base threshold for health and long-term care insurance: EUR 52 200/year (EUR 4 350/month) – high earners above the "assessment threshold" (*Versicherungspflichtgrenze*) can opt out of the statutory health and long-term care insurance and insure themselves privately (EUR 57 600/year or EUR 4 800/month in 2017); contribution base threshold for pension and unemployment insurance: EUR 76 200/year (EUR 6 350 per month) in old states and EUR 68 400/year (EUR 5 700/month) in the new states. Numbers in brackets indicate that the bracketed rates only apply to those who opt into the statutory system – the self-employed have the option to choose a private provider, which may charge a different fee.

* for part-time jobs with earnings between EUR 450 and EUR 850 per month employee contributions are lower (starting with half of regular rates and gradually increasing to full rates at EUR 850 per month).

** if employed in private households, employees pay 13.7% and private households pay only 5% for pension insurance; private households pay 5% for health insurance.

*** alternatively regular monthly contribution of EUR 556.33 in the old states or EUR 497.42 in the new states, with the possibility of a 50% reduction for the first three years of self-employment.

**** additional surcharge for childless people of 0.25%.

+ minimum of EUR 84.15 per month (based on marginal part-time earnings threshold of EUR 450 per month), maximum of EUR 1 187.45 in the old states (based on maximum contribution base threshold).

++ except for Saxony where employees pay 1.775% and employers only 0.775%.

Growing numbers in self-employment in particular led to the establishment of different public insurance options for those not working in traditional dependent employment. All self-employed are now obliged to take either statutory or private health and long-term care insurance. Furthermore, all self-employed occupations have been granted opportunities to voluntarily join the statutory pension insurance system while others have been obliged to enrol. However, while some of those obliged to enrol have to pay the full social insurance contribution themselves, artists and writers only pay half, due to a special regime called the Artists' Social Security Fund, which is incorporated into the German Statutory Pension Insurance Scheme (Table 5.1). Those who are statutorily insured include craftsmen, midwives, sea pilots, coastal mariners and fishermen, teachers and educators as well as carers with no compulsorily insured employees, homeworkers, and self-employed people with one customer and no compulsorily insured employees.

The German old-age social security system consists of three pillars – a statutory pension scheme, company-based pension plans and private provisions. The first pillar, the public pension scheme, is built on the idea of an inter-generational contract and covers most economically active people due to compulsory membership regulations. Certain groups of self-employed such as artists and craftsmen are compulsorily insured, while others can be insured in the public system on a voluntary basis. Only civil servants, farmers and some professions such as lawyers and doctors are covered by different systems. Dependent employees cannot opt out of this first pillar of public old-age pensions, but there is a maximum contribution threshold.

Company pension plans, the second pillar, are dependent on employers' voluntary payments into specific pension plans which cannot be cancelled even if the employee leaves the company. In such cases the company has to guarantee the capital that has already been paid in and the contract can be transferred to a new employer under certain circumstances but not converted into a private pension plan. The third, private pillar is made up of various private provisions, including private capital formation plans, which often benefit from favourable tax treatment.

The first pillar still provides the most important source of old-age income in Germany. However, the second and particularly the third pillar have grown in significance. Those in self-employment can access the first pillar, albeit on different terms, have no access to company plans but can sign up to private pension schemes.

5.2. Artists' social security insurance

5.2.1. The development of a special regime for writers and artists

The German Artists' Social Security Act (*Künstlersozialversicherungsgesetz, KSVG*) came into effect in 1983 and has since guaranteed a special form of insurance support for artists and writers. Although self-employed musicians, art educators and performers were required to be insured in the statutory health insurance scheme before this reform, it had become apparent that artists' comparatively low wages meant that they were insufficiently protected from the risks of illness and old-age poverty. The new law was based on the idea that the special character of artists' and writers' work makes them heavily dependent on users of their services – marketing and sales people – in a way that is similar to the relationship between employers and employees. Companies that make use of artistic services have thus been obliged to make a contribution to the Artists' Social Security Fund (*Künstlersozialkasse).* To compensate for the difficulties of collecting contributions from private users of artistic services, the state pays an additional federal subsidy. Self-employed artists and writers are thus left having to pay only half of their contributions to the statutory health insurance, pension and (since 1995) also long-term care insurance schemes.

5.2.2. Who is covered?

All self-employed artists and writers are obliged to join the Artists' Fund if they fulfil three main conditions.[1]:

- They are practising their artistic profession commercially, not just temporarily, and do not have more than one employee.
- Applicants' artistic work fits into the occupational definitions: The Artists' Social Security Act defines artists as those who create, practise or teach music, or applied or visual arts. Writers are defined as those who work as authors, journalists, publish in any other form or teach journalism. Due to the fast-changing nature of the arts, the fund continuously updates the list of eligible occupations. In case of ambiguity, the Federal Social Court of Germany is asked to judge the individual case.
- They earn at least EUR 3 900 from their artistic or publishing work per year, with the exception of recent market entrants who pay low fixed monthly contributions for the first three years.

All those covered by the Artists' Social Security Fund have full enitlement to insurance for the three main social security risks:

- Statutory pension insurance, covering old age, invalidity and surviving dependents.
- Statutory health insurance, including maternity allowance (Mutterschaftsgeld).

Statutory long-term care insurance.

Like other self-employed workers, artists are not entitled to unemployment insurance unless they apply within the first three months of starting their self-employed work and have made unemployment insurance contributions for at least 12 months within the last two years, either as dependent employees or while receiving unemployment benefit (*Arbeitslosengeld I*). But self-employed artists and writers as well as other self-employed people are entitled to the tax-financed standard jobseeker allowance (*Arbeitslosengeld II*) if they become unemployed, if their household has insufficient income or disposable assets.

Self-employed workers and artists have no entitlement to statutory accident insurance, but can take out private insurance on a voluntary basis. Since maternity leave benefit (*Elterngeld*) is financed from taxation, all dependent employees and self-employed people including artists and writers are eligible for this regardless of their type of health insurance. Self-employed workers and dependent employees with private health insurance are in general not eligible for maternity allowance, although they may have supplementary private insurance cover.

The statutory health insurance scheme provides a basic level of prevention, diagnosis and treatment of diseases, medical rehabilitation, sickness benefits, pregnancy and maternity care. Various company, local, guild and substitute health insurance funds may offer different benefit rates for health and long-term care costs, but always have to guarantee the statutory basic health insurance provisions. Those insured in the Artists' Fund are entitled to sickness benefits (*Krankengeld*) from the seventh week of being unable to work, as are dependent employees. Voluntary contributions to health insurance providers (not administered by the Artists' Fund), can give artists and writers entitlements to sickness benefits also for the first six weeks which are comparable to entitlements for dependent workers (*Entgeltfortzahlung im Krankheitsfall*). Long-term care insurance is also provided by health insurance schemes, covering domestic and in-patient nursing benefits, as well as in-kind and cash benefits for those needing care.

All those covered by the statutory pension insurance scheme are entitled to the same benefits. These include sickness prevention and rehabilitation benefits and old-age benefits such as subsidies for health insurance contributions, pensions for surviving dependents, partial disability pension and the regular old-age pension. The level of statutory old-age pension income depends on the number of earnings points that have been built up collected during the insurance period. Earnings points are calculated on the basis of the ratio between the average earnings of all employees in a given year, which translates into one earnings point, and the earnings of the individual insured.

5.2.3. Exemptions from statutory insurance obligations and treatment of multiple income sources

Lower rates for the newly insured and favourable insurance conditions compared to other private options for the self-employed make the Artists' Fund very attractive. Those in the first three years of their careers as self-employed artists or writers can opt for private instead of statutory health insurance. Those opting for such private health insurance receive a subsidy of up to half of the contributions for the statutory health insurance or half of the contributions for the chosen private insurance, whichever is lower. In 2016, only 5 803 persons were registered for such a subsidy, indicating low incentives for artists to choose private insurance over the statutory one.

If artists with longer experience as self-employed artists join the Artists' Fund they are obliged to join the statutory health insurance scheme as long as they are not high earners. The rationale for this is to avoid giving incentives to experienced, privately insured artists to join the Artists' Fund just to get a subsidy. Therefore it seems very unlikely that experienced self-employed artists who have private health insurance will join the Artists' Fund, except to benefit from subsidised statutory pension insurance payments.

If previous experience as an artist or writer was built up during dependent employment with private health insurance, this restriction does not apply as these people are considered to be artists at the beginning of their self-employed career. Experts assume that the main incentive for artists and writers to opt for the Artists' Fund is to obtain low-cost health insurance.

Those with earnings above annual limits may also be exempted from statutory health insurance. Those who have been exempted from statutory health insurance are also free from long-term care insurance obligations. A decision to opt out of statutory insurance cannot be reversed. An artist who wants to make an application for exemption in 2017 must have earned more than EUR 164 700 over 2014-16. This regulation and the underlying rationale is similar to the one for dependent employees who can also opt out irreversibly if their gross yearly earnings exceed the assessment threshold for statutory health insurance (*Pflichtversicherungsgrenze*), which was EUR 54 900 in 2015.

If artists and writers engage in other forms of employment, further exceptions to their insurance obligations apply depending on the main occupation and the nature of the other work. The main occupation or primary work in these cases is defined as the activity that is economically more significant (higher earnings) and more time consuming (working hours). In general, self-employed artists and writers are exempted from statutory pension insurance if their earnings as a dependent employee or a non-artistic self-employed person exceed half of the maximum contribution base threshold (*Beitragsbemessungsgrenze*). Artists and writers are exempted from health care and long-time care insurance via the Artists' Fund if they are statutorily insured because additional dependent employment is their primary work or because of regular non-artistic self-employment paying more than EUR 450 per month or more than EUR 5 400 per year. The statutory insurance obligations for non-artistic self-employed work follows the same regulations as for other self-employed people.

5.2.4. Contributions

Self-employed artists and writers pay a percentage of monthly income as insurance contributions to the Artists' Fund, at half of the statutory insurance rates set out in the annual social security statute book, just like dependent employees (Table 5.1). If the insured person notifies the fund that earnings are lower than expected, adjustments to the rates are made.

All those who make use of artistic and publishing work are required to contribute to the fund, based on the principle that there is a special symbiotic relationship between artists and users. These include publishers, theatres, orchestras, television companies, galleries, museums and similar entities. The contributions by users are supposed to account for roughly 30% of artists' and writers' insurance costs. Users are obliged by law to notify the fund of the sum of all payments made to artists and writers at the end of the year. In 2014 around 181 000 companies were registered with the Artists' Fund as users, but 95 000 did not pay contributions because they did not make use of artists' work in the year concerned.

The German Statutory Pension Insurance Scheme (*Deutsche Rentenversicherung*), the public institution responsible for co-ordinating the statutory pension insurance system, has been inspecting employers' contributions to the fund since 2007. In January 2015, the German Act on the Stabilisation of Artists' Social Security Contributions (*Künstlersozialabgabestabilisierungsgesetz, KSAStabG*) extended the inspection of user companies to all companies that are subject to a general inspection of their social security contributions every four years. The German Statutory Pension Insurance Scheme also provided more information to companies on the use of artistic and publishing work, leading to greater acceptance of the need to contribute to the Artists' Fund among user companies. This led to an enormous increase of about 50 000 in the number of user companies making contributions over 2015 and 2016 (Bundesministerium für Arbeit und Soziales, 2017, p. 138[11]).

Contributions by users are paid as a percentage of their total payments to artists and writers. In order to avoid distortion of competition, this sum must also include payments to artists who are not eligible for Artists' Fund insurance because of minimal secondary, non-commercial artistic activities or living abroad. Since 2014 there has been a minimum limit of EUR 450, below which companies do not have to pay contributions. In the first half of 2015, 32 950 companies made use of this exemption.

Contribution rates are calculated each year by the German Ministry of Employment and Social Affairs, depending on the numbers of insured people and users of artistic services. In recent years these have fluctuated between 3.8% and 5.8% of the sum of payments made to artists and writers (Table 5.2).

Table 5.2. Contribution rates payable by user companies of artistic services fluctuate to cover 30% of overall costs

Contribution rates for user companies, as a percentage of all payments made to artists and writers, 2000-17

2000	2001	2002	2003	2004	2005	2006	2007	2008	2009	2010	2011	2012	2013	2014	2015	2016	2017
4.0	3.9	3.8	4.3	5.8	5.5	5.1	4.9	4.4	3.9	3.9	3.9	3.9	4.1	5.2	5.2	5.2	4.8

Source: Künstlersozialkasse 2017.

User companies have to make a monthly pre-payment to the Artists' Fund equivalent to one-twelfth of their payments to artists the year before multiplied by the current contribution rate. After the end of the year, there is an adjustment to take account of the real amount of services used. Fees paid to artists as declared by users to the fund have quadrupled since 1991 (Figure 5.1).

If a company fails to declare its total payments, fines and penalties apply. In 2007 maximum fines were raised from EUR 5 000 to EUR 50 000 to increase the deterrent effect. Companies' insurance liabilities for artists have been inspected by the German Statutory Pension Insurance Scheme in the course of their regular audits of companies with dependent employees since 2007. The scope of these inspections has been extended since 2015, bringing in extra payments of more than EUR 30 million that year alone. This led to a decrease in the contribution rate.

Companies subject to contributions can form compensation associations to simplify the administrative process. Common rates for all members of the associations can be set and payments administered jointly. In 2008 there were only 15 such associations with around 2 000 members.

Figure 5.1. Artists' fees have quadrupled over the last two decades

Total fees paid to artists as declared by user companies, 1991 to 2013 (in Millions of Euros)

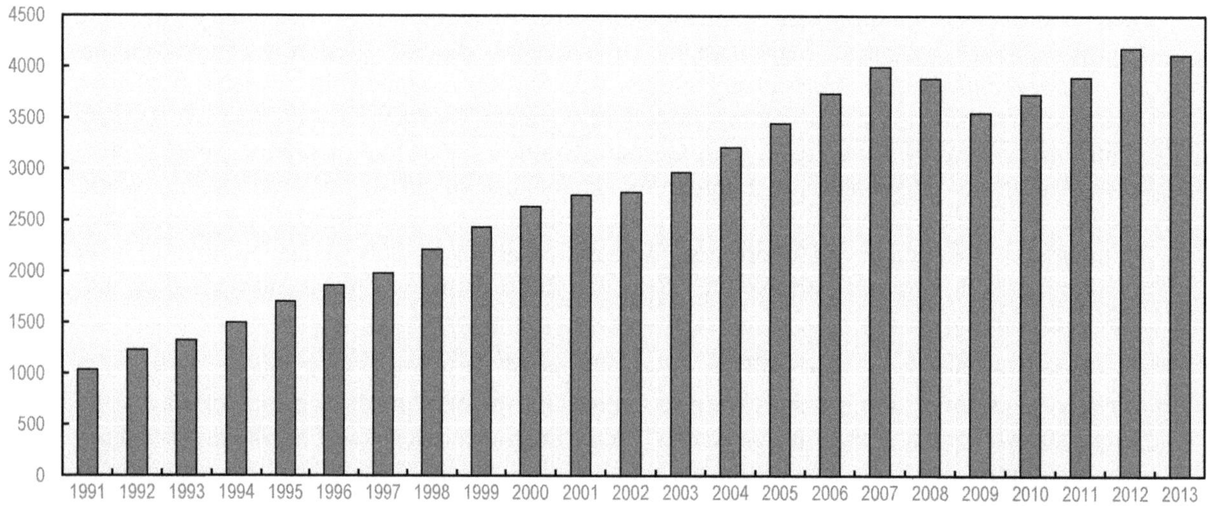

Note: Artists' fees include all payments to self-employed artists and writers as declared by user companies irrespective of whether the contracted artists and writers are insured via the Artists' Social Security Fund.
Source: Künstlersozialkasse 2017 (own depiction using data as of April 1, 2015)

5.2.5. Government subsidies

The government pays a subsidy to the Artists' Fund which is supposed to account for roughly 20% of the insurance contributions for insured artists and writers. The sum is based on estimates of the private consumption of artistic services, which is regarded as the justification for this tax-based state contribution. The sum has increased significantly from EUR 58 million in 1995 to more than EUR 200 million in 2017 (Table 5.3).

Table 5.3. Government subsidies to the Artists' Fund are increasing

Government subsidy for the Artists' Fund, 1995-2019

Year	1995	1997	1999	2001	2003	2005	2007	2009	2011	2013	2015	2017	2019
EUR mln	58.0	78.0	89.1	80.0	91.6	100.7	119.3	139.7	157.1	170.9	188.3	204.5	226.1

Note: the years 2017-19 are projections
Source: Künstlersozialkasse; Bundestagsanfrage 2015 Drucksache 18/6304.

Overall, contributions to the fund are made up, roughly as targeted, of 50% from artists' contributions, 30% from user contributions and 20% public subsidy (Figure 5.2).

Figure 5.2. The public subsidy should cover 20% of the scheme's overall costs

Budget composition of the Artists' Insurance Fund (target distribution of funding), in percentages

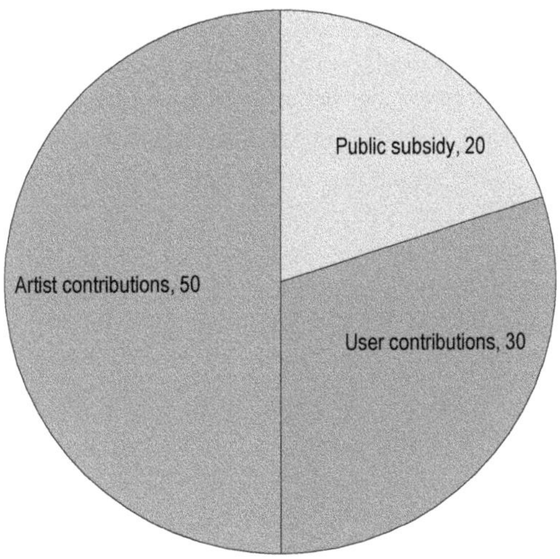

Source: Künstlersozialkasse 2017 (own depiction).

5.2.6. Description of members, earnings and coverage rates

As of June 2016, there were 183 796 artists and writers registered for insurance in the Artists' Fund of which 48% were women. More than a third of all insured were visual artists (63 834), in contrast to only 25 271 in the performing arts (Table 5.4).

Only 8 282 overall were exempted from the pension insurance, which means they were either engaged in financially significant dependent employment or profitable self-employment. Around 25 200 artists and writers were not obliged to pay contributions to the statutory health and long-term care insurance, either because they were privately insured, had high earnings from art, primary dependent employment or non-minor other self-employment. A precise breakdown is currently impossible due to a lack of data.

Table 5.4. Distribution of insured in areas of activity and types of insurance (2016)

	Writing	Visual Arts	Music	Performing Arts	Overall
Total insured	42 923	63 834	51 768	25 271	183 796
Of which female	22 645	31 312	20 830	13 301	88 088
Of which male	20 278	32 522	30.983	11 970	95 708
Statutory pension insurance	40 597	60 513	49.783	24 621	175 514
Statutory health insurance	36 374	56 081	44.490	21 621	158 566
Statutory long-term care insurance	36 365	56 074	44.485	21 619	158 543

Source: Deutscher Bundestag (2016[2]).

Current data show that declared earnings (salaries less operating expenses such as materials or studio rent) remain low on average, but also vary greatly by gender, occupation and age. Notably the vast majority of artists and writers have high levels of qualifications (Brenke, 2013[3]).

According to the most recent data for the Artists' Fund, the top earners among registered artists and writers are male writers aged 40-50 with average earnings of EUR 24 000 per year, which is less than two-thirds of average full-time dependent gross earnings. The lowest earners are female performing artists under the age of 30 with earnings of EUR 8 522 per year (Table 5.5). On average, male artists and writers earn only EUR 18 100 and women EUR 13 600 per year. Those who only recently entered the artists' market have even lower average yearly earnings of EUR 12 700. Once social security has been paid, they are at the lower end of the overall German income distribution with median net earnings of EUR 1 100 to EUR 1 300 per month. For comparison, German average gross earnings were EUR 33 396 in 2016 which leaves the average single full-time employee without children with EUR 21 631 of net yearly earnings after social security contributions and taxes.

Table 5.5. Declared average earnings of insured people by occupation, gender and age (as of 1 January 2017)

Occupations and gender	under 30	30-40	40-50	50-60	over 60	overall
Occupations:						
Writing	16 612	17 621	19 708	20 867	18 886	19 603
Visual arts	13 151	15 213	16 682	16 431	13 463	15 740
Music	10 955	12 367	13 421	13 994	13 818	13 317
Performing arts	9 609	12 895	17 008	17 330	16 672	15 581
Gender						
Men	12 940	16 339	19 359	19 823	16 823	18 079
Women	10 926	12 577	13 909	14 858	12 891	13 621
Overall	11 960	14 406	16 568	17 000	15 382	15 945

Source: Künstlersozialkasse 2017.

Heterogeneity exists within and between groups: As noted above, average incomes vary between occupational groups. But at the same time, income disparities within occupational groups seem to be very high, with for example only 1 in 12 visual artists but 1 in 10 jazz musicians earning over EUR 20 000 per year from artistic work (Priller, 2016[4]; Renz, 2016[5]).

Employment patterns also differ between occupations, which can affect insurance coverage. For example, it is common for performing artists to work on temporary contracts which they combine with self-employment. This mix of self-employment and dependent artistic employment means that performing artists often lose their entitlement to be in the Artists' Fund (Keuchel, 2009[6]). Musicians, in contrast, seem to have more stable insurance histories but still have low incomes, as they are traditionally primarily self-employed musical performers or teachers (Renz, 2016[5]).

Membership has drastically expanded since the establishment of the Artists' Social Security Fund. From 12 000 insured members in 1982, the number has risen to almost 184 000 in 2016. Increases can be found in all segments, but most newly insured people work in music and visual arts (Figure 5.3).

Figure 5.3. Membership in the Artists' Social Security Fund is increasing, especially in music and visual art

Number of actively insured in the Artists' Insurance Fund, 1991 to 2016

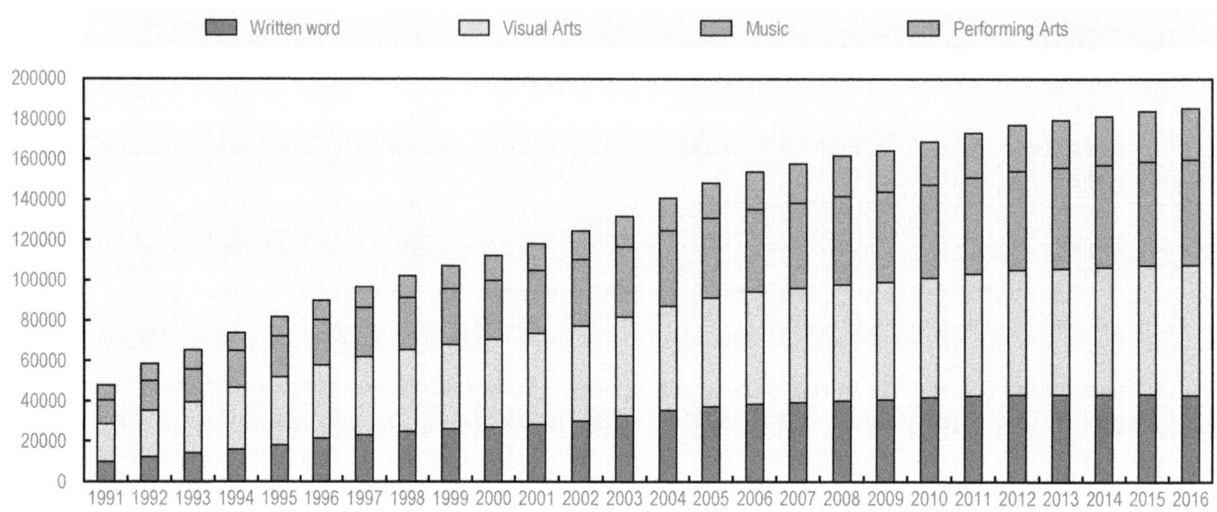

Source: Künstlersozialkasse 2017 (own depiction).

Coverage rates are uncertain because artists and writers eligible to be insured by the Artists' Fund are difficult to identify in surveys and there are no register data available in Germany. Furthermore, the group of artists eligible to join the Artists' Fund is difficult to measure because artists tend to have multiple economic activities. Statistics show that in 2011 around 20% of all male artists and half of all females worked in part-time self-employment (Brenke, 2013[3]).

Based on official microdata (*Mikrozensus*) for the year 2013 there are about 1.3 million people doing artistic and creative work, accounting for 3.1% of the total labour force. Of these, 40% are self-employed, which leads to a rough estimate of about 500 000 self-employed people in artistic and creative occupations (Statistisches Bundesamt, 2015, p. 28f[7]). If we assume that all of these are eligible to join the Artists' Fund (although this would depend on their earnings and other activities, for which there is a lack of data), this would suggest that about 36% of self-employed artists are covered by the Artists' Fund.

5.3. Efficiency and effectiveness

5.3.1. Implementation

The Artists' Social Security Fund acts as a co-ordinator for the insurance of writers and artists. Based in Wilhelmshaven, it is responsible for making decisions on entitlements to social security insurance and for managing funding. It determines responsibility for the payment of contributions, signs up artists to social insurance, takes in contributions from insured people and user companies as well as the federal subsidy. Then the fund makes payments to insurance providers.

The Artists' Fund only collects contributions, passes them on to the chosen statutory health and long-term care insurance providers, and provides information to the data bank of the statutory pension scheme. Insurance benefits are managed by the pension insurance authorities and the health and care insurance institutions themselves. In general, the procedure is the same as for dependent employees where companies are obliged to pass on employers' and employees' social security contributions.

When artists want to register for insurance, they have to notify the fund and prove eligibility by filling in a questionnaire and providing additional documents. Once accepted, the insured have to declare their expected annual earnings for the next year before 1 December of the current year. Artists and writers that fail to do so will be asked to pay contributions based on an earnings estimate made by the fund.

In the first years of the Artists' Fund, declared earnings were cross-checked with the income tax returns of artists and writers, but this was dropped due to legislative changes. Instead, since 2007 the fund has been required to check the real incomes of previous years for a random sample of at least 5% of those insured each year.

Since 2007 the German Statutory Pension Insurance Scheme (*Deutsche Rentenversicherung*) is responsible for the inspection and checking of user companies. The new regulation that came into force in 2015 has led to an increase in the number of registered users and their contributions. According to information from the German Statutory Pension Insurance Scheme, the inspection of a random selection of all companies every four years has been unexpectedly effective. Although no data are available, it is estimated that the additional costs are very low compared with the costs of the regular inspection of companies for social security contributions and therefore the increased number of registered user companies can be regarded as a success. The increased number of user companies in turn has led to a decrease of the contributions rate for users.

5.3.2. Costs and acceptance by users

In 2013, the latest year for which information is available, there were 45 people employed at the fund (plus 10 team leaders) responsible for 177 000 registered artists and writers and 16 000 applicants per year. The acceptance rate for applications was about 75% in 2012 and has risen slightly since then. This means that about 4 000 artists and writers are administered per employee. This compares with a ratio of 500 to one at one of the biggest private insurance companies in Germany (Allianz), so the Artists' Fund seems to work efficiently, although its tasks are not really comparable (Hörtz, 2013[8]).

The fund's administrative costs are funded from taxation and amount to about EUR 11 million per year. This cannot be compared with the costs for dependent employees as there is no budget breakdown. Processes for checking entitlements and collecting contributions do not apply for dependent employees and the costs for signing up to social insurance and forwarding the contributions are covered by companies in the case of dependent employees and there are no comparable data for these costs. As other self-employed people have to sign up and pay contributions without assistance, one could argue that the administrative costs of the Artists' Fund represent an additional government subsidy to self-employed artists and writers. However, the administrative costs are low compared with the government contributions subsidy.

The government contributions subsidy of about 20% of the total budget of the Artists' Fund has increased over time, according to the budget, and in 2017 the expected subsidy was about EUR 205 million for artists' and writers' health and long-term care as well as pension insurance. The administrative costs of the Artists' Fund, which are about EUR 11 million per year, are also covered by the government. Further administrative costs at the German Statutory Pension Insurance Scheme, for inspecting users and taking care of pension accounts, cannot be estimated. There is also an additional regular subsidy to the German Statutory Pension Insurance Scheme, but this subsidy also concerns dependent employees and it is not possible to estimate artists' and writers' share of this. The government pays a subsidy into the pension scheme to balance income and expenditure and this totalled EUR 64.5 billion in 2016.

User acceptance of the Artists' Fund remains low, according to employers' associations who are arguing for its abolition (Bundesvereinigung der Deutschen Arbeitgeberverbände (BDA), 2017[9]). But currently there is no public or political discussion on the possibility of changing the system.

Reliable data on user costs are not available but employers' associations claim that costs for administration at user companies are too high, with administrative costs estimated to equate to 70-100% of the cost of contributions (Müller, 2016[10]; Astheimer, 2016[11]; Institut der deutschen Wirtschaft (iwd), 2013[12]). It remains unclear whether this is a realistic estimate and how it compares with administrative costs for dependent employees. Resistance to registration seems to have declined due to regular inspections and information from the German Statutory Pension Insurance Scheme since 2007 and the new regulation in 2015.

5.3.3. Incentives and risks

Concerns about low average earnings of artists and writers led to the establishment of the Artists' Fund in the 1970s and 1980s. The contribution system of the Artists' Fund was put in place to guarantee that self-employed artists and writers have access to the same health and long-term care insurance and receive the same pension entitlements as dependent employees with the same earnings. Yet as declared earnings by artists and writers tend to be lower than average dependent employees, this is reflected in lower pension incomes from their artistic work too.

One can assume that declared earnings do not reflect the full picture of artists' earnings. Incentives to declare total actual earnings from artistic work are relatively weak. Anecdotal evidence suggests that artists' main motivation for joining the Artists' Fund lies in the fact that it gives full access to health care irrespective of the amount of contributions paid (above a minimum level of contributions).

Although most evidence is based on case studies, self-employed artists seem to remain characterised by low wages and fluctuating demands for artistic work. While health and long-term care insurance is guaranteed regardless of the contributions paid, pension insurance is more problematic.

If artists and writers only opt in to the Artists' Fund to get health and long-term care insurance, those with low earnings would have the strongest incentives to join the scheme. Low earnings can be either the result of under-declaration of earnings – which enables the insured to enjoy low contributions to health and long-term care insurance while being fully covered, but also leads to very low pensions – or of low prices for self-employed artistic work. Representative empirical evidence is not available, but based on information from the German Statutory Pension Insurance Scheme, declared earnings of artists are indeed mainly found at the lower end of the distribution – slightly above minimum entrance earnings. This suggests that the scheme attracts bad risks and that there are insufficient contributions for pension insurance, which do not guarantee pension incomes above the social minimum unless there are other assets, private insurance or savings.

5.3.4. Comparison with the standard pension scheme

In 2015 there were 37 million people actively insured in the German Statutory Pension Insurance Scheme (*Deutsche Rentenversicherung*), meaning that they were building up credits in their pension accounts. The vast majority, about 77% (28.4 million), were dependent employees. The remaining were people in marginal part-time employment (3.34%), voluntarily insured (0.65%), those in credit periods such as education, parental leave or unemployment (7.4%), other compulsorily insured and those in self-employment.

Some 294 000 self-employed people were registered for insurance, and 60% of them were artists and writers. However, the number of insured self-employed is likely to be higher as some choose to become voluntary insured because of cheaper conditions. Almost 241 000 were registered as voluntarily insured in 2015 but the number of self-employed within this total is unknown.

Contributions to the public pension scheme are shared in equal parts by employees and employers in dependent employment relationships. At average gross yearly earnings of EUR 36 267, monthly contributions would be EUR 283. Yet as two-thirds of employees earn less than the average, most contributions will be lower.

Levels of average pensions paid to the retired differ significantly between eastern and western Germany, as well as gender. Whilst men in the eastern German federal states receive EUR 1 124 monthly pension on average, the figure only stands at EUR 1 040 for men in the western federal states. Not only do women have much lower pension income, but there are also greater regional difference : Women receive on average EUR 846 in the east but only EUR 580 in the west. Longer employment records in the east and gender differences in employment patterns account for these gaps. Lower wage levels in the east are likely to reverse this trend in the future.

On average, artists and writers pay monthly contributions of EUR 197 in the new states and EUR 235 in the old states. Other compulsorily insured self-employed people pay EUR 252-301 in the new states and EUR 282-424 in the old states. Rates for the voluntarily insured self-employed are much lower – they only pay EUR 127 into the pension scheme on average (Table 5.6).

Consequently, pension incomes from artistic activities are very low too. Although the fund was established to provide sufficient pension incomes for artists, irregular and low incomes are not enough to secure contributions that lead to an adequate old-age income. Outdated studies found that pension incomes derived from Artists' Fund contributions for self-employed artists were around EUR 90 per month. Interestingly, this only represented 11.7% of the pension incomes of self-employed artists who have built up their pensions mainly though other compulsorily insured employment (Bruns 2004, cited in (Haak, 2008[13])). Current data are not available, but it is likely that whilst artists' incomes from pensions administered by the Artists' Fund might have grown due to longer contribution periods, patterns of pension income combinations from different forms of employment remain. This is also in line with surveys of performance artists and musicians that report high concerns with old-age poverty due to low-paid artistic work (Norz, 2016[14]; Renz, 2016[5]).

Table 5.6. Few self-employed opt in to the public pension system

German standard pension scheme by groups of insured, 2015

Groups of insured*	Compulsorily insured				Voluntarily insured (non-compulsorily insured self-employed, freelancers, homemakers, ...)
	Dependent standard employees	Marginal part-time employees (<EUR 450 /month)**	Self-employed artists and writers	Other self-employed (insured statutorily and upon request)	
Percentage of all actively insured (overall total 37 million people)					
	76.9%	3.34%	0.48%	0.31%	0.65%
Average monthly contributions					
	~EUR 566	No official data	~EUR 235 (old states) ~EUR 197 (new states)	~EUR 282-424 (old states) ~EUR 252-301 (new states)	~EUR 127
Average monthly pension income					
New states					
Men	EUR 1 124	No official data	No official data	No official data	No official data
Women	EUR 846	No official data	No official data	No official data	No official data
Old states					
Men	EUR 1 040	No official data	No official data	No official data	No official data
Women	EUR 580	No official data	No official data	No official data	No official data

Note: *Not included here: 18.1% in training, old-age marginal part-time employment, unemployment, employees in marginal part-time employment exempt from statutory insurance contributions, other non-self-employed compulsorily and voluntarily insured, and those in non-employment credit periods such as education or unemployment.

** Compulsory pension insurance for marginal part-time employees *(Minijobs)* since 1 January 2013, for whom insurance was previously optional. Insurance conditions for marginal part-time contracts signed before 2013 remain.

Source: Rentenversicherung in Zahlen 2017, p. 28.

However, while detailed information on the incomes of artists is scarce, existing case studies paint a picture of precarious artistic work. Artists seem to increasingly take up non-artistic secondary work to secure a living (Keuchel, 2009[6]; Renz, 2016[5]; Priller, 2016[4]). Although official data on artists' combinations of employment are not available, surveys have highlighted that concerns with insecure employment and income situations are widespread among different groups of artists (Norz, 2016[14]; Renz, 2016[5]), which suggests that low incomes from artistic work are an incentive to take up non-artistic dependent work and reduce artistic working time. Statistics show that in 2011 around 20% of all male artists and half of all females were working on a part-time self-employment basis (Brenke, 2013[3]). A survey of jazz musicians showed that two-thirds of jazz musicians were using up to 40% of their working time for non-artistic work and one-fifth were even spending more than half of their working time on non-artistic work (Renz, 2016[5]).

5.4. Conclusion and assessment

The Artists' Fund was established in 1983 aiming to guarantee a special form of insurance support for artists and writers to protect them from the risks of illness and old-age poverty. The Artists' Fund is neither a separate insurance scheme nor an autonomous system. It can rather be described as a special regime within the German statutory social security scheme, supporting artists and writers who work in precarious employment involving irregular and low earnings.

Artists and writers covered by the Artists' Fund only pay half of their overall contributions for pension, health and long-term care, which is analogous to the position of dependent employees. The remaining contributions are shared between user companies (30%) and government (20%). However, they are exempt from unemployment insurance and occupational accident insurance, as are other self-employed people. Health and long-term care of artists and writers in the Artists' Fund is fully covered and is not related to the level of contributions, while pensions are linked to the amount of contributions paid, as for other dependent employees.

Self-employed artists and writers who mainly do artistic work and do not employ more than one employee are entitled to join the Artists' Fund. Since 1991 membership of the fund has almost quadrupled. In 2016 about 180 000 artists and writers were actively insured, accounting for about 0.4% of the total active labour force in Germany. In 2013 the Artists' Fund received about 16 000 applications per year of which about 75% were accepted but access is still limited to certain occupations.

It can be assumed that the main motive for artists and writers to be covered by the Artists' Fund is to get health insurance since average declared earnings are comparably low and thus result in low pensions from self-employed artistic work. Empirical studies show that self-employed artists and writers often combine multiple economic activities, such as other self-employed work or part-time dependent work. State subsidies and the low-income assessment basis of the artists' insurance fund creates an incentive for artists to access to the full range of the German healthcare system at a very low cost.

The Artists' Fund based in Wilhemshaven itself is an administrative government agency, formally an operational division of the German occupational insurance for public services (*Unfallversicherung Bund und Bahn*). Whereas health and old-age care insurance funds and the German Statutory Pension Insurance Scheme manage the insurance benefits themselves, the Artists' Fund only administers entitlements and contributions, signs up to social insurance and forwards the contributions to the respective insurance funds. The resulting administrative costs, currently about EUR 11 million per year, are financed from taxation.

The state levy raised from companies using content provided by artists and writers has increased over time as a result of the increase in membership and artists' fees declared by user companies. The government subsidy increased to over EUR 200 million in 2017 and can be seen as a compensation for the art consumption of private households that are not subject to the levy.

Acceptance of the fund by user companies seemed to be rather limited during its first decades, leading to higher contribution rates which are set by the government in order to receive social security contributions to the targeted share of user companies of about 30%. The number of registered user companies has increased in recent years also due to inspections by the German Statutory Pension Insurance Scheme since 2007 and a new regulation in 2015. Currently there are 180 000 registered user companies. The contribution rate by users is based on fees paid to artists and writers irrespective of whether they are covered by the Artists' Fund and is currently 4.8%.

Even though employers claim that the Artists' Fund is costly and therefore should be abolished, there is currently no discussion of a change to the system. If artists and writers were forced to pay the same full contributions to health and long-term care as other self-employed people, this would probably mean that artists and writers would have to ask for higher fees. This could lead to more unemployment or higher prices for user companies and in turn for end users, too. The government's 20% subsidy for health and long-term care contributions as well as for pension insurance thus could be seen as a subsidy to end users and user companies in order to keep arts, music and writing at a reasonable price for everyone. Alternatively, the subsidy could be used for grants and scholarships for artists and writers or for any other form of direct participation for artists and writers. Whether this would be more efficient or effective in terms of social security is unclear.

In the press and media the Artists' Fund has been mentioned as a model for new forms of work such as online labour or crowdworking, but there is little detailed discussion on how this would work. According to the German Statutory Pension Insurance Scheme, extending the Artists' Fund to self-employed online workers would be rather difficult because the identification of user companies is highly problematic, whereas for artists and writers the definition of user companies is quite simple. Furthermore, if the intention is to avoid social benefits for self-employed persons with low earnings during old age, the results of the comparison of the standard pension scheme rather suggests that the contributions for artists and writers are too low – not guaranteeing a level of pension income above social allowance level in the future. Hence, the model of the Artists' Insurance Fund cannot ensure sufficient pension entitlements given low (declared) earnings of artists.

Note

[1] Gig or platform workers are not yet covered by the Artists' Fund, there has also not been any application by online workers to get entitled and therefore no practical experience has been gathered so far (Deutscher Bundestag, 2015, p. $12_{[15]}$).

References

Astheimer, S. (2016), *Wirtschaft läuft gegen die Künstlersozialkasse Sturm*, http://www.faz.net/aktuell/wirtschaft/kuenstlersozialversicherung-verursacht-hohe-kosten-14410014.html. [11]

Brenke, K. (2013), *Solo-Selbständige*, https://www.diw.de/documents/publikationen/73/diw_01.c.415654.de/13-7.pdf. [3]

Bundesministerium für Arbeit und Soziales (2017), *Sozialbericht 2017*. [1]

Bundesvereinigung der Deutschen Arbeitgeberverbände (BDA) (2017), *Künsterlsozialversicherung*, https://www.arbeitgeber.de/www/arbeitgeber.nsf/res/C83F0C6D29502C94C1257D07005757B5/$file/Kuenstlersozialversicherung.pdf. [9]

Deutscher Bundestag (2016), *Antwort der Bundesregierung auf die Große Anfrage der Abgeordneten Sabine Zimmermann (Zwickau), Herbert Behrens, Matthias W. Birkwald, weiterer Abgeordneter und der Fraktion DIE LINKE. Soziale Lage und Absicherung von Solo-Selbstständigen.*. [2]

Deutscher Bundestag (2015), *Sachstand. Rechtsfragen zum Crowdworking.* [15]

Haak, C. (2008), *Berufsrisiko Künstler. Geringe Einkünfte und drohende Altersarmut*, http://www.kupoge.de/kumi/pdf/kumi123/kumi123_78-79.pdf (accessed on 27 July 2017). [13]

Hörtz, M. (2013), *Die Künstlersozialkasse in Zahlen*, http://blog.zeit.de/open-data/author/michaelhoerz/. [8]

Institut der deutschen Wirtschaft (iwd) (2013), *Subventionierte Kreativwirtschaft*, https://www.iwd.de/artikel/subventionierte-kreativwirtschaft-113067/. [12]

Keuchel, S. (2009), *Report Darstellende Künste. Erste Berichte zur Datenlage*, http://www.kupoge.de/kumi/pdf/kumi125/kumi125_28-29.pdf (accessed on 27 July 2017). [6]

Müller, J. (2016), *Künstlersozialkasse: Wirtshcaft fordert Abschaffung aufgrund hoher Verwaltungskosten*, https://www.versicherungsbote.de/id/4844917/Kunstlersozialkasse-Verwaltungskosten-Wirtschaft/. [10]

Stiftung, H. (ed.) (2016), *Faire Arbeitsbedingungen in den darstellenden Künsten und der Musik?! Eine Untersuchung zu Arbeitsbedingungen, Missständen sowie Vorschlängen, die zu besseren Arbeitsbedingungen beitragen können.*. [14]

Priller, E. (2016), *Die wirtschaftliche und soziale Situation Bildender Künstlerinnen und Künstler 2016*, Bundesverband Bildender Künstlerinnen und Künstler. [4]

Renz, T. (2016), *Lebens- und Arbeitsbedingungen von Jazzmusiker/-innen in Deutschland*, http://jazzstudie2016.de/jazzstudie2016small.pdf (accessed on 27 July 2017). [5]

Statistisches Bundesamt (2015), *Beschäftigung in Kultur und Kulturwirtschaft*. [7]

Chapter 6. Italy: Para-subordinate workers and their social protection

Michele Raitano (Sapienza University of Rome)

This chapter focuses on para-subordinate workers in Italy, i.e. individuals who are legally self-employed but who are often "economically dependent" on a single employer. The chapter first presents the welfare provisions that para-subordinate workers are entitled to receive, pointing out that the disadvantages facing para-subordinate workers relative to employees have been recently reduced. Afterwards, making use of the most suitable available longitudinal data, statistics about the evolution over time of the number and characteristics of para-subordinate workers are shown and the first phase of the working career of para-subordinate workers is observed, assessing vulnerability in terms of earnings level, employability and accrual of pension contributions over a ten-year period.

6.1. Introduction

The term "para-subordinate worker" is used in Italy to describe individuals who are self-employed in legal terms – they work at their own risk and are not formally the subordinate of an employer – but are often "economically dependent" on an employer since, in most cases, their activity is reliant upon one or a small number of clients.

In practical terms, the term covers categories of workers who are mandatorily enrolled in a special public fund called *Gestione Separata,* established by Law No. 335/1995, which is managed by the Italian Social Security Institute (INPS). They are obliged to pay pension contributions to this fund and – when they only work as a para-subordinate – additional contributions to finance sickness, unemployment and family benefits and allowances for maternity and parental leave. However, the group of workers enrolled in the *Gestione Separata* is heterogenous along many dimensions and welfare guarantees differ accordingly (see Section 6.2).

First, two main groups of workers are enrolled in the *Gestione Separata*: various types of "collaborators" – e.g. co-ordinated and continuous collaborators, occasional or project collaborators[1] and so-called "additional workers" (also named "workers on vouchers") – and professionals who perform their activity in an unlicensed sector not regulated by a specific professional register (e.g. web-designers, archaeologists).[2] Those who work as a professional in a licensed sector regulated by a professional register – e.g. lawyers, architects, accountants, physicians – are not enrolled in the *Gestione Separata* and are not regarded as para-subordinate workers.[3]

Second, para-subordinate jobs can be associated with other types of employment or self-employed activities (in both the public and the private sector) or can be performed by retired persons. Therefore, a distinction can be made between exclusive para-subordinate workers (i.e. those only working as a para-subordinate) and non-exclusive para-subordinate workers (i.e. pensioners and those with another non-para-subordinate job).

Third, the category of collaborators is also heterogenous, since it includes generally low-paid workers hired under short-term arrangements (the types of collaborators mentioned above and workers on vouchers), relatively high-paid workers obliged by the law to enrol in the *Gestione Separata* – namely, company accountants, administrators and executives – and some high-skilled workers at the beginning of their careers (PhD students, postdoctoral fellows and physicians attending a postgraduate qualification course).

In the economic policy debate, especially before the outbreak of the economic crisis, many worries about the growing number of para-subordinate workers emerged (Berton et al. 2012), since, in most cases, these workers suffered low wages, frequent unemployment spells and were entitled to lower welfare guarantees than employees, with respect to both pension benefits and other payments (maternity, sickness, family and unemployment allowances). Furthermore, these worries were exacerbated by the feeling that many para-subordinate arrangements (for both collaborators and professionals) hid true employment relationships, which the employer organised as para-subordinate arrangements to save labour costs thanks to the lower social contributions levied on these arrangements.

A specific concern relates to the expected pensions of para-subordinate workers, because in the past they have paid a reduced contribution rate (and for professionals a reduced rate is still in force; see Section 6.2) and in the Italian notional defined-contribution public pension (NDC) scheme, introduced in 1995 and mandatory for those enrolled in the *Gestione Separata*, future pensions depend on the success of the working career, i.e. on lifetime earnings, on the frequency of unemployment spells (a risk worsened when notional contributions[4] are not paid in the event of unemployment) and on the contribution rate (Palmer, 2006; Jessoula, 2012; Jessoula and Raitano, 2017). As a consequence, if para-subordinate workers are disadvantaged along these three dimensions, they risk receiving low pensions when retired. Furthermore, para-subordinate workers tend not to enrol in private pension funds due both to liquidity constraints (they very often receive low wages and are exposed to short-term unemployment risks) and administrative constraints: waiting and vesting rules requiring minimum enrolment periods hamper the participation of workers with insecure employment prospects. Moreover, occupational funds – defined by contractual agreements – usually do not include para-subordinate workers. And para-subordinate workers are not entitled to TFR (*Trattamento di Fine Rapporto*, a form of severance pay that can be used to finance contributions to private pension funds) (Jessoula and Raitano, 2017).

To deal with these issues the Italian government has followed a three-pronged strategy over the past decade: i) a process of gradual increases in contribution rates and welfare guarantees for para-subordinate workers to improve coverage for certain events (e.g. retirement, unemployment, maternity) and to reduce the advantage to employers – in terms of lower labour costs – of para-subordinate arrangements; ii) the introduction of stricter regulations aimed at detecting "false" para-subordinate arrangements for both collaborators and professionals[5] (Law No. 92/2012); iii) the abolition of some types of contractual arrangements, namely, apart from some exceptions, project collaborations and continuous and co-ordinated collaborations (since 2016 and 2018 respectively; Decree No. 81/2015) and "vouchers" (replaced by a new type of arrangement for additional workers since July 2017; Decree No. 50/2017).

The debate about para-subordinate workers has been complicated also by the difficulty of finding comparable data to provide an extensive picture of the phenomenon. In fact, confusion about the extent of para-subordinate jobs emerged in the past due to the different procedures followed by various institutions to record the phenomenon (Raitano 2007). Indeed, while, on the one hand, survey data (e.g. the Labour Force Survey) identify as a para-subordinate those who self-report as "exclusively" working under such an arrangement at the time of the interview, administrative data (managed by the INPS) record all individuals who paid at least one contribution as a para-subordinate collaborator or professional over a period of a year (even if, during that year, these individuals also performed non-para-subordinate activities). As a consequence, the number of para-subordinate workers is higher when assessed through administrative data than through survey data. However, INPS data have the advantages of being based on an objective status rather than individual self-reporting, precisely recording the type of activity performed by a para-subordinate worker, and distinguishing between collaborators and professionals, on the one hand, and exclusive and non-exclusive para-subordinate workers, on the other hand. In this chapter we will therefore rely on administrative data from the INPS to describe the extent and characteristics of para-subordinate workers.

This chapter is organised as follows. After having described the welfare provisions that para-subordinate workers are entitled to receive (Section 6.2), we present the main evidence on trends relating to individuals working in the various types of para-subordinate arrangements (Section 6.3) and on their characteristics (Section 6.4). Afterwards, we make use of an innovative sample dataset, called AD-SILC, built by merging INPS data with the Italian version of the EU-SILC (European Union Statistics on Income and Living Conditions), to compare distributions of earnings and weeks worked for para-subordinate workers and employees (Section 0), and to observe, in a dynamic perspective over a ten-year period, employment trajectories (Section 6.7) and the accrual of pension contributions (Section 6.7) by a cohort of younger workers in order to assess whether para-subordinate workers are disadvantaged in the early phase of their careers[6]. Section 6.8 summarises the main evidence and proposals raised to improve conditions for para-subordinate workers.

6.2. Welfare entitlements for para-subordinate workers

This section briefly discusses the various welfare benefits which different groups of para-subordinate workers are entitled to. Table 6.1 and Table 6.2 summarise these welfare benefits and how they are financed for para-subordinate workers and employees.

Table 6.1. Labour costs are still lower for para-subordinate workers

Contribution rates and welfare benefits by type of employment arrangement, 2018

			Pension contribution rate	Contribution rates other than pensions
Para-subordinate	Collaborator	Exclusive	33%	0.72% for financing sickness, maternity and family benefits + 0.51% for financing unemployment benefits.
		Non-exclusive	24%	0
	Professional	Exclusive	25%	0.72% for financing sickness, maternity and family benefit.
		Non-exclusive	24%	0
Additional workers – "workers on vouchers"			33%	0
Employee			33%	Total contribution rate depends on firm's size and sector and on workers' qualification. Total rate (including pensions) is around 40% plus 6.91% to finance TFR.

Note: TFR is *Trattamento di Fine Rapporto*, a form of severance pay entitlement. Data about para-subordinate workers provided by the INPS in the *Osservatorio sui lavoratori parasubordinati* include collaborators and professionals but not workers on vouchers, whose information are collected in another archive, the *Osservatorio sul lavoro accessorio*. Therefore, the table lists workers on vouchers separately.

Table 6.2. Social protection coverage of para-subordinate workers

			Unemployment	Maternity	Sickness	Family Benefits	TFR
Para-subordinate	Collaborator	Exclusive	Yes, but lower maximum duration*	Yes	Yes	Yes	No
		Non-exclusive	No	No	No	No	No
	Professional	Exclusive	No	Yes	Yes	Yes	No
		Non-exclusive	No	No	No	No	No
Additional workers – "workers on vouchers"			No	No	No	No	No
Employee			Yes	Yes	Yes	Yes	Yes

Note: TFR is *Trattamento di Fine Rapporto*, a form of severance pay entitlement.

* The unemployment benefit for para-subordinates, DS-COLL, is payable for half of the months worked between 1 January of the previous year and the end of the contract, up to six months. The standard unemployment benefit is payable for half of the months worked over the previous 48 months, up to 24 months.

In line with the classification used in the previous section, based on the categorisation of para-subordinate workers used by INPS in the administrative archives, we distinguish between collaborators (e.g. continuous, project and occasional collaborators plus other workers included as collaborators such as the administrators and accountants of firms and postgraduate and postdoctoral students) and professionals. We also divide both groups into "exclusive" para-subordinate workers when only the para-subordinate activity is performed during the year by a worker who is not retired – and "non-exclusive" para-subordinates – when the worker is a pensioner or also performs non-para-subordinate activities, as an employee (in the public or in the private sector) or as a self-employed person. Note that, in line with normal procedures, we do not include "workers on vouchers" in the para-subordinate category, even if these workers pay contributions to the *Gestione Separata*. However, at the end of this section, the characteristics and welfare guarantees of "workers on vouchers" – a contractual arrangement that has been substantially revised in 2017 after an intense debate about their misuse by employers – will be also discussed.

Regarding pensions, para-subordinate workers are obliged to pay contributions to the public fund *Gestione Separata* which (like the whole Italian public pension system) is financed on a pay-as-you-go basis. Workers enrolled in the *Gestione Separata* will receive a pension calculated through the NDC formula (introduced in Italy by the Law No. 335/1995), which is based on principles of actuarial neutrality: pension benefit is based on the notional accrual of individual contributions over the whole career (a notional rate of return linked to nominal GDP growth is paid annually on the accumulated amount of contributions) and, at retirement, the accumulated amount is converted into an annuity based on average life expectancy at retirement age (Franco and Sartor, 2006).

The NDC formula can thus be considered as a reflection of a worker's career: for a given set of macroeconomic conditions and demographic trends, and for a given retirement age, individuals' pensions will depend on contributions paid during their whole working life, i.e. on earnings, the length of (effective or figurative) contribution periods and the contribution rate applied to earnings – in a NDC scheme, lower contribution rates mean lower future pensions. Furthermore, since it both lacks a minimum pension level and applies the same rate of return on contributions to every individual, the Italian NDC scheme has no explicit redistributive features. Consequently, the actuarial public pension pillar systematically transfers labour market inequalities at working age to pension differences at retirement (Jessoula and Raitano, 2017).

In this framework, a specific concern relates to para-subordinate workers, since they often experience low wages and frequent spells of unemployment (see Section 0) and until 2018 paid a lower contribution rate than that levied on employees. Contributions for employees stood at 32.7% in the period 1996-2006 and 33% since 2007 (23.81% is paid by the employer, 9.19% by the employee). Pension contribution rates for para-subordinate workers were much lower, especially in past years.

For exclusive collaborators, the contribution rate was just 10% in 1996 and 1997 and increased very gradually to 13.5% in 2002, then to 17.3% in 2004, 23.0% in 2007 and, then by around 1 percentage point per year until it equalled the 33% levied on employees in 2018 (Figure 6.1, Panel A). Pension contributions are not the only contributions paid by the client, however: since 1998 an additional rate (0.50% until 2007, 0.72% afterwards and 1.23% since July 2017) is paid to finance sickness, maternity and family benefits and, since July 2017, unemployment benefits.

Except in 1996 and 1997, contribution rates for non-exclusive collaborators have been lower than those paid by exclusive collaborators and are currently fixed at 24% (in 2003-06 retired people paid a contribution rate higher than non-exclusive collaborators performing a "second job", but the rates have been equal since then; Figure 6.1, Panel A). Additional contributions for other welfare guarantees are not levied on earnings of non-exclusive collaborators, who are not entitled to receive welfare benefits other than pensions (Table 6.1). For both exclusive and non-exclusive collaborators one-third of the contribution rate is paid by the worker, and two-thirds by the client.

Contribution rates for exclusive professionals were equal to those levied on exclusive collaborators up to 2013 when the process of gradual increases for professionals stopped. In fact, this rate has been reduced to 25% (plus 0.72% for financing the other types of benefits, apart from unemployment benefits that do not cover professionals) since 2017 (Figure 6.1, Panel B). Non-exclusive professionals have instead been subject to the same contribution rates as non-exclusive collaborators since 1996.

Figure 6.1. Contribution rates for para-subordinates mostly rose since the 1990s

Contribution rates levied on para-subordinate workers, by contractual arrangement, 1996-2018, in percentages

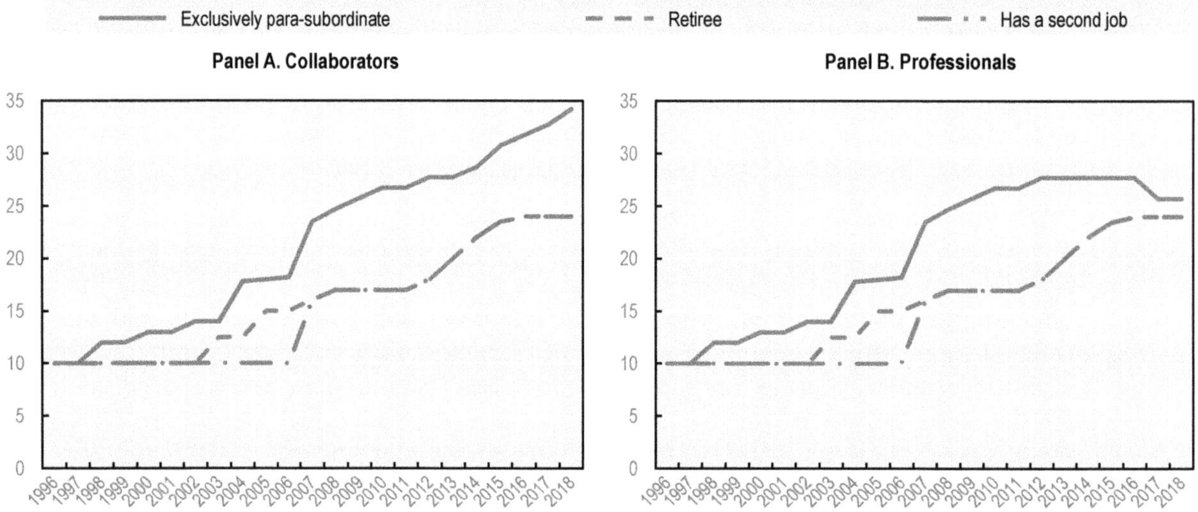

Note: Panel A: Since 1998 the contribution rate is made up of the pension contribution rate plus an additional contribution paid by exclusive collaborators for financing sickness, maternity, unemployment and family benefits. This additional contribution rate was 0.5% in the period 1998-2007, 0.72% since 2008 to June 2017, while since July 2017 the additional rate has been increased to 1.23% to finance the increasing coverage of unemployment benefits for collaborators (DIS-COLL). The rest of the contribution rate is devoted to finance the pension system. Note that the contribution rate is paid for one-third by the worker and two-thirds by the client.

Panel B: Since 1998 the contribution rate is made up of the pension contribution rate plus an additional contribution paid by exclusive professionals for financing sickness, maternity, unemployment and family benefits. This additional contribution rate was 0.5% in the period 1998-2007 and 0.72% since 2008 to June 2017. The rest of the contribution rate is devoted to finance the pension system.

In spite of the steep increase in contribution rates, social contributions on para-subordinate arrangements are still lower than those levied on standard employees. Indeed, while para-subordinate arrangements are subject to a 34.23% contribution rate at the most in 2018, total contribution rates levied on private employees for pensions, maternity, sickness, family benefits and the *Cassa Integrazione* allowance (paid to an employee when the job relationship is temporarily suspended by the firm) are around 40%, depending on occupation, sector and size of firm (pension contribution rates are, however, constant across sectors, size of firm and occupations).[7] Furthermore, private firms also pay an additional compulsory contribution of 6.91% to finance a worker's TFR (a form of severance payment), which can also be used to finance contributions to private pension funds (Jessoula and Raitano, 2017).

Para-subordinate workers were not entitled to unemployment benefits until recently. An unsuccessful means-tested lump sum benefit was paid on an experimental basis in the 2009-11 period to those working as an exclusive collaborator with a single client and a low gross annual income (no higher than EUR 20 000). This benefit amounted to 30% of earnings with a EUR 4 000 ceiling). An unemployment benefit scheme for para-subordinate exclusive collaborators – named DIS-COLL – was introduced as an experiment by the Jobs Act reform (Decree No. 22/2015) and its provision was made permanent in 2017 (Law No. 81/2017), when an additional 0.51% contribution rate on exclusive para-subordinate earnings was established (Table 6.1). Professionals and non-exclusive collaborators are not entitled to DIS-COLL. A few categories of exclusive collaborators are also not entitled to DIS-COLL and therefore do not have to pay the additional contribution e.g. administrators of local authorities, occasional collaborators, postgraduate training physicians (after intensive discussions DIS-COLL has however been extended to PhD students and postdoctoral fellows).

DIS-COLL is paid for a period equivalent to half of the months worked between 1 January of the previous year and the end of the contract, up to a maximum of six months. The duration of payment is therefore lower than for the ordinary unemployment benefit for employees (NASPI), which is half of the months worked in the previous 48 months, but with a maximum duration of 24 months. The amount of the monthly DIS-COLL is, however, the same as the NASPI benefit: 75% of the average monthly income before the period of unemployment for incomes below EUR 1 195, with 25% of the difference between average monthly incomes and EUR 1 195 added in case of higher incomes, up to a maximum benefit of EUR 1 300. After the fourth month, the amount of the DIS-COLL payment is reduced by 3% per month. Unlike the NASPI, individuals receiving DIS-COLL are not entitled to notional pension contributions.

Exclusive collaborators and professionals (paying the additional 0.72% contribution rate; Table 6.1) are entitled to sickness, maternity and family benefits[8].

Annual sickness allowance entitlement is at least 20 days and at most one-sixth of the total duration of the employment contract or 61 days, whichever is lower. The amount of sickness allowance is based on previous earnings and on the length of the contract.

In case of maternity, the contract is suspended for a five-month period and an allowance equal to 80% of the previous wage is paid if the worker paid contributions for at least three months in the previous year. Parental leave amounting to 30% of the previous wage is also available when the child is less than one year old.

Para-subordinate exclusive workers are also entitled to family allowance (ANF, *Assegno per il Nucleo Familiare*), a contribution-based scheme in which payments depend on household income and size (e.g. in 2017 the monthly benefit for a two-parent household with one child was EUR 137.50 if the household annual income was below EUR 14 383.37).

Finally, we should also focus on additional workers – usually termed "workers on vouchers", since workers are paid by the client through a pre-printed form sold in shops – a further category that pays contributions to the *Gestione Separata*. This type of arrangement was introduced in 2003 (Decree No. 276/2003), to reduce the scale of the informal economy, to pay for some occasional jobs performed in a few cases (e.g. domestic care, private home lessons) by a limited number of categories (e.g. housewives, students, long-term unemployed) and with strict limits on the total amounts received every year and from a single client in the form of vouchers. Vouchers were very rarely used until 2008 when they were allowed in agriculture and a EUR 10 gross value for each voucher was established. This equates to a net wage of EUR 7.50 for the worker after taking account of a 13% pension contribution rate, while no other welfare guarantee is provided[9].

Subsequently, several deregulations of the economic sectors and categories of workers entitled to use vouchers were introduced, especially in 2012 (Law No. 92/2012), when the usage of vouchers was extended to all sectors and all types of workers (including employees doing additional jobs) and in 2015 (Decree No. 81/2015) when the limits on voucher payments were increased (a worker can receive no more than EUR 7 000 in overall annual voucher payments and a maximum of EUR 2 020 from the same client).

The number of workers paid with vouchers increased strongly in recent years (see Section 6.3), possibly suggesting that the arrangement was being misused to replace regular employment or to pay some working hours performed by informal workers in case of administrative checks, and the left-wing trade union CGIL proposed a referendum on the abolition of vouchers. The government reformed the rules concerning additional jobs, limiting the type of firms allowed to use vouchers and increasing the pension contribution rate to 33% (16.5% for domestic activities), while no further welfare guarantees have been introduced (Decree No. 50/2017, phased in July 2017). The "new vouchers" can only be used by firms with up to five employees and by the public sector in some limited cases and a firm cannot pay vouchers for more than EUR 5 000 anually; a worker can annually receive as a voucher no more than EUR 5 000, with a limit of EUR 2 500 from a single client. Net hourly wage cannot be lower than EUR 9 and the daily net wage has to be equal to at least EUR 36.

6.3. Para-subordinate workers: the extent of the phenomenon

Using administrative data from the INPS which record workers paying at least one contribution a year to the *Gestione Separata* fund, a picture about the evolution over time of the number of para-subordinate workers is provided in this section, which also distinguishes between the different types of para-subordinate workers and highlights the evolution over time of additional "workers on vouchers".[10]

The number of para-subordinate workers (collaborators and professionals, irrespective of whether they are exclusive or non-exclusive; Figure 6.2) hugely increased between 1996 and 2007: during that period the total number of contributors to the *Gestione Separata* increased 126% (129% for collaborators and 106% for professionals), while, in the same period, according to Eurostat figures, based on the Labour Force Survey, the mean number of employees and total workers over a year increased, respectively, by 19% and

14%. In 2007 around 1.9 million workers had a para-subordinate arrangement, and the number of collaborators was very large too (around 1.67 million workers versus around 220 000 professionals).

Afterwards, while the number of professionals increased almost constantly over the whole observation period to reach around 327 000 in 2016, the number of collaborators fell sharply to around 917 000 in 2016 (Figure 6.2). The number of collaborators is expected to decrease further in future years since, as mentioned, the Jobs Act reform of 2015 banned new project collaborations from 2016 and new co-ordinated and continuous collaborations from 2018. The only exclusive collaborations still allowed are occasional collaborations and collaborations in which the worker is clearly independent from the client (for instance, to be counted as an "independent collaboration" there can be no working hours schedule and the collaborator cannot be obliged to work in the client's office).

Figure 6.2. The number of para-subordinate collaborators follows an inverted U-shape

Number of workers paying contributions to the *Gestione Separata, 1996-2016, in 1 000s*

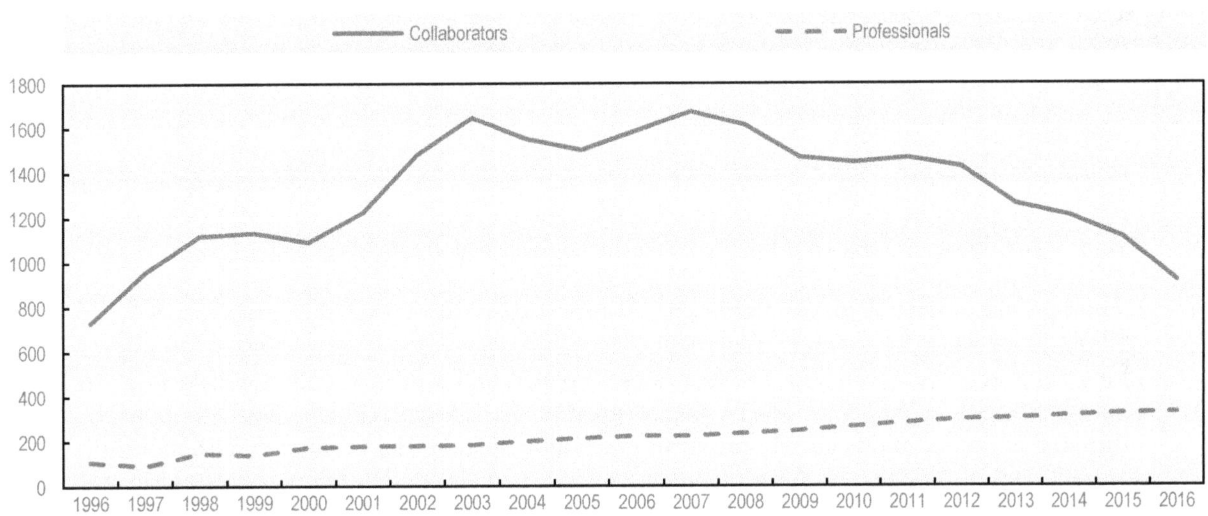

Source: Own calculations based on INPS data "Osservatorio sui lavoratori parasubordinati".

Distinguishing between para-subordinate workers on the basis of whether they are exclusive or non-exclusive, there has been a clear reduction in the number of exclusive collaborators, which has only been partially offset by an increase in the number of exclusive professionals (Figure 6.3). In the period 2011-16 the number of exclusive collaborators declined 49.6%, while the number of exclusive professionals increased 23.6%.

Therefore, it has to be emphasised that the decrease in the extent of exclusive collaborations came before the more binding regulatory constraints introduced by the 2012 reform and particularly by the 2015 reform. The decline started after 2007, when, as shown in the previous section, a process of gradual increases in the pension contribution rates for para-subordinate workers started.

As a consequence, in 2016 the number of exclusive collaborators is almost equal to that of non-exclusive collaborators (484 972 versus 432 535, respectively) while exclusive and non-exclusive professionals amount, respectively, to 241 338 and 85 600 individuals (Figure 6.3). This evidence is therefore consistent with the idea that the widespread use of para-subordinate collaborations of the previous decade was mainly due to the lower cost of these arrangements rather than to a real need to use collaborators rather than employees.

Figure 6.3. The number of exclusive para-subordinate collaborators fell in recent years

Number of workers paying contributions to the *Gestione Separata*, by contractual agreement, in 1 000s

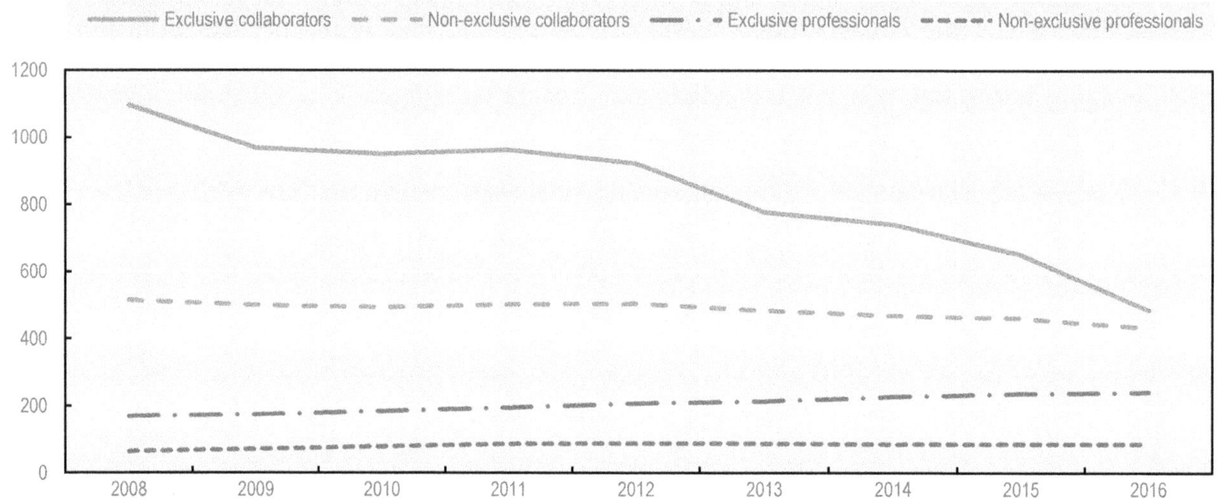

Source: Own calculations based on INPS data "Osservatorio sui lavoratori parasubordinati".

Detailed data collected in the INPS (2017) report also show that the large majority of collaborators work for a single client (89.6%) while only 2.1% have at least three clients in a year. There were 174 035 collaborators who still had a project collaboration in 2016 (compared with 376 774 in 2015), while around 34 455 individuals worked in a co-ordinated and continuous collaboration in the public sector. The number of collaboration contracts based on the definition of "independence" of the collaborator according to the content of the Decree No. 81/2015 was 48 671 in 2016. Within the category of exclusive collaborators, there were 51 665 PhD and postdoctoral students, 34 376 postgraduate physicians in training and 504 315 administrators and accountants are also included.

This latter category is, as expected, paid more than other categories: on average, para-subordinate collaborators working as administrators and accountants had gross earnings of EUR 32 682 in 2016, compared with mean earnings for all collaborators of EUR 22 813.

Finally, it is interesting to report that, among the 432 553 non-exclusive collaborators in 2016, 19.3% were pensioners and 20.1% employees (in the public or the private sector), with the remainder accounted for by self-employed people (especially craftsmen and dealers). Interestingly, consistent with the evidence that pensioners who combine pensions and labour income were often high-skilled workers, mean annual earnings from non-exclusive collaborations performed by pensioners were in 2016 around EUR 30 000.

Finally, data on the trend of the number of vouchers sold to pay additional workers confirm the dramatic rise of the usage of this type of arrangement (Figure 6.4, Panel A). In 2016 over 130 million vouchers were sold to pay 1 765 810 individuals. From 2012 to

2016 the number of vouchers increased by 482%. This trend has reversed following the substantial reform of the voucher scheme, see Section 6.2).

Figure 6.4. The number of vouchers increased rapidly, and incomes on vouchers are low

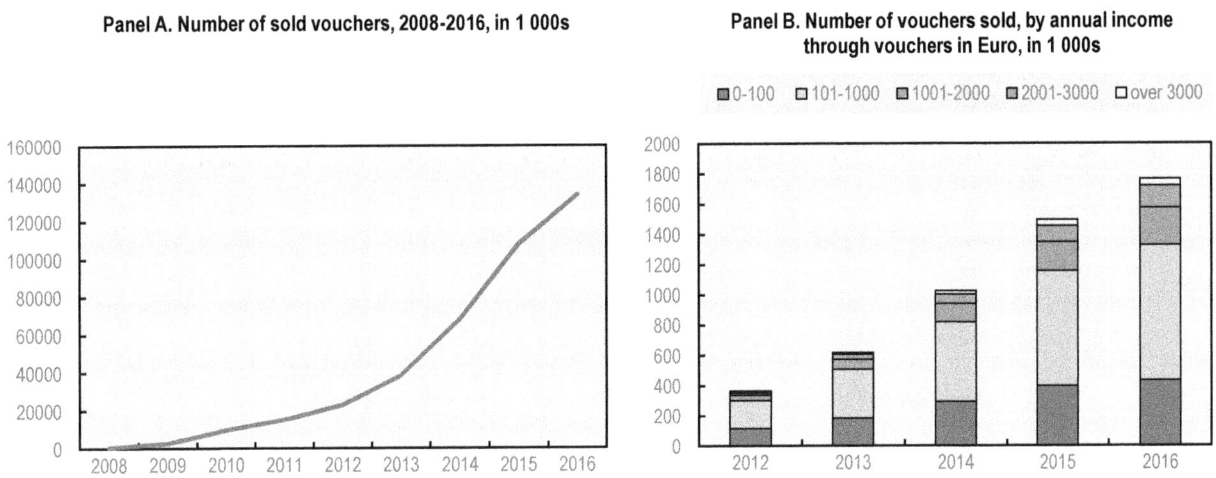

Source: Calculations based on INPS data "Osservatorio sul lavoro accessorio".

The distribution of the yearly amounts received in vouchers (Figure 6.4, Panel B) shows that very few individuals received more than EUR 3 000 annually (2.6% in 2016), while the large majority earn very low incomes: 75.1% of additional workers received less than EUR 1 000 in 2016. These figures clearly show that if work paid by vouchers is the only activity performed in a year by a worker, the amount received is totally inadequate to provide a decent wage. And if individuals are only working through vouchers, this points to them working more hours informally than they are paid through vouchers (Anastasia et al., 2016).

6.4. The main characteristics of para-subordinate workers

A disadvantage of INPS data is that, because they are based on administrative forms filled in by employers when contributions are paid, detailed workers' characteristics are not recorded (e.g. education, marital status, number of children, parents' background; INPS data, instead, record sex, age and area of work). In particular, information about the education of those working as a para-subordinate is crucial to better assess the characteristics of these workers.

To this end, in the rest of the chapter we will mainly rely on the micro-data collected in the AD-SILC dataset, a longitudinal dataset built by adding INPS data to the IT-SILC waves 2004-2012. Thus, the individual information recorded in IT-SILC has been enriched by the longitudinal information about the working history of each individual in the sample (e.g. recording for each working relationship, the type of arrangement, identified by the specific INPS fund where the workers pay contributions – which allows us to distinguish between para-subordinate collaborators and professionals – weeks worked and gross earnings).

Because individuals may have various contractual arrangements during a year, we recognise the working status at a point in time (31 December), thus identifying those exclusively working as a para-subordinate at that moment (if at 31 December an individual also has an employment or a self-employment arrangement or is retired he/she is therefore not classified as a para-subordinate worker).

Interestingly, data at our disposal show that the use of para-subordinate arrangements is much wider among those with a tertiary education qualification than among those with a lower level of education. Indeed, on the one hand, the distribution by education of private employees, para-subordinate collaborators and professionals in 2013 (Figure 6.5) shows that the share of those with a tertiary education is much higher in the two para-subordinate categories (34.0% and 46.8% of collaborators and professionals, respectively) than among private employees (11.2%), and conversely the share of low-skilled individuals (those with at most a lower secondary educational qualification) in para-subordinate arrangements is small. Similarly, 7% of tertiary graduates were para-subordinates at the end of 2013 (compared with a peak of over 10% in 2003), while the corresponding shares of those with at most upper secondary or lower secondary educational qualifications, respectively, 3.4% and 1.7% (not shown).

Figure 6.5. Para-subordinate workers are well educated on average

Share of workers by contractual arrangement and education, percentages, in 2013

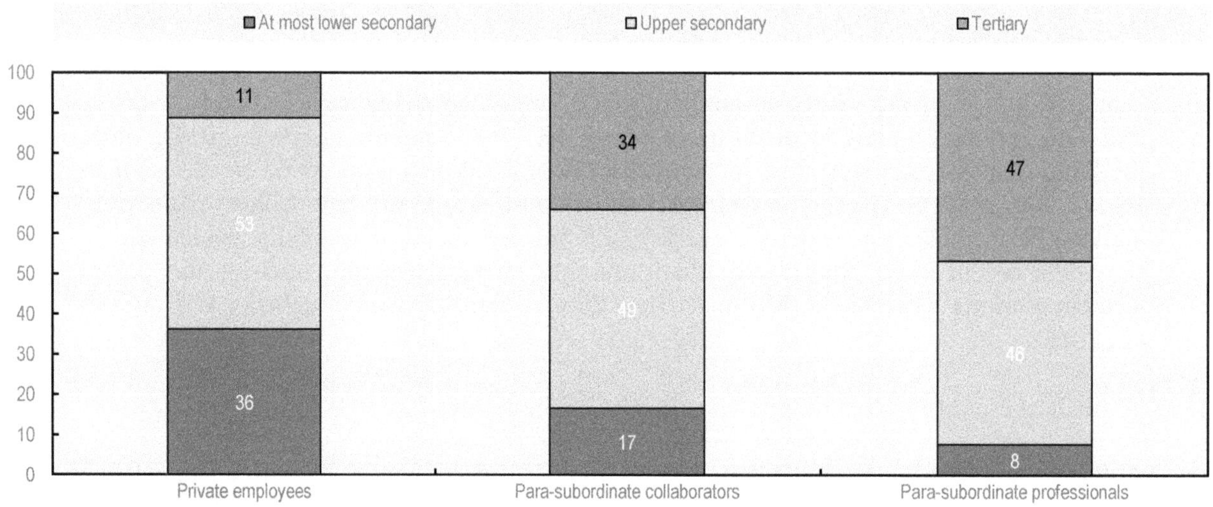

Source: Own calculations based on AD-SILC data.

The use of para-subordinate arrangements among the well-educated may be due to compositional effects (e.g. para-subordinate arrangements are often used in the case of younger workers who are, on average, more educated) and to the fact that some specific activities performed only or mostly by tertiary education graduates (e.g. postgraduate fellows, administrators or accountants) are classified as para-subordinate jobs. However, multivariate econometric estimates confirm that, even after controlling for the type of job and characteristics of workers, the probability of working in a para-subordinate arrangement is much higher for tertiary graduates than for less educated individuals (Raitano, 2007). This might be driven by the specific characteristics of some highly skilled jobs, which mean that these jobs are more frequently carried out via para-subordinate work arrangements. Since survey data do not contain detailed job descriptions, this cannot be confirmed in this analysis.

As argued above, para-subordinate arrangements might mask – among both collaborators and professionals – actual employment relationships in which the employer uses a para-subordinate arrangement to save labour costs. The 2012 and 2015 reforms tried to avoid the misuse of these arrangements by adding requirements confirming that the para-subordinate worker is really independent.

To assess how many para-subordinate arrangements concealed what are effectively subordinate relationships between the employer and the worker before the recent reforms, a specific survey carried out by the ISFOL (*Istituto per lo sviluppo della formazione professionale dei lavoratori* – Institute for developing workers' lifelong learning) on a sample of workers in 2010 is very useful. Indeed, this survey recorded how many para-subordinate workers reported in interviews that their job had some features that should not be typical of para-subordinate jobs, which suggests that there was actually a subordinate relationship between the employer and worker.

The figures in the ISFOL survey are worrying since they show that the large majority of para-subordinate workers performed activities similar to those of employees, which suggests that many para-subordinate arrangements masked subordinate relationships (Figure 6.6): indeed, the large majority of those interviewed reported having accepted a para-subordinate arrangement at the client's request (70.5%), to work in the client's office (71.7%), to follow prearranged working hours (67.0%) and because of a desire to convert their flexible para-subordinate arrangement into an open-ended employment contract (75%). Thus, rather than choosing this type of arrangement voluntarily, many workers seem to have been forced by employers to accept a very flexible arrangement, offering lower welfare guarantees and, very often, lower wages than employees.

Figure 6.6. Para-subordinates report working under conditions similar to those of employees

Share of para-subordinate workers who report that their working arrangement fulfils characteristics of dependent employment relationships, in percent, 2010

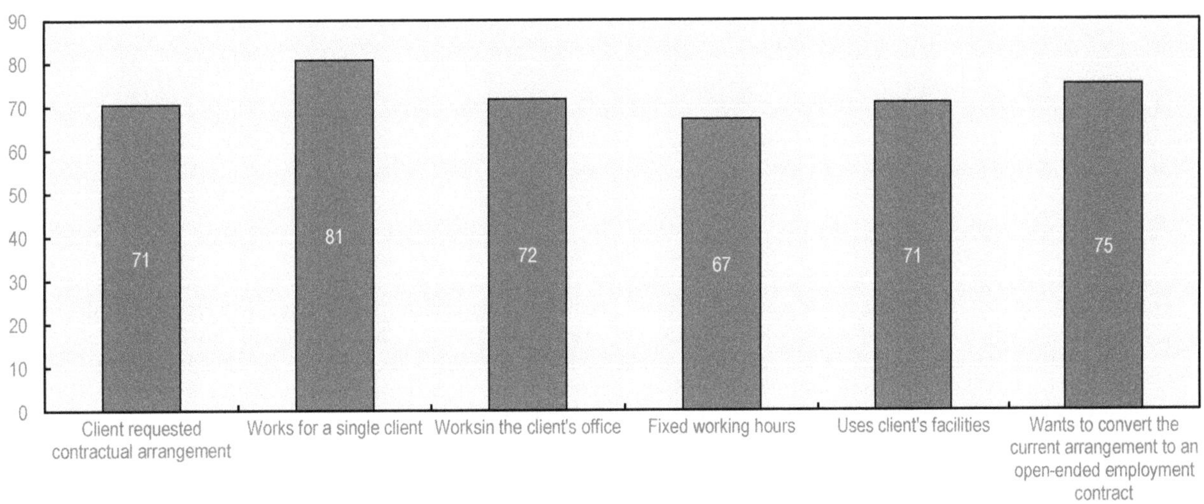

Source: Own calculations based on ISFOL-PLUS 2010 data.

6.5. Earnings distribution by contractual arrangements

As pointed out in previous sections, para-subordinate workers have less generous welfare entitlements than employees, or none at all. It is therefore interesting to analyse whether this disadvantage is compensated for by higher rewards – in terms of earnings or less frequent unemployment spells – or whether, on the contrary, lower welfare guarantees are associated with shorter working periods and lower earnings on average over a year.

To this aim, in AD-SILC we have identified the "main" working condition during a year as the contractual arrangement accounting for the highest number of working weeks in a year.

Focusing on total annual working weeks as the main working condition experienced during a year, a clear gap in terms of weeks worked emerges (Figure 6.7). While, on average, in the period 1996-2013 the mean number of weeks worked by private employees was fairly constant at around 44, total weeks worked by collaborators and professionals never reached this level. The gap in weeks worked between employees in the private sector and para-subordinate collaborators and professionals amounted to 7.5 and 7.0 weeks respectively in 2013.

Figure 6.7. Para-subordinates are less likely to work year-round than dependent employees

Average total number of annual weeks worked, by main contractual agreement, 1996-2013

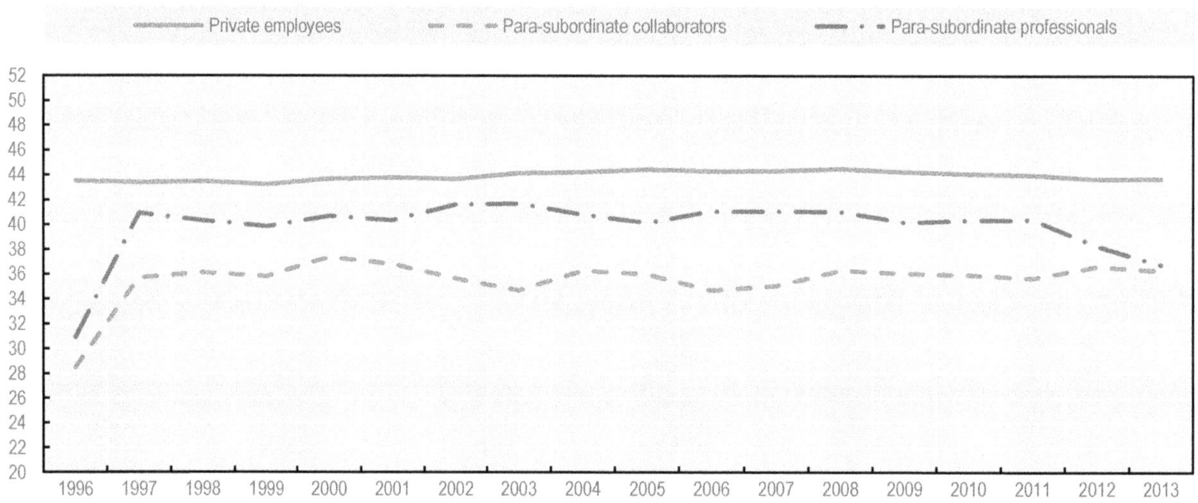

Note: All workers in the sample are assigned a "main" contractual agreement in any given year (the one with the highest number of weeks worked). Number of weeks worked are then calculated irrespective of contractual agreement. Retirees are excluded from the analysis. The low value in 1996 is related to the fact that the *Gestione Separata* fund was introduced in that year and, therefore, many workers started to work as a para-subordinate during the year. Annual weeks worked exclude paid annual leave.
Source: Own calculations based on AD-SILC data.

Para-subordinate workers also receive lower wages than employees (Figure 6.8, Panel A). Focusing on median earnings (which allows us to exclude the impact of possible outliers at the top of the earnings distribution) a large gap between private employees and collaborators emerges, while the gap between employees and professionals grew in 2012 and 2013, probably due to the effects of the economic crisis. In 2013, a median collaborator's annual gross earnings were 33.8% lower than the median private employee wage, while professionals' earnings were 31.8% lower.

Figure 6.8. Para-subordinate earnings are lower and more dispersed than those of employees

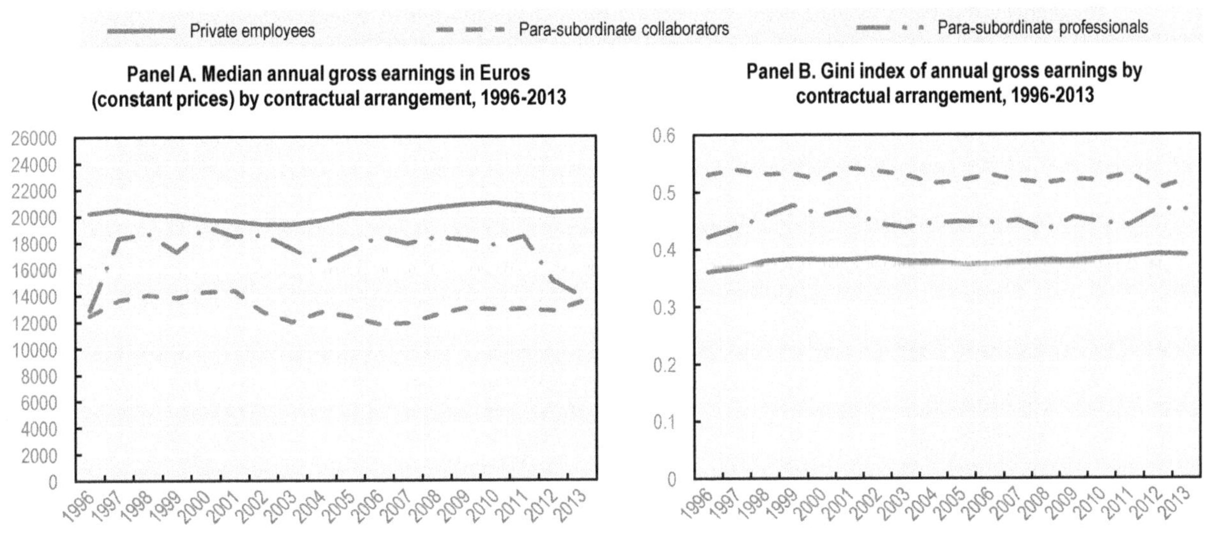

Note: This analysis only includes earnings from the main earnings source in any given year; that is, collaborators' earnings refer to annual earnings from work as a para-subordinate collaborator, received by those who worked prevalently as a collaborator in that year. Earnings from other contractual arrangements, as well as the earnings of those who have a contractual arrangement as a para-subordinate collaborator as a secondary earnings source, are disregarded.
Source: Own calculations based on AD-SILC data.

However, median incomes do not provide a full picture of para-subordinate living standards since, as already noted, para-subordinate arrangements are very heterogenous and include, for instance, both well-paid activities (such as those performed by administrators and accountants) and low-paid and short-term occasional collaborations.

The evidence of a large heterogeneity emerges when calculating the Gini income of inequality of gross earnings received in a year by those mainly working under the various contractual arrangements (Figure 6.8, Panel B). Gini coefficient values were fairly constant over the period observed, but the level of earnings inequality between para-subordinate professionals and, particularly, para-subordinate collaborators is much higher than inequality between private employees.

The picture of large inequalities between para-subordinate workers is also confirmed when looking at the distribution by income brackets of annual earnings in 2013 (Figure 6.9). Indeed, 39.2% and 36.6% of those "mainly" working as collaborators and professionals, respectively, earned less than EUR 10 000 in 2013, while the corresponding share was 24.8% among private employees (part-time and fixed-term employees are in the bottom tail of the employed earnings distribution). Conversely, the share of high-paid workers – i.e. those earning more than EUR 75 000 in 2013– is higher among collaborators (5.3%) and professionals (2.3%) than among private employees (1.3%).

Figure 6.9. Among para-subordinates, both high and low earners are overrepresented

Breakdown of workers by main employment arrangement and annual gross income, percentages, 2013

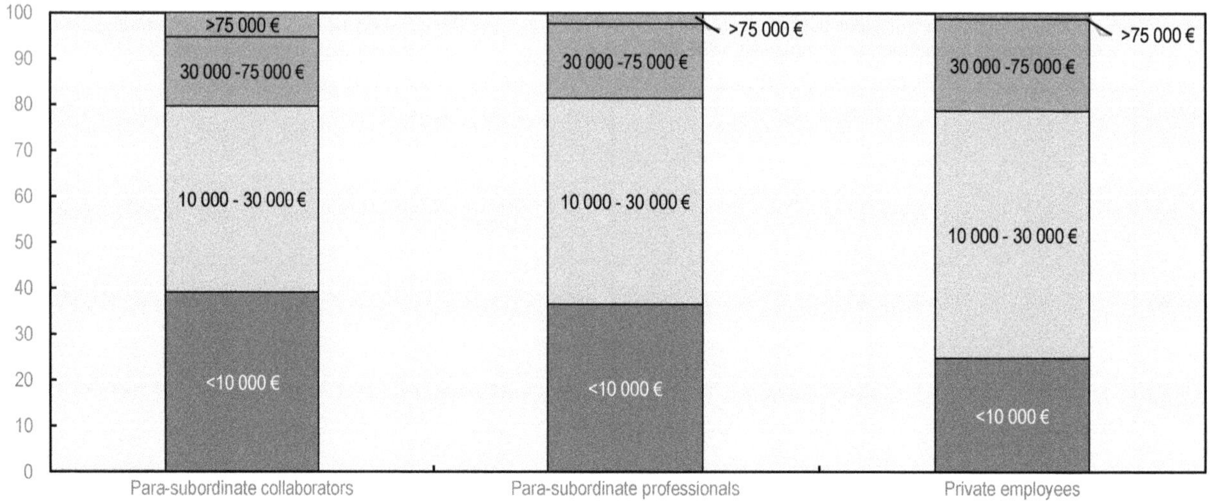

Note: This analysis only includes earnings from the main earnings source in any given year; that is, collaborators' earnings refer to annual earnings from work as a para-subordinate collaborator, received by those who worked prevalently as a collaborator in that year. Earnings from other contractual arrangements, as well as the earnings of those who have a contractual arrangement as a para-subordinate collaborator as a secondary earnings source, are disregarded.

Source: Own calculations based on AD-SILC data.

6.6. Para-subordinate workers' working lives: a dynamic perspective

Risks related to para-subordinate arrangements cannot be assessed simply by looking at individuals' labour market situations at a particular point in time, because individual employment trajectories need to be assessed over a longer time span. To this purpose, we have made use of the longitudinal AD-SILC dataset and observed the employment trajectories of individuals who entered the labour market in the 1996-2001 period over the ten years following the year of entry, using some indicators of poor careers related to unemployment spells and periods spent working in para-subordinate arrangements. In Section 6.7 we will also assess risks related to the starting phase of the working career by calculating total contributions accumulated in the NDC scheme over a ten-year period, which acts as both an indicator of the success of the early phase of the career and, in the case of limited accumulation of pension contributions, as a signal of a possible risk of old-age poverty in the future if the working career does not improve over the subsequent decades.

We first focus on new labour market entrants and show the share of individuals who started working in a para-subordinate arrangement (Figure 6.10, Panel A). This can only be calculated until 2011, since those working in the public sector are not recorded in AD-SILC after that year. The share of new entrants working as para-subordinate collaborators steadily increased over time until it reached a peak of 15.5% in 2008 and then declined to 11.1% in 2011 – maybe as an effect of the aforementioned rise in social security contributions for para-subordinate workers – while the share of new entrants who were professionals remained fairly constant in the 1-1.5% range.

Consistent with the evidence of Section 6.4, it is mostly tertiary education graduates who start working in a para-subordinate arrangement, while the share of workers with a lower level of education entering the labour market through a para-subordinate arrangement is much lower, since many para-subordinate jobs require high-skilled workers (Figure 6.10, Panel B). For instance, in 2009 the first working contracts of 29.3% of tertiary graduates were as para-subordinates, compared with peaks of 18.2% in 2008 for those with an upper secondary education and 6.0% in 2007 for those with at most a lower secondary qualification.

Figure 6.10. The number of labour market entrants working as para-subordinates peaked in 2009

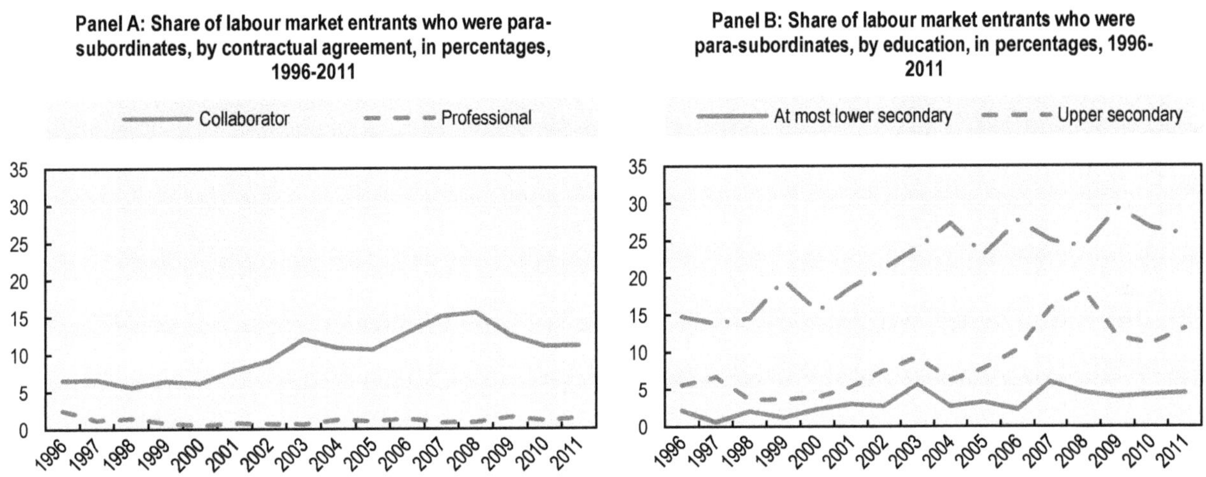

Note: Labour market entrants are under 35-year-olds who, in a given year, worked 13 weeks or more for the first time.
Source: Own calculations based on AD-SILC data.

However, para-subordinate arrangements at entry might either represent a stepping stone towards a better paid and guaranteed arrangement or a sort of trap (a "dead end") in less advantaged jobs (Muehlberger and Pasqua, 2006; Picchio, 2008; Berton et al., 2011).

The employment trajectories tracked in INPS data show that the persistency of para-subordinate arrangements is not too high: among new entrants in 2000, 19.2% still worked as para-subordinates in 2005, while 36.4% moved towards private dependent employment and 20.2% towards other self-employed activities. However, the share of those who were unemployed or inactive was very high (21.3%).

To better assess employment trajectories, we have used AD-SILC data – which, as mentioned, precisely record the number of weeks worked each year under the various types of contractual arrangements – to extract a sub-sample of around 13 000 individuals, and followed those entering activity in 1996-2001 over a ten-year period (i.e. 1997-2006 for entrants in 1996, 1998-2007 for entrants in 1997 etc.), distinguishing by types of arrangement at entry (Figure 6.11).[11] On average, the share of workers spending periods working as a para-subordinate is low: only 2.3% of all workers and 0.9% of those who started on a non-para-subordinate contract spent at least five of the ten years as a para-subordinate worker. However, the number of years spent as a para-subordinate worker for those who started working as a collaborator or a professional is higher: indeed, 32.7% of these spent at least three of the ten years working as a para-subordinate.

Figure 6.11. Those who start their careers as para-subordinates often continue on this path

Breakdown of 1996-2001 labour market entrants by weeks spent working as a para-subordinate over the first 10 years after labour market entry, by contractual arrangement at labour market entry, in percent

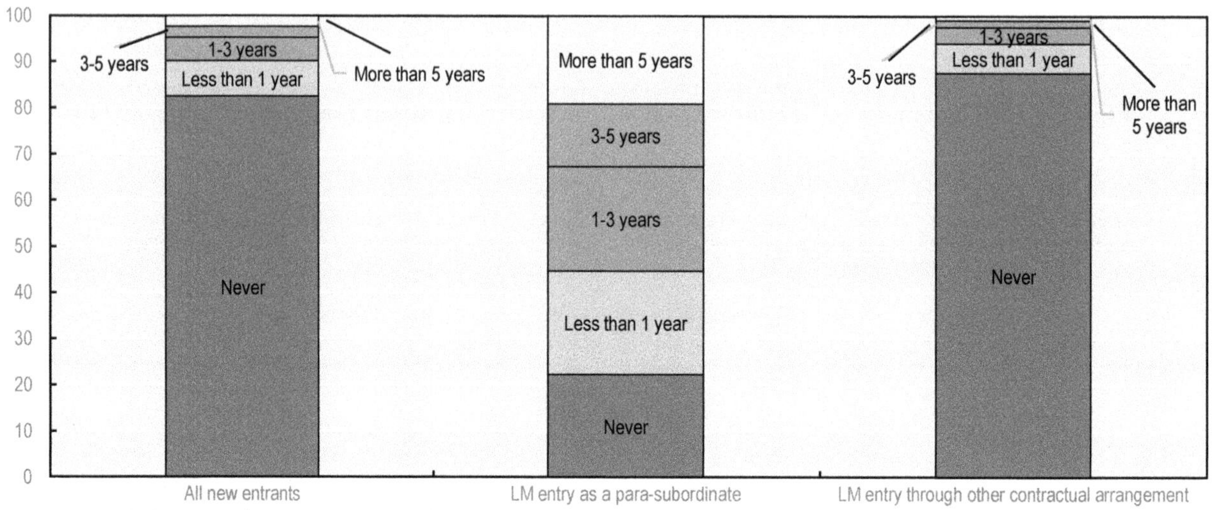

Note: Labour market entrants are under 35-year-olds who, in a given year, worked 13 weeks or more for the first time. The first 10 years start in the year after labour market entry.
Source: Own calculations based on AD-SILC data.

In general, what clearly emerges from the AD-SILC data is that the early phase of a career is characterised by frequent periods spent not working, irrespective of the contractual arrangement at entry, thus confirming a picture of widespread vulnerability among younger workers in Italy since the mid-1990s (Figure 6.12, Panel A). On average, new entrants in 1996-2001 spent around a quarter of the following ten-year period (i.e. 2.5 years) not working and not receiving unemployment benefit (the share of young workers receiving unemployment benefit in Italy is rather limited).

However, while unemployment risks are similar irrespective of the initial contract, those who start out as a para-subordinate worker do spend a much higher share of their weeks worked in para-subordinate jobs.

Figure 6.12. Those who start as para-subordinates do not work less than others

Share of weeks worked, and share of worked weeks worked as a para-subordinate, over the first 10 years after labour market entry, by contractual arrangement at labour market entry, labour market entrants 1996-2001, in percent

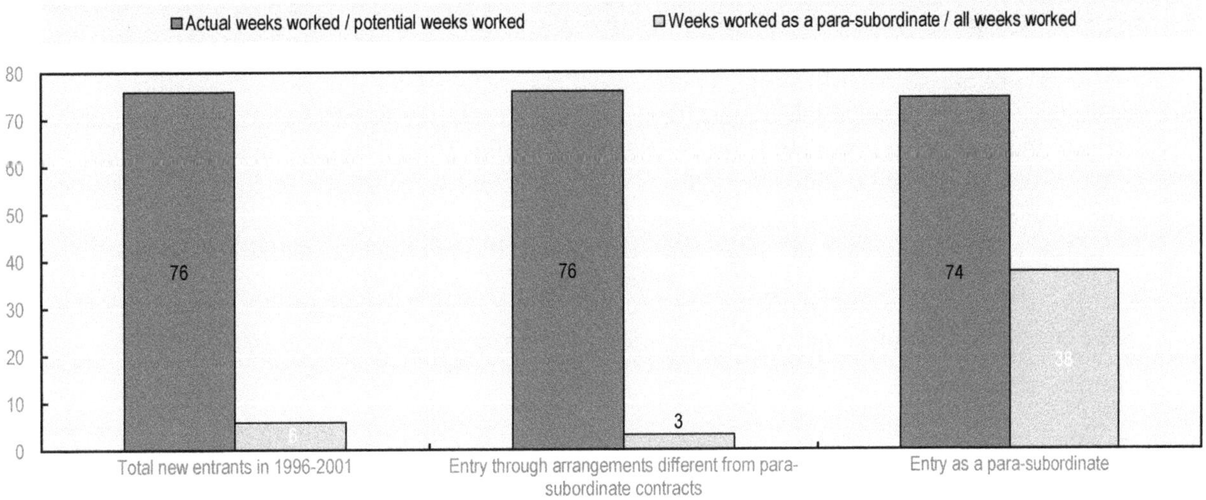

Note: Labour market entrants are under 35-year-olds who, in a given year, worked 13 weeks or more for the first time. The first 10 years start in the year after labour market entry.

Source: Own calculations based on AD-SILC data.

6.7. Actual accumulation of pension contributions by para-subordinate workers since 1996

The success of a working career over a certain period can be evaluated by measuring total pension contribution accrued over that period (according to the rules of the Italian NDC pension system, the annual rate of return on accrued contributions is equal to the five-year average of the GDP nominal growth rate). This is a useful indicator that summarises both the outcomes of various dimensions of a career over a period of several years (i.e. earnings, which are also influenced by the frequency of periods of part-time working, periods spent not working or receiving unemployment benefit, periods spent working in contractual arrangements that pay a reduced contribution rate, such as para-subordinate arrangements) and to highlight possible risks of inadequate future pensions due to a poor accrual of contributions in the early phase of the career in the NDC pension system where, it should be noted, future pensions strictly depend on contributions paid over the whole working life.

To assess the size of pension contribution accrued over the ten-year period following labour market entry for new entrants in 1996-2001 we used a relative approach, i.e. we calculated the relative accumulation with respect to the accumulation potentially achieved by a representative worker. We then chose as a benchmark an individual who worked continuously over the ten-year period as a full-time dependent employee in the private sector (thus paying the 33% contribution rate) and always earning the gross median wage (amounting, in real terms, to around EUR 20 000 per year). Consistent with the relative poverty approach, we then identified those who accumulated less than 60% of the potential accumulation of the ideal full-time, never unemployed median private sector employee over the ten-year period as poor in terms of pension contributions.

Our calculations clearly show that the ten-year period after labour market entry has not been successful for a high share of Italian workers in previous years. Indeed, just under half of workers that entered the labour market in the period 1996-2001 accumulated less than 60% of the hypothetical median employee (Figure 6.13): for those who started work as a para-subordinate, the share of those with poor contributions accumulation – which can be also regarded, as mentioned, as an indicator of a risk of a poor future pension – is 46.7%, but it is also extremely high among those who started work as an employee in the public or private sector (40.9%). As expected, the risks of an unsuccessful career are higher for females than for males and for workers with a lower level of education than for tertiary education graduates, but these risks are also fairly high among males and high-skilled workers (Figure 6.13).

Figure 6.13. Many have low pension contributions, but para-subordinates are more vulnerable

Share of workers at-risk of low future pension, by contractual arrangement and other characteristics, labour-market entrants 1996-2001, in percent

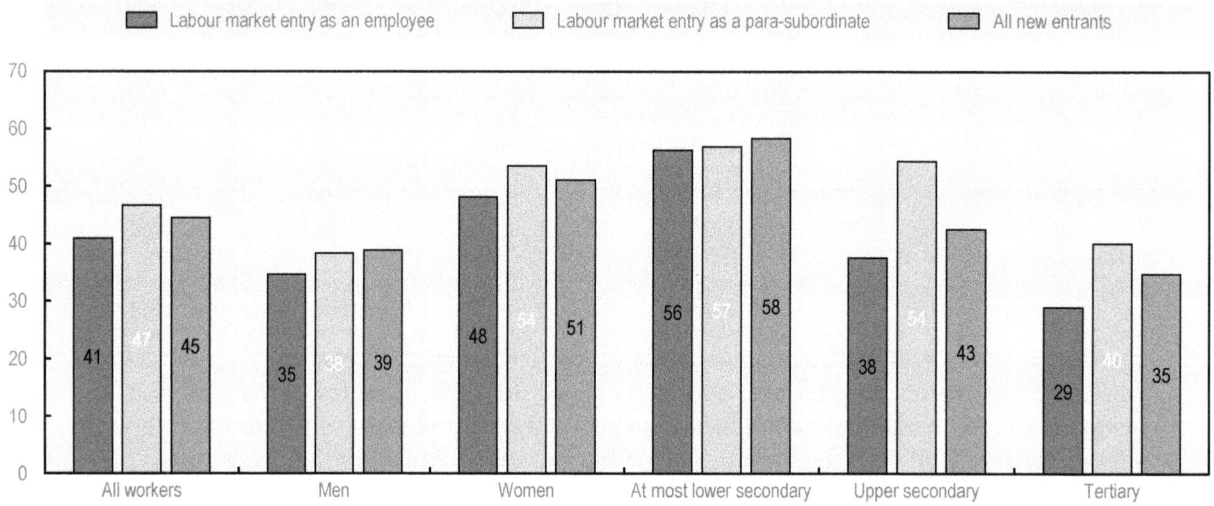

Note: Labour market entrants are under 35-year-olds who, in a given year, worked 13 weeks or more for the first time. The first 10 years start in the year after labour market entry. Workers "at-risk of low future pension" have, during the first 10 years of their career, accumulated less than 60% of the amount a person who has worked consistently on a full-time basis over 10 years at the median wage would have contributed.
Source: Own calculations based on AD-SILC data.

A crucial factor in the success of the starting phase of the career is the continuity of the employment period. As expected, indeed, risks of low accumulation (and potential pension inadequacy in the future) reduces when the number of years effectively worked increases, even if a worrying 20.6% were rated "poor" in terms of accumulated contributions over the 10-year period among those who worked at least eight of the ten years, due to low earnings and periods spent working in arrangements with reduced contribution rates (left panel in Figure 6.14).

Conversely, consistent with the heterogeneity of the types of para-subordinate workers, risks of poor accumulation do not increase linearly with the number of years spent working as a para-subordinate. Indeed, the share of workers with poor accumulation, while always very high, is lower among those who worked at least five years as a para-subordinate – both "strong" para-subordinates such as accountants and administrators and very disadvantaged workers belong to this group – than within the group of those who worked a lower number of years as a para-subordinate – poor workers with very fragmented careers may, indeed, belong to this group (right panel in Figure 6.14).

Figure 6.14. Low pension accruals are mainly driven by disrupted employment histories

Share of workers at-risk of low future pension, by number of years worked and number of years worked as a para-subordinate during the first 10 years after labour market entry, in percent, LM entrants 1996-2001

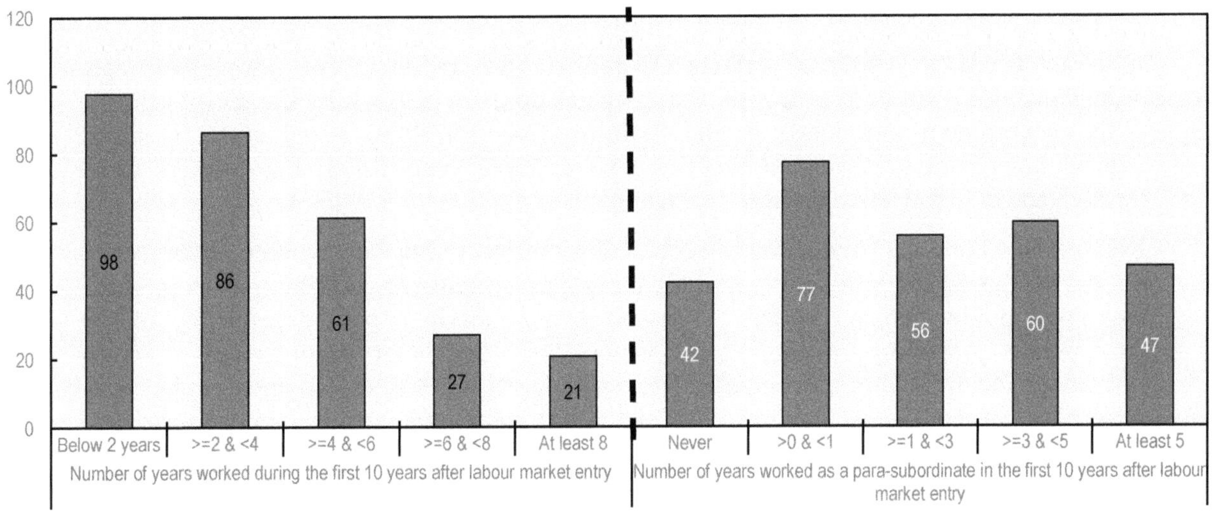

Note: Labour market entrants are under 35-year-olds who, in a given year, worked 13 weeks or more for the first time. The first 10 years start in the year after labour market entry. Workers "at-risk of low future pension" have, during the first 10 years of their career, accumulated less than 60% of the amount a person who has worked consistently on a full-time basis over 10 years at the median wage would have contributed.
Source: Own calculations based on AD-SILC data.

6.8. Concluding remarks

Using administrative data from the INPS, in this chapter we have surveyed the evolution over time of the number of individuals working in para-subordinate arrangements in Italy, in light of the evolution of the rules governing hiring through the various types of arrangements and the welfare guarantees applied to them, which clearly affect the relative labour cost of para-subordinate workers and employees.

The disadvantages in terms of welfare guarantees for para-subordinate workers have been reduced by the recent reforms, even if some gaps still exist, particularly concerning unemployment benefit. However, those who worked as a para-subordinate in previous years were clearly disadvantaged by the reduced contribution rates applied to such contracts (below 20% until 2007) which will have a major impact on future pensions from the Italian public pension scheme where, being based on an NDC formula, pensions depend on contributions paid during the whole career.

Recent reforms have also tightened the requirements for clients signing a para-subordinate arrangement and have ended the very disadvantageous – in terms of wages and welfare guarantees – "voucher arrangement" which has been replaced by a more favourable and less deregulated arrangement since the middle of 2017.

There has probably also been a reduction in the use of para-subordinate collaborations in recent years due to fiscal incentives (i.e. a strong reduction in social contributions paid by firms) introduced by the 2015 Jobs Act reform for those who hired new workers through open-ended employment contracts in 2015 and 2016.

However, as pointed out by the dramatic increase in the number of "workers on vouchers" before the 2017 reform – also due to limits on hiring through para-subordinate collaborations – Italian firms continue to search for opportunities to hire less costly and more flexible workers and are liable to use these contracts even when they mask what are effectively subordinate working relationships.

Also to avoid the adverse effects related to the existence of para-subordinate arrangements – even if, as noted, their use was made more difficult by the recent reforms – the government introduced in the Stability Law for 2018 a reduction in social contributions paid by firms for the first two or three years for young workers hired through an open-ended employment arrangement.

Relying on a temporary reduction in social contributions to improve workers' prospects – a measure that is costly for the public finances since it reduces contributions to the pay-as-you-go public pension system[12] – assumes a belief in a path dependency of the employment trajectory, according to which the contractual arrangement at entry influences the following career path. However, in past years, employment trajectories have often varied widely irrespective of the initial contractual arrangement (Fabrizi and Raitano, 2012). While young people who started their careers as para-subordinates in the late 1990s were more likely to continue to work as para-subordinates, they are not significantly less likely to work *overall* than those who started out in other contractual arrangements. Therefore, reducing the cost of the employment arrangement at labour market entry might not be sufficient to improve employment trajectories that, as summarised in Sections 6.6 and 6.7, have proved to be unsuccessful for a very high share of workers in past years.

A particular concern relates to the future pensions of those with unsuccessful career patterns over a long period (in terms of earnings, unemployment spells, atypical and less guaranteed contractual arrangements). Indeed, in an NDC scheme (as the Italian public pension system is for those who started work since 1996) less successful careers will be exactly mirrored by lower pensions and there are no redistributive tools, apart from personal income tax progressivity and the existence of means-tested welfare benefits for the elderly poor. Even if Italian labour market conditions suddenly improve from 2018 onwards, as shown in Section 6.6, a high share of individuals have so far only accumulated low contributions in the NDC pension scheme – partly due to periods spent working as para-subordinates – and will therefore risk receiving a low pension at retirement if their career pattern does not significantly improve.

Some measures to improve expected NDC pensions of workers with fragile careers have been proposed recently by some scholars and have been discussed by the government and the main trade unions (for a survey, see Raitano, 2017). Some proposals are based on the introduction of a flat "citizenship" pension to be associated with an NDC scheme with a reduced contribution rate (to cut labour costs), but these proposals would be very expensive for the public budget due to the immediate reduction in pension contributions in the pay-as-you-go system. Some relate to the possibility of extending the amount of social assistance benefits paid in future years to poor pensioners, while other proposals suggest introducing a "minimum pension" in the NDC scheme with the amount increasing with the length of the individual career, in line with the principle of "making contributions pay". These last two types of measures would have the advantage of increasing public spending only after around 2040, when the first cohort of individuals wholly enrolled in the NDC scheme start to retire. However, after an intense debate following the agreement between the government and the trade unions signed in September 2016 and the promise of measures to improve the pension prospects of younger workers, discussions about how to provide future guarantees for poor pensioners in the NDC scheme have stopped and no measure on this is going to be included in the Stability Law for 2018.

Notes

[1] To be considered as continuous the contract duration shall be at least 30 days per year. If this requirement is not fulfilled the collaboration is considered "occasional". Project collaborations are based on a specific project to be carried out by the worker (i.e. the worker cannot simply carry out repetitive tasks).

[2] Note that data about para-subordinate workers provided by INPS in the *Osservatorio sui lavoratori parasubordinati* include collaborators and professionals but not workers on vouchers, whose information are collected in another archive, the *Osservatorio sul lavoro accessorio*. As a general rule, if not differently specified, we thus refer to collaborators and professionals when we refer to para-subordinate workers.

[3] Collaborators' contributions are paid by the client to the *Gestione Separata*, while professionals pay contributions on their own. Note also that in Italy liberal professionals with a professional association pay pension contributions to specific social security funds privately managed by their professional association.

[4] Within the regular unemployment insurance system (e.g. NASPI), the government pays notional (or imputed) pension contributions for the unemployed, see Section 6.2.

[5] Law 92/2012 introduced an "assumption of a subordinate job" – for both collaborators and professionals – when at least two of the three following conditions are fulfilled: i) the arrangement for the same client lasts at least eight months over a two-year period; ii) the workers receives at least 80% of his/her earnings from the same client in a two-year period; iii) the worker has a regular workstation in the client's office. When two of these conditions are fulfilled the worker is considered to be an employee and the firm is fined.

[6] I thank Fondazione Giacomo Brodolini for allowing me access to the AD-SILC dataset.

[7] For instance, the total contribution rate is 41.57% for blue-collar workers and 39.35% for white-collar employees in industrial firms with at least 50 employees; 40.07% and 37.85% respectively for firms with up to 15 employees; and 39.37% for both groups in commercial services companies of over 200 employees.

[8] All Italian workers are also insured against workplace and occupational injuries through a specific contribution to INAIL (*Istituto nazionale Assicurazione Infortuni sul Lavoro*). All workers participating in the social insurance system, are also entitled, in the case of disability, to the "ordinary disability allowance" (if the percentage of disability is at least 66%) or to the "disability pension" (if the percentage of disability is 100%).

[9] Additional workers are guaranteed against workplace injuries as they pay a 3.5% contribution rate to INAIL (7% before the 2017 reform). The gross value of vouchers also includes EUR 0.50 to cover administrative costs.

[10] As already mentioned, because these data record the number of individuals who paid, at least once, a contribution to the *Gestione Separata*, the figures are different from those provided by survey samples (e.g. the Labour Force Survey) which record the number of individuals who self-report as performing a para-subordinate activity at the time of the interview.

[11] The analysis does not distinguish between non-para-subordinate contractual contracts, such as temporary vs. permanent contracts because, (i) no significant differences between different non-para-subordinate contractual arrangements persist in the medium term (after five years; Fabrizi and Raitano, 2012) and (ii), the INPS only provides information on permanent vs. temporary contracts since 1998, reducing the sample size of our exercise.

[12] Raitano et al. (2017) estimate that the contribution reliefs introduced by the Jobs Act reform in 2015 cost around EUR 15-20 billion (according to the various scenarios) in terms of missed revenues for the pension system in the 2015-18 period.

References

Anastasia B., Bombelli S., Maschio S. (2016). Il Lavoro accessorio dal 2008 al 2015. Profili dei lavoratori e dei committenti. WorkINPS papers, n.2.

Berton F., Devicienti F., Pacelli L. (2011). Are temporary jobs a port of entry into permanent employment?: Evidence from matched employer-employee. International Journal of Manpower, vol. 32(8), pp. 879-899.

Berton F., Richiardi M., Sacchi S. (2012). *The Political Economy of Work Security and Flexibility: Italy in Comparative Perspective*, Policy Press.

Fabrizi E., Raitano M. (2012). Rigido, flessibile o liquido? L'immagine del mercato del lavoro italiano dal dataset AD-SILC, Economia e Lavoro, n.3/2012.

Franco D., Sartor N. (2006). NDCs in Italy: unsatisfactory present, uncertain future. In Holzmann R., Palmer E. (eds.), Pension reform: issues and prospects for ndc schemes, Washington: World Bank Publishing.

INPS (2017). Il lavoro parasubordinato. Aggiornamento all'anno 2016. Rome.

Jessoula M. (2012). A risky combination in Italy: selective flexibility and defined contribution pensions. In Hinrichs K., Jessoula M. (eds.), Labour market flexibility and pension reforms, Palgrave Macmillan.

Jessoula M., Raitano M. (2017). Italian pensions from "vices" to challenges: assessing actuarial multi-pillarization twenty years later. In Natali D. (eds.), The New Pension Mix in Europe. Peter Lang Publishing.

Muehlberger U., Pasqua S. (2006). The "Continuous Collaborators" in Italy. Hybrids between Employment and Self-employment?. CHILD Working Papers no. 10/2006.

Palmer E. (2006). What Is NDC?. In Holzmann R., Palmer E. (eds.), Pension reform: issues and prospects for NDC schemes, Washington: World Bank Publishing.

Picchio, M. (2008). Temporary jobs and transition to stable jobs in Italy, Labour, Vol. 22 No. 1, pp. 147-74.

Raitano M. (2007). I lavoratori parasubordinati: dimensioni del fenomeno, caratteristiche e rischi. Economia e Lavoro, n. 3/2007, pp. 135-160.

Raitano M. (2017). Poveri da giovani, poveri da anziani? Prospettive previdenziali e vantaggi della pensione di garanzia. OCIS Social Cohesion Papers No. 3.

Raitano M., Fana M., Patriarca F. (2017). Il costo e l'efficacia degli sgravi contributivi connessi al Jobs Act. In Pizzuti F.R. (eds), Rapporto sullo Stato Sociale 2017, Sapienza University Press, Roma

Chapter 7. Netherlands: non-standard work and social protection

Marloes de Graaf-Zijl, Bas Scheer and Jonneke Bolhaar

Over the last decades, the share of non-standard work in The Netherlands has grown substantially and it is now among the highest of all OECD-countries. Approximately one in three workers work in a non-standard work arrangement (including own-account or temporary work, variable hours contracts and agency work). In the current Dutch institutional setting, firms can save social contributions, severance payments, re-integration obligations and tedious administrative procedures by hiring people as own account workers or, to a lesser extent, through one of the other non-standard work arrangements. By using temporary work arrangements, for example, employers can circumvent employment protection legislation – i.e. severance payments and time-consuming procedures to ask for permission to dismiss – and sickness related payments and re-integration obligations that end upon the end date of the contract. If policy makers wish to reduce the share of non-standard work arrangements, they should aim to reduce incentives to hire workers on non-standard contracts, by reducing differences in taxes and social security coverage between non-standard and standard work.

7.1. Introduction

In recent decades, the share of non-standard work in the Netherlands has grown substantially and it is now among the highest of all OECD countries. One of the potential reasons for this can be found in Dutch institutional settings that allow employers to circumvent various welfare state obligations attached to open-ended contracts by hiring people on various alternative forms of employment. The Netherlands is therefore an interesting case for studying the social protection of workers in these various work arrangements.

Part-time employment is not regarded as non-standard employment in the Dutch context. The share of part-time work is high, but mostly voluntary, and is treated by labour law in exactly the same manner as full-time employment. We therefore restrict this section to other flexible work arrangements, among which we distinguish between temporary contracts, agency work, own-account work and variable hours contracts (including own-account workers on variable hours contracts).

Figure 7.1. Forms of non-standard employment in the Netherlands

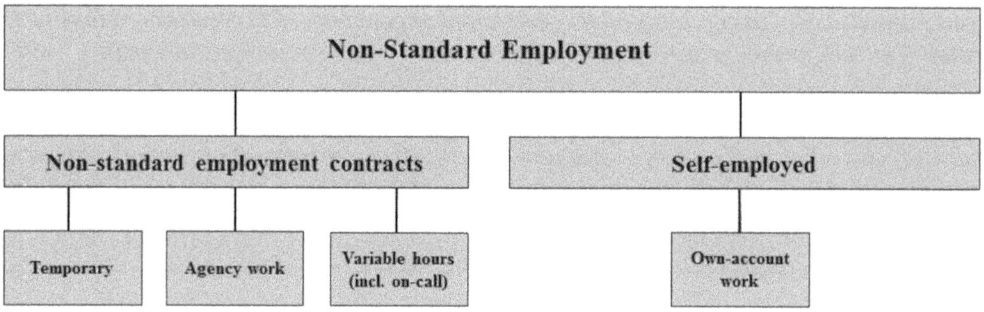

7.2. The incidence of various forms of non-standard employment

The number of non-standard jobs has increased steadily over the last 14 years, with only a brief slowdown during the great recession of 2008. However, the number of standard jobs did not increase between 2003 and 2009 and even declined after that period. . This decline came to a halt at the end of 2015, but there has still not been any significant growth in standard work (see Figure 7.2, Panel A). As a result, the share of standard work still declined (see Figure 7.2, Panel B). More recently (first quarter of 2018), with the increase of labour market tightness, the share of standard work has stabilised and even increased slightly. However, it is uncertain how this share will develop in the future, for example when the current economic boom comes to an end.

Figure 7.2. Employment has shifted from standard to non-standard employment relations

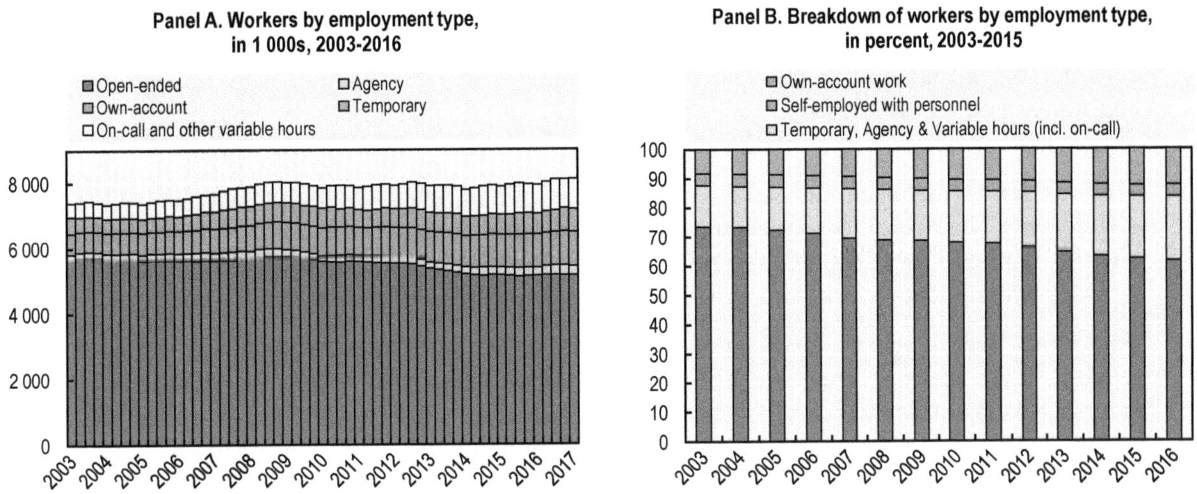

Note: non-standard is the sum of variable hour contracts (incl. on-call), temporary work, agency work and own-account work. Non-standard consists only of open-ended employment contracts. Self-employed with personnel are excluded from this graph.
Source: Statistics Netherlands.

Currently, approximately one-third of all workers are employed on a non-standard work arrangement. The share of workers employed in temporary work, agency work and on-call work has risen from 14% in 2003 to 22% in 2016 (23% in the third quarter of 2017, not in the figure), while the share of own-account workers has increased from 8% to 12% (Figure 7.2, Panel B). This increase came entirely at the expense of regular open-ended contracts, since the share of self-employed people with personnel hardly changed (Figure 7.2, panel A).

Among those in non-standard employment, own-account workers are the largest sub-group. Those on variable hours contracts (including on-call work), are currently the second largest sub-group. Their share nearly doubled, from roughly 6% in 2003 to 11% in 2016. The third largest sub-group is formed by those on temporary contracts (without variable hours), whose share increased from 6% in 2003 to 8% in 2016. The smallest sub-group is accounted for by agency work, which has been broadly stable at around 2.5% of total employment, increasing when economic activity expands and decreasing when it contracts (de Graaf-Zijl and Berkhout, 2007[1]).

We can subdivide temporary contracts (without variable hours) further into temporary contracts of one year or more, shorter than one year and temporary contracts that from the start are intended to be converted into open-ended contracts. Even though all temporary contracts can be converted into open-ended contracts, those in the latter category specifically envisage such an outcome, if the employee performs well and the financial situation of the firm allows it. [1] Even though there is no thorough legal basis for this conversion, around one-third of all temporary contracts are agreed on this basis. Their share of all temporary contracts varies over the business cycle, but they became more prevalent over the 2003-16 period and 3.5% of all workers are currently on such contracts. Temporary contracts of one year or more recorded the largest increase (from 1.3% to 2.1%). The share of temporary contracts for shorter periods (less than one year) has remained broadly stable at around 2%.

7.3. Which groups work on a non-standard work arrangement?

Non-standard work is not equally distributed across the working population. Figure 7.3 presents descriptive statistics based on Dutch Labour Force Survey data. There are considerable differences in the share of non-standard work by gender, age, educational attainment and ethnicity. Differences are especially pronounced between age groups, but differences between educational levels and ethnic groups are substantial as well.

The differences between men and women are relatively small compared with the other differences. The overall shares of men and women in non-standard work are comparable, but the type of work differs. Temporary and on-call work are more prevalent among women, while agency work and own-account work are more prevalent among men.

Temporary work, agency work and on-call work are more prevalent among younger workers[2] than among prime-age and older workers. The share of these types of non-standard workers decreases with age. However, for the 65-74 year-old post-retirement group, these shares increase again, especially for on-call work. This is most likely caused by a decrease in open-ended contracts, since many of these contracts end at the statutory retirement age (which until recently was 65). The share of own-account work increases with age: only 5% of 15-24 year-olds work as own-account workers, compared with 16% of 55-64 year-olds. After retirement age, this share increases to almost 50%.

Workers with a low level of education are more likely to work in agency work or on variable hours contracts than those with a higher level of education. There is a particularly marked difference for on-call work, which accounts for 20% of workers with a low level of education but only 5% of workers with a higher level of education. The share of temporary work, however, does not differ much across education levels. Own-account work is more common among highly educated workers (14%) than among those with a lower level of education (11%).

Regarding ethnicity, second generation non-western immigrants are particularly more likely to be temporary, agency or on-call workers and less likely to be own-account workers. This difference is at least partly due to the fact that this group consists of relatively young workers.

Figure 7.3. Nonstandard work most strongly associated with age

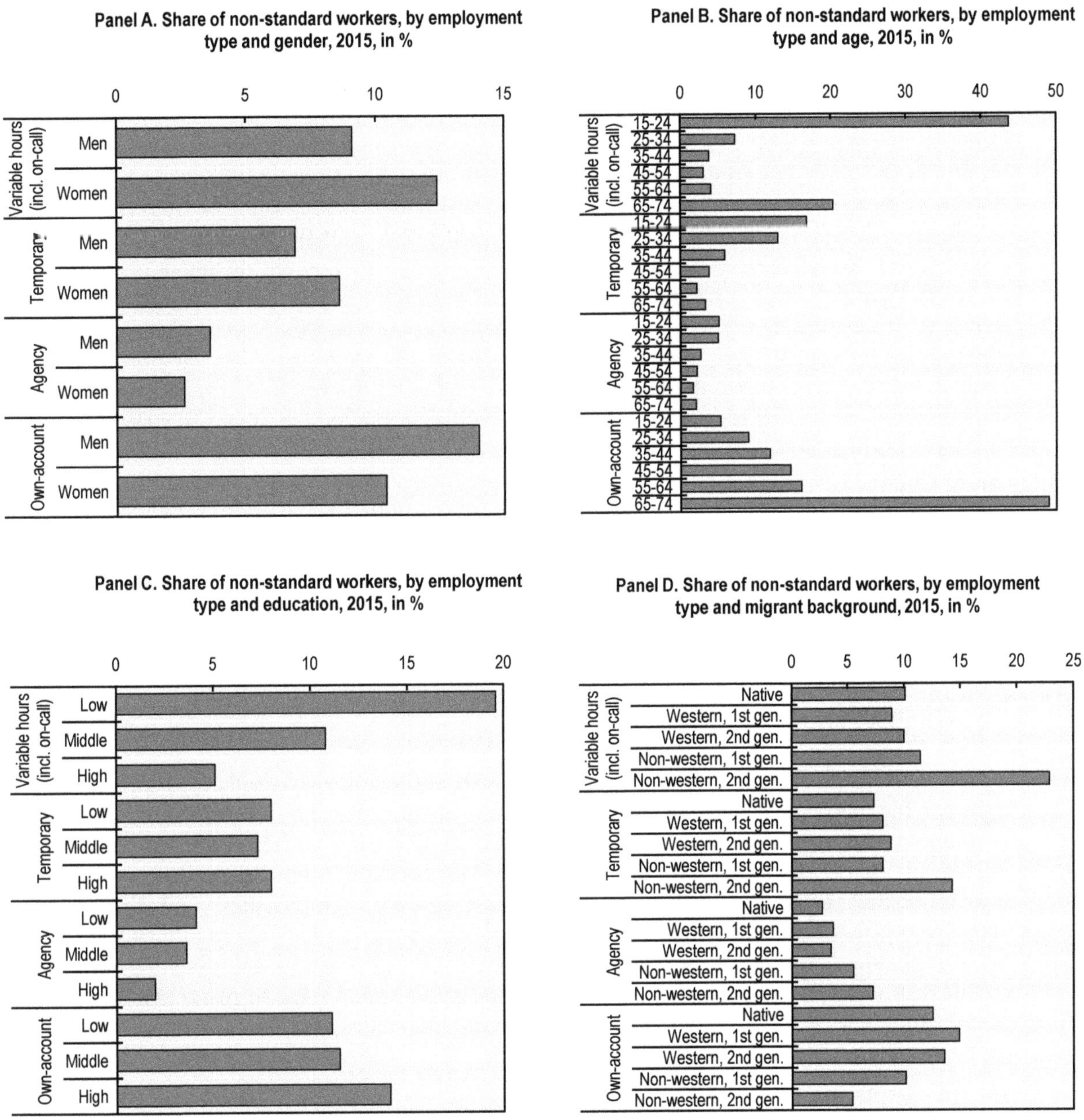

Note: Western countries include Europe, north-America and Oceania, Indonesa and Japan. Non-western countries include Africa, Central and South America, and Asia, excluding Indonesia, Japan, Morocco and Turkey (Morocco and Turkey are not shown).
Source: Own calculations based on Dutch LFS-Data.

The descriptive statistics presented above consider only one dimension at a time, and do not take possible correlations between gender, age, education and ethnicity into account. After controlling for correlations with other characteristics by means of regression analysis, age appears to be by far the most important determinant of the probability of working in non-standard employment (Bolhaar, Brouwers and Scheer, 2016[2]). The probability of working in all types of non-standard employment contracts decreases with age, whereas the share of own-account work increases with age. There are differences between men and women, between educational groups and between ethnic groups as well, but these differences are smaller than those between age groups. In some cases these differences appear to be almost fully driven by the variation in the age of the different groups.

Bolhaar, Brouwers, and Scheer (2016[2]) show that the gender of those in non-standard employment varies according to the unemployment rate. When unemployment is low, the difference between men and women for the probability of working on a flexible contract is largest. When economic circumstances improve, women remain in flexible employment, while men move to open-ended contracts. So far, we do not know what drives this pattern. It may be the result of better bargaining power or skills among men: possibly women are in a worse position to negotiate a better contract when the economic situation improves. It does not appear to be driven by preferences for flexible work arrangements. According to the Dutch Working Conditions Survey of 2015, working on a non-standard contract is a positive choice (i.e. they like arrangements that offer flexibility and have no need for security) for roughly 35% of men, compared with 29% of women. An alternative explanation is that women enter and leave the workforce more often than men, which means they have shorter tenure and are therefore less likely to move to open-ended contracts.

7.3.1. A snapshot of the social protection system in the Netherlands

This section presents the social protection of workers on open-ended contracts and other work arrangements in terms of employment protection, unemployment benefits, disability benefits, sickness pay, minimum wages, collective labour agreements, active labour market policies, pensions and the taxes they pay (including work-related deductions).

Dutch labour law regards employees as those who depend mostly on their employment contract for their income and are therefore in an unequal bargaining position with the employer. The employee is therefore protected against any unfair treatment by the employer, such as dismissal without notice, very long working hours, dangerous working conditions and so on. Employees are also insured against unemployment and disability risks by social security. And there are sectoral collective labour agreements that stipulate wage schedules, on-the-job-training rights and pension rights, and sometimes top-ups to sickness or unemployment benefits. There is a legal minimum wage in place that applies to all employees (not for own-account workers), and many sectoral collective labour agreements impose higher wage levels.

By law, employers in the Netherlands are obliged to treat all employees equally: they are not allowed to make a distinction based on the number of working hours in the contract or the permanency of the employment contract. Part-time and full-time workers therefore have the same rights by labour and social security law. This is also the case for workers on temporary contracts, with the exception of employment protection, and for variable hours contracts except on the matter of their working hours.

Since hiring firms are not regarded as the legal employer of agency workers, they fall under a different collective labour agreement. Therefore, their working conditions may differ from workers hired directly by the firms at whose workplace they are based.

Since own-account workers are not regarded as employees, they are not covered by labour law or collective sickness, disability and unemployment insurance systems. Their social protection therefore differs substantially from that of all other workers.

7.3.2. Social protection of workers on open-ended contracts

In labour law, employees on open-ended contracts are protected against involuntary termination of their contract. Without the consent of the employee (i.e. except in cases of mutual agreement), an employer can only terminate the employment contract if he can show fair grounds for dismissal and the employee cannot be reassigned to another position within the firm.[3] These fair grounds need to be approved by the public employment office when the contract is ended for economic reasons or by a court if the termination is based on individual factors, before the termination can actually take place. Upon termination, the employer is obliged to make a transition payment to the employee (i.e. severance payment), if the worker was with the employer for two years or more. This severance payment is based on the years of service and gross salary. The employer is only exempt from these transition payments if the employee was fired on the grounds of gross misconduct.

All employees are protected against dangerous or unhealthy working conditions by the Working Conditions Act (*Arbowet*). The employer is responsible for the provision of proper working materials and is legally accountable for any harm that employees suffer on the job. There are rules for the minimum number of holidays, and holiday payments of 8% of the gross wage.

There is a statutory minimum wage that applies to all employees. The current minimum wage for adults aged 22 years or older is EUR 8.96 per hour worked. For younger people the minimum wage increases in steps from EUR 2.69 per hour for 15-year-olds to EUR 7.61 per hour for 21-year-olds. The minimum wage is adjusted on 1 July every year.

Collective labour agreements (CLAs) are concluded on a sectoral base between employers' organisations and unions. Wage schedules, pension rights and training rights are all included in these arrangements, as well as the negotiated wage rise for the sector as a whole. Some CLAs also include top-ups of unemployment benefits or sick pay.

Social security law protects employees against income loss resulting from unemployment by the Unemployment Benefits Act (*Werkloosheidswet*) and afterwards by the universal means-tested social assistance and Act on Income Provisions for Older Unemployed (IOW or *Wet Inkomensvoorziening Oudere Werklozen*). The Unemployment Insurance Act (WW) provides insurance against involuntary job loss for employees. Eligible workers can receive unemployment benefits for a minimum of three months, while the maximum duration depends on the number of weeks the worker was employed before the job loss. For the first two months workers receive 75% of the monthly base wage, which is a function of their previously earned wage up to a certain ceiling, and 70% afterwards.

Employees are protected against income loss resulting from sickness by the Sickness Benefits Act (ZW, or *ZiekteWet*). Employers are obliged to keep sick employees on the payroll for two years. By law, the employer has to pay 70% of the wage during this period. In most collective bargaining agreements this is increased to 100% in the first year. Employers are required to attempt to reintegrate sick workers in their organisation or at another organisation. If employers cannot prove that they have made a reasonable attempt at reintegration, the period of continued wage payment can be extended to three years.

After these first two years, sickness becomes a fair ground for dismissal. Employees who have been on sick leave for more than two years are eligible for WIA disability benefits – WIA is the Work and Income (Capacity for Work) Act. The WIA is aimed at reintegration into the workforce, unless people are fully and permanently disabled. For older (partially) disabled unemployed people who are not eligible for the IOW there is another programme: Income Provisions for Older and Partially Disabled Unemployed Employees (IOAW).

Besides these employment-related social protection benefits, there is also a universal means-tested social assistance (*Bijstand*), which is not dependent on a person's employment history. The means test consists of a wealth test and a household income test. The maximum income is 70% of the minimum wage for single person households and 100% for multi-person households.

7.3.3. Social protection of workers on temporary contracts

In the Netherlands, the same labour and social security laws, minimum wages and youth minimum wages apply to workers on temporary contracts as to workers on open-ended contracts. The same protection against unsafe or unhealthy working conditions and rules for holidays, vacation days and holiday allowances also apply. Temporary workers fall under the same collective agreement as their colleagues on open-ended contracts, but these agreements may stipulate different on-the-job-training rights or pension rights for the two categories. Unfortunately, there is no recent study on these specific exceptions in CLAs for temporary workers (De Beer and Verhulp, 2017[3]).

The fact that the coverage of many of the social security schemes depends on employment history means that temporary workers enjoy more limited benefit rights than workers on open-ended contracts. Like workers on open-ended contracts, temporary workers build up insurance against involuntary unemployment under the Unemployment Benefits Act. However, as discussed in the section above, the duration and amount of unemployment benefit depends on the prior wage and employment history. As a result, temporary workers are not only more likely to become unemployed (Van der Werff, Kroon and Heyma, 2016[4]; De Beer and Verhulp, 2017[3]), but also have shorter maximum benefit durations due to a shorter employment history (Van der Werff, Kroon and Heyma, 2016[4]).

Subject to certain restrictions the Public Employment Service (PES) compensates workers who move frequently between employment and unemployment. If an unemployed worker finds a job, but loses it again within 26 weeks, the unemployment benefit that the workers received before finding this job is reinstated if the new base wage[4] is below 87.5% of the old base wage. This is done to compensate for the loss of benefit income due to accepting a lower-paying job. However, if the new job lasts longer than 26 weeks or pays more than 87.5% of the old job, reinstatement of benefit is not possible and the worker needs to start a new unemployment benefit application procedure. Only the employment history and wage of the new job counts towards this new unemployment benefit.

In essence, temporary workers also receive the same insurance against sickness and disability. However, the obligation to keep sick employees on the wage bill ends at the pre-specified end of the contract. From that moment, the PES pays the sickness benefit (ZW benefit or *Ziektewet-uitkering*) and is responsible for the reintegration of the sick employee into the labour market. Like workers on open-ended contracts the benefit is determined by the base wage: the default amount is 70% of the base wage.

The most important difference between open-ended and temporary contracts is that temporary contracts end at a prespecified date or event. This means that the employer is not obliged to provide a fair ground for dismissal at the end of the contract. By employing workers on temporary contracts, employers can thus avoid the need for a dismissal procedure and, in most cases, also the need to make a severance payment. The employee only receives a transition payment at the end of the contract if the duration of the contract (or consecutive contracts) exceeded two years. Most temporary contracts are shorter than that.

According to EU Directive 1999/70/EC, European countries are obliged to adopt regulations that restrict the use of temporary contracts. The Netherlands has chosen not to place restrictions on the reasons used to justify the use of temporary contracts, but rather on their maximum duration and the maximum number of consecutive temporary contracts with one employer. In 1999 the Dutch government introduced the *Wet Flexibiliteit en Zekerheid (Flexwet)* law, which set the maximum duration of consecutive temporary contracts at three years. A contract was considered consecutive if the period between the end of a contract and start of a new contract was less than three months. A temporary contract was automatically converted into an open-ended contract if the duration of consecutive contracts exceeded the maximum of three years. This regulation of consecutive fixed-term contracts was called the chain rule.

In 2015 the regulation of these "chains of temporary employment" became stricter with the introduction of the Work and Security Act (WWZ or *Wet Werk en Zekerheid*). Contracts are now considered consecutive if the period between the end of a contract and start of a new contract is less than six months, and the maximum duration of such consecutive contracts has been lowered to two years. In addition to the maximum duration of consecutive contracts, the WWZ stipulates that an employee can be on a maximum of three consecutive fixed-term contracts. Thus, a temporary contract is automatically converted into an open-ended contract if the total number of contracts in a chain exceeds three or the total duration of the chain exceeds two years. For example, if an employee renews a fixed-term contract and this takes the total duration of the contracts to more than two years, then the new contract is regarded as an open-ended contract by law. Note that this rule only applies to a chain of contracts. A single fixed-term contract for a period of more than two years is possible, but it cannot be extended with a second temporary contract. In that case, any extension must be an open-ended contract.

The effectiveness of these measures in reducing the share of temporary work is not evident. There is no thorough study yet on the effects of the WWZ. Causal inferences are difficult to find, because it is hard to disentangle the effect of various elements of the very broad act and changing economic circumstances. In addition, the new law introduced an incentive to hire people for shorter periods. Circumstantial evidence shows that a sequence of three temporary contracts lasting seven and eight months each (23 months in total) has become much more popular since the introduction of the WWZ law, because this so-called 7-8-8 scheme maximises the total length and number of consecutive temporary contracts.[5]

Since 1999 firms have been able to deviate from the standard chain rule in their CLAs for jobs that require more flexibility due to the nature of the work. The maximum number of consecutive fixed-term contracts can be extended to six (at most) and the maximum total duration of these contracts can be extended to (at most) four years. In addition, the required six-month break between contracts that is necessary to break the chain can be shortened to three months, but only when the work is of a seasonal nature. The most recent detailed study of these deviations dates from 2014, before the introduction of the stricter WWZ regulation. However, these older CLAs still show whether the chain rule was made stricter or less strict in the bargaining process. For 71% of workers covered by a CLA there was a deviation from the default chain rule that either applied to all employees or specific groups of employees covered by the CLA. A deviation for specific groups of employees was most prevalent: this applied to 60% of employees covered by a CLA (e.g. those aged 65 and over, seasonal workers or apprentices). For 17% of employees covered by a CLA the deviation applied to all employees.[6] (De Beer and Verhulp, 2017[3]).

CLAs that included a deviation from the chain rule tended to decrease the maximum total duration of the chain, which effectively made the chain rule stricter. However, the rules for the maximum number of contracts and the minimum gap between chains were more often made less strict. So, overall it seems that unions were most interested in decreasing the total possible duration of the chain, but were less concerned about the maximum number of contracts and the minimum gap between chains.

For specific groups of employees (e.g. those aged 65 and over and apprentices) it is possible to agree to exclude specific groups from the chain rule completely. 18% of employees in such groups are not covered by the rule due to such an exemption (De Beer and Verhulp, 2017[3]). In these cases an indefinite number of consecutive temporary contracts can be offered.

Unfortunately, relatively little is known about deviations in CLAs after the introduction of the WWZ. In 2015 roughly 25% of employees covered by a newly created CLA were in agreements covered by a CLA that deviated from the WWZ chain rule. However, the exact nature of these deviations is currently unknown (De Beer and Verhulp, 2017[3]).

7.3.4. Social protection of agency workers

In the Netherlands, the same labour and social security laws apply to agency workers as to open-ended contracts, with a few exceptions. The same minimum wage and youth minimum wages apply as to workers on open-ended contracts or temporary contracts. Agency workers also build up rights for unemployment benefits and disability benefits in the same way as other workers, but like temporary workers their rights are usually shorter due to interrupted work histories (see below). Furthermore, agency workers have the same protection against unsafe or unhealthy working conditions and the same rules for holidays, vacation days and holiday allowances apply.

In short, employment conditions are the same for agency workers and other employees, as stipulated in the WAADI law on the provision of employees by intermediaries (*Wet Allocatie Arbeidskrachten door Intermediairs*). This also means that agency workers must be paid on an equal basis to other workers at the user company. However, this equal pay rule is difficult to apply in practice and Dutch unions complain that is not well respected (PPMi, 2017[5]). Finally, pension rights are not included in the WAADI law. Agency workers automatically enrol in a separate pension fund after 26 weeks under contract at the agency firm.

The rules concerning temporary work differ between standard employment agreements and agency agreements. By law, the chain rule for temporary contracts does not apply during the first 26 weeks of an agency agreement, as a result of which an indefinite number of temporary contracts can be put in place during this time, without any requirement for a trial period.[7] Afterwards, a maximum of six consecutive temporary agency agreements is allowed (instead of three for standard employment contracts) with a maximum total duration of four years (instead of two for standard employment contracts). In addition, during the first 26 or 78 weeks, temporary agency contracts automatically end if the hiring firm ends the hiring. This is the case if the contract between the worker and the temporary employment agency contains a so-called "*uitzendbeding*" clause. Most contracts have this clause during the first 26 or 78 weeks, depending on the CLA.[8] Dutch politicians and policy makers regard the temporary agency sector as an important means of getting unemployed workers back into the work force. The agency sector has therefore been granted these exceptions to the rules.

Only 13% of agency workers are employed for more than 26 weeks by the same temporary employment agency and 2% beyond 78 weeks (Vermeulen et al., 2016[6]).

Regarding unemployment benefits, disability benefits and social assistance, the same rules apply for agency agreements and standard employment agreements. However, due to interrupted work histories agency workers less often meet the eligibility criteria and if they are eligible, their entitlement to benefits is usually shorter. The difference in inflow to unemployment and unemployment benefits between standard and non-standard contracts will be discussed in Section 7.3.3.

Rights during periods of sickness are different for temporary agency workers than for other employees, though this depends on their contract with the temporary employment agency. If their contracts contains a "*uitzendbeding*" clause, which is usually the case during the first 26 or 78 weeks, the employment contract ends upon the start of a period of sickness. In that case the UWV employee insurance agency pays sickness pay of 70% of the base wage, and is responsible for the reintegration into the labour market. If the contract does not contain a "*uitzendbeding*" clause, which is usually the case if the contract with the employment agency exceeds 26 or 78 weeks (depending on the CLA), sickness regulations are the same as for regular employment. Recall thatonly 13% of agency workers are employed for more than 26 weeks by the same temporary employment agency and 2% beyond 78 weeks (Vermeulen et al., 2016[6]).

7.3.5. Social protection of on-call workers and those on other variable hours contracts

In the Netherlands, the same labour and social security laws apply to contracts with variable working hours as to other employment contracts. The same protection against unsafe or unhealthy working conditions and rules for holidays, vacation days and holiday allowances apply. The same hourly minimum wage and youth minimum wages also apply. In order to protect on-call workers against employers calling on them for only a very short amount of time, the employer is obliged by law to pay at least three hours' wages every time he uses the worker for less than three hours of work.

On-call contracts and other contracts with variable hours can be either an employment contract or agency contract. Furthermore, this contract can be open ended or on a temporary basis. Basically, workers on variable hours contracts have the same social protection as other workers on the corresponding contracts with fixed working hours. So the employment protection of, for example, on-call workers on open-ended contracts is the same as the employment protection for other workers on open-ended contracts. And for on-call workers on temporary contracts the same chain rule applies as for temporary workers. On-call workers on an employment contract have the same pension rights as workers on a standard employment contract. The amount of pension rights is determined by the actual number of hours worked.

The employer is not free from obligations when deciding to call upon an on-call worker. If the employee is willing to work, and the employer has suitable work available, then the employer is obliged to offer the expected number of hours' work to the on-call worker. If the employer does not adhere to this rule, the on-call worker can demand payment for the number of hours that could have reasonably been expected in a particular month. The on-call worker, on the other hand, is obliged to respond to the employer's calls if he is available. The employer and employee are allowed to deviate from these rules, by agreeing at the start of the on-call contract that this rule does not apply, but only for the first 26 weeks.

Upon dismissal, the same rules apply as to other workers. A firm cannot just stop calling upon an on-call worker. The same grounds for dismissal are allowed and need to be proven in court or at the public employment office before dismissal can take place. Also, the same rules apply for severance payment, which is based on years of service and gross salary.[9] Naturally, workers need to be aware of these rights for them to be effective. It is unclear whether all workers in these types of on-call arrangements are aware of these rights.

However, in certain cases the employer and on-call worker do not agree on the hours of work an on-call worker can reasonably expect. Or firms suddenly stop calling upon a worker, even though that is not allowed. In those cases the on-call worker may have to go to court to ascertain these rights (e.g. Rb. Amsterdam 3 February 2014, ECLI:NL:RBAMS:2014:522). It is unclear how many on-call workers are not aware these rules.

After having worked three months, the same rules for unemployment benefits and disability benefits apply to workers with variable hours contracts as to other employees. UWV calculates the rights for benefits based on the wage earned in the year before the start of the period of unemployment or sickness.[10]

Sick pay differs. Firms are obliged to pay at least 70% of the wage during the first two years of sickness (or until the end of the temporary contract), for the usual hours worked, or the hours for which the worker was already scheduled to work. However, if explicitly stipulated in the employment contract, firms may pay only for the actual hours worked (i.e. excluding sick days) during the first six months of on-call or other variable hours work. If a worker has worked for at least six months on a regular schedule, he has the right to receive sick pay of at least 70% of the wage based on this schedule.

7.3.6. Social protection of self-employed and own account workers

The social protection of self-employed and own-account workers differs substantially from the social protection of all employees mentioned above. Only protection against unsafe or unhealthy working conditions is the same as for employees.[11] For all other social protection the situation for own-account workers is completely different due to the fact that the contract between a hiring firm and an own-account worker is, according to the law, not a labour contract. As a result, labour law does not apply. This implies that there is no employment protection, no employee insurance against unemployment, disability or sickness and no minimum wages. Own-account workers do not fall under any collective labour agreement either, so they have no training rights or obligatory pension savings. There are no rules for vacation days and holiday allowances.

Unlike employees, own-account workers are not automatically insured against unemployment, disability and sickness. They do not pay contributions to the public unemployment insurance or disability funds, and therefore have no rights to these types of benefits. Social assistance is therefore their safety net, unless they arrange disability insurance or pension savings by themselves.[12]

Additionally, there is a social assistance act specifically for the self-employed (*Besluit bijstandverlening zelfstandigen,* Bbz). Self-employed workers who experience a temporary income shortfall can get social assistance to supplement their income (up to the level of a regular social assistance benefit). It is also possible to receive a zero- interest loan instead of the social assistance. If the person's wealth exceeds EUR 186 498, they are only eligible for a zero-interest loan. A number of criteria need to be met to be eligible for the Bbz. First, the loss of income must be temporary, with an expectation that the self-employed person will regain a sufficient level of income in the future. Moreover, the person must spend a minimum of 1 225 hours per year working at his own company and it is not possible to receive funding from a private party. The default maximum duration of this assistance is 12 months, but this can be extended for an additional 24 months if necessary.

Last, for elderly self-employed people with a low income, there is another separate benefits act (*Wet Inkomensvoorziening oudere en gedeeltelijk arbeidsongeschikte gewezen zelfstandigen*, IOAZ). This provides an income supplement to poor self-employed people who are older than 55 but not yet at statutory pension age (65)[13].

Own-account workers are not insured against unemployment, disability and sickness through the social security system, but they can opt for private insurance. In practice 25% of own-account workers are insured against disability (Berkhout and Euwals, 2016[7]). Roughly 25% of own-account workers report that they have not made any arrangement for their pension (including savings, firm/house equity or pension funds). The most prevalent reasons are that they cannot afford to make pension contributions (53%), they have not gotten to it yet (27%) and that the pension age is still a long time away (20%). Another 10% report that they have a partner with adequate pension arrangements (Statistics Netherlands & TNO, 2017[8]).

In case of pregnancy, female own-account workers receive benefits equivalent to the minimum wage for 16 weeks. This duration is the same as for female employees, but the benefit level is lower.

Own-account workers pay much lower taxes and do not pay any social insurance contributions. The net income of an own-account worker is therefore much higher compared with an employee with the same gross income while the wedge of taxes and social security contributions is smaller (Figure 7.4). On average own-account workers pay 20% less tax from the same gross income (Bosch, De Graaf-Zijl and Van Vuuren, 2015[9]). Also they do not pay contributions for unemployment and disability insurance, and saving for an occupational pension is voluntary.

In certain situations a worker is not allowed to be classified as an own-account worker, because he matches the definition of an employee in Dutch labour law[14] (see Section 7.4.2. for more information on the misclassification of own-account workers). However, employers have faced legal uncertainty regarding the classification of own-account workers. In order to clarify these rules a law was passed in 2016, called the Deregulation Labour Relations Assessment Law (*Wet Deregulering Beoordeling Arbeidsrelatie*, the DBA law). This required both the employer and the own-account worker to assess whether the worker is actually allowed to be classified as an own-account worker (rather than as an employee). If the parties are unsure about the classification, sector specific template agreements are available that define criteria for the correct classification of own-account work. If these criteria apply, the worker and employer can sign the agreement and both parties can be sure that the own-account worker has not been misclassified.

However, this law did not have the desired effect. Legal uncertainty increased even more, due to confusion about how strictly these new agreements would be monitored. Many employers and own-account workers reported that this made hiring own-account workers less attractive. Due to these protests and fears of job losses, the government decided to postpone monitoring the template agreements: no companies or own-account workers will be fined before 2020 (except in clear-cut cases of fraud or malicious intent). This is supposed to provide the necessary time for the government to redraft the laws concerning own-account workers and increase legal certainty.

Figure 7.4. The tax wedge is significantly higher for dependent employees

Marginal (left) and average (right) tax wedges in percent as a function of annual income in thousands of euros, single person households, 2014

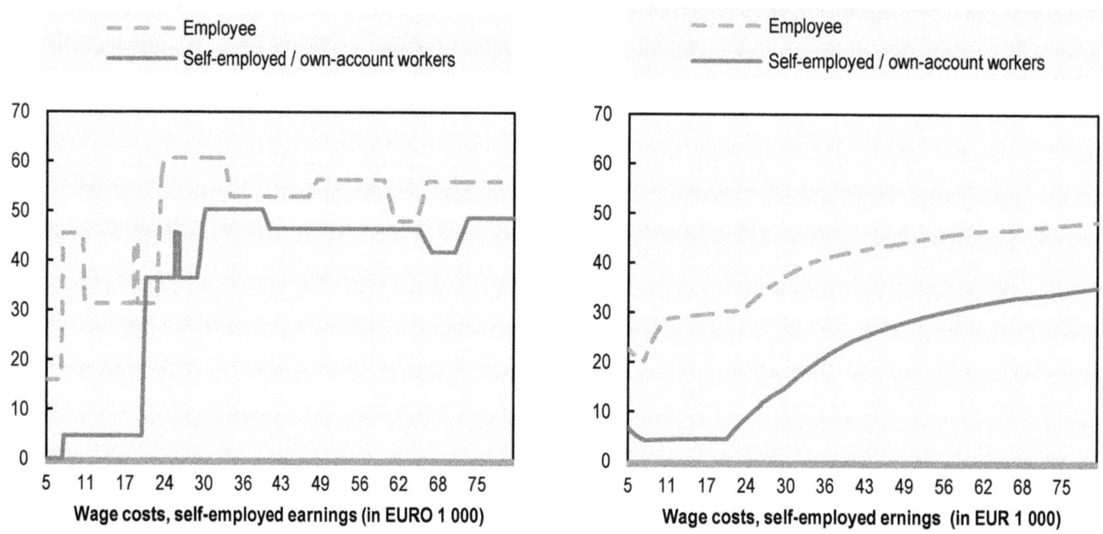

Note: The wedge is defined as the difference between labour cost and disposable income. Taxes and premiums for the unemployment benefits sickness/disability benefits are included in this wedge, whereas pension premiums are not. Self-employed earnings are the profits from self-employment as reported for tax purposes. The kinks in the marginal tax rates are caused by the phasing in and out of tax credits.
Source: Bosch, De Graaf-Zijl and Van Vuuren (2015[9]).

7.4. Incentives created by the system and implications for the financing of social protection

The different entitlements associated with different forms of employment (employment protection legislation, sickness benefit, unemployment and disability benefits, collective labour agreements and minimum wages) influence incentives for employers to hire people on temporary contracts, agency work, on-call work and own-account work as alternatives to open-ended contracts. In general, firms can save on social contributions, severance payments, reintegration obligations and burdensome administrative procedures by hiring people as own-account workers or on one of the flexible employment arrangements. The use of all these types of flexible work arrangements instead of regular open-ended contracts with fixed working hours is a much debated topic in the Netherlands. Dutch unions claim that employers use these types of contracts for the sole purpose of circumventing the social protection of open-ended contracts.

This section discusses the incentives the Dutch system of social protection, employment protection legislation and collective bargaining generates for employers and workers, looks at the evidence on whether these incentives actually influence firm and worker behaviour and at the incomes of non-standard workers and their reliance on tax-funded assistance compared with non-standard workers.

7.4.1. Incentives resulting from the system

By using temporary work arrangements, employers can circumvent employment protection legislation – i.e. severance payments and time-consuming procedures to obtain permission for dismissal – and avoid sickness-related payments and reintegration obligations which end on the termination date of the contract. So even though in principle temporary workers have the same social security rights and fall under the same labour law and collective labour agreements as workers on open-ended contracts, employers can avoid costly and onerous dismissal procedures and obligations to reintegrate sick workers if they hire people on a temporary basis. The WWZ law made the use of a chain of temporary contracts less attractive in 2015, with the aim of limiting the use of temporary employment contracts. However, its effectiveness is unclear (see Section 7.3.3).

However, establishing such a set-up with the purpose of avoiding the automatic transition to an open-ended contract can be unlawful, and in some cases, such structures are penalised in court. The temporary contract can then be converted to an open-ended contract, even if the employer adhered to the chain rule (e.g. Rb. Utrecht 12 December 2008, ECLI:NL:RBUTR:2008:BG9194). In other cases the contract is not converted to an open-ended contract, but the employee is compensated, for example, by being guaranteed an extension of the temporary contract (e.g. Rb. Groningen 14 March 2007, ECLI:NL:RBGRO:2007:BA1435). However, agreeing a pause in employment contracts to avoid having to offer an open-ended contract is not in itself a sufficient condition for the court to rule in the employee's favour (e.g. HR 29 June 2007, ECLI:NL:HR:2007:BA2504). A decision to compensate the employee depends on the context of the case. For example, a ruling in favour of the employee is more likely if the employee has repeatedly worked on temporary contracts with the same employer for a long time.

By hiring temporary agency workers, employers can limit costs and risks, due to the fact that the hiring firm can end a hiring period without notice and is not responsible for reintegration obligations and sickness payments. In addition, in some sectors temporary agency workers are cheaper for employers than regular workers, because they fall under a different collective labour agreement with lower wage scales.

Moreover, employers can save on wage payments by hiring people on contracts with variable working hours because this means they do not have to pay for unproductive hours. Also, sickness payments can be avoided during the first six months of on-call work.

By hiring own-account workers, employers can avoid risks and costs. They are not subject to employment protection obligations, regulations in cases of sickness or collective labour agreements with their ensuing pension and training rights if they hire own-account workers. In addition, own-account workers pay considerably lower taxes due to tax reductions that are specifically aimed at self-employed workers and small companies, and firms may capture part of this benefit. Firms that hire own-account workers negotiate a fee with the worker. Whether lower taxes and social security contributions benefit the firm or the worker depends on their respective bargaining positions.

A report by senior civil servants from various Dutch ministries (2015[10]) indicated that own-account workers at the higher end of the wage distribution can use their bargaining power to gain benefit from the lower costs, while firms profit from the tax advantages at the lower end of the wage distribution by negotiating low fees. At the lower end of the wage distribution, they calculated that firms can save 30% of wage costs by hiring an own-account worker and capturing all the cost advantages, compared with hiring the same worker on an employment contract at the minimum wage level. On the other hand, at the higher end of the wage distribution (roughly two times the median wage) they calculated that own-account workers can earn a 43% higher net income than employees in cases where the hiring firm has the same wage costs, if the workers can capture all benefits for themselves.

Another topic under debate in the Netherlands is the position of workers employed by payrolling firms. Much like agency workers, workers on payrolling contracts work for a hiring firm, whilst under contract at another firm. However, the main difference between agency and payrolling firms is that agency firms actively search for suitable workers and match them with hiring firms. Payrolling firms do not perform such tasks; workers are recruited by the hiring firm and that firm then contacts a payrolling firm that formally employs the worker. Payroll contracts have a separate CLA, which means that firms that prefer the payrolling CLA over their sector-specific CLA have an incentive to hire workers on payrolling contracts. However, this does not allow employers to offer lower wages, because payroll workers must be paid on an equal basis to other workers doing similar jobs at the hiring firm; because payrolling is covered by the WAADI law (see Section 7.3.4). The incidence of payrolling is difficult to quantify, because payrolling workers are currently not included as a separate category in the labour market statistics.

7.4.2. Is there evidence that firms misclassify workers to save contributions?

In the Netherlands, the discussion on misclassification of workers is mostly focused on false self-employment. By hiring own-account workers instead of (temporary) employees, firms can save on social security contributions, which provides an incentive to opt for the former classification. Alternatively a worker can save on both taxes and social security contributions by performing a task as an own-account worker instead of on a labour contract. However, in certain situations a worker is not allowed to be classified as an own-account worker, because he matches the definition of an employee in Dutch labour law. If in such a case an employer nevertheless decides to hire someone as an own-account worker, this is called false self-employment. From a social protection viewpoint such structures are undesirable, since no social contributions are made for these own-account workers even though they are in fact employees. From an individual viewpoint this can be beneficial for both the employer and worker, since both the wage cost and net wage can increase due to the lower wedge.

Researching false self-employment is a difficult task, because it is not always clear whether an own-account worker is actually a misclassified employee[15]. As such, estimates of the size of the group of false self-employed generally have a large margin of error. In a 2013 study an attempt was made to estimate the share of false self-employment in four sectors: construction, health care, transport and management and organisation (including ICT) (SEOR, 2013[11]). By surveying own-account workers within these branches, the researchers estimated that roughly 3-15% of own-account workers should have been classified as employees.

According to the SEOR report, misclassified own-account workers do not necessarily earn less than actual own-account workers. The average gross hourly earnings of the misclassified group are higher, because they spend less time on unpaid tasks (administration, acquisitions etc.). However, employers do not pay a higher hourly rate to the misclassified group – overall their compensation is comparable. The transport and management branches are an exception, with misclassified own-account workers being paid more than their correctly classified counterparts and even more than the wage costs of an employee. This suggests that in these branches false self-employment is a benefit for the own-account worker (at the expense of the employer). In other branches misclassified own-account workers are paid comparable or lower amounts than correctly classified workers (employees and own-account workers), which suggests that either the employer or both the employer and the own-account worker benefit from the misclassification.

7.4.3. Incomes, risks and reliance on tax-funded assistance

It is hard to determine the causal relationship between working on non-standard work arrangements and income. The reason is that the people working in these arrangements differ substantially from workers on regular open-ended contracts. As shown above, workers in flexible work arrangements are in general younger, have a lower level of education and more often come from a non-native background. These characteristics generally correlate with human capital and work experience and workers on non-standard work arrangements are therefore expected to earn lower wages, have lower incomes and less wealth, for these reasons alone.

That being said, we do observe differences in standardised household income by contract type. People on open-ended contracts on average have the highest standardised household income, roughly EUR 33 000, followed by own-account workers (EUR 32 000, see Figure 7.5). People on non-standard employment contracts generally have a lower income, of which agency work has the lowest average (EUR 25 300). These differences may result from various factors, not only the wage/personal income as an own-account worker, but also partner income and the number of people in the household. Personal characteristics differ between the various groups as well (see Section 7.4).

Figure 7.5. Those working on standard contracts enjoy the highest incomes

Average standardised annual household income in Euro, 2015

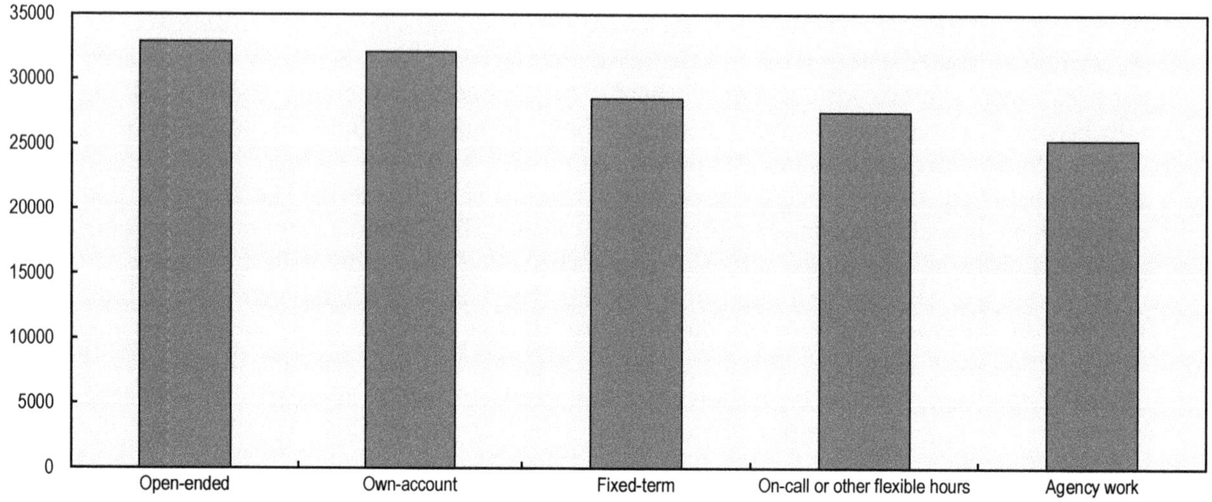

Note: Standardised income is the disposable income corrected for differences in household size and composition. This adjustment is done using equivalence factors. These factors represent the economy of scale realised by sharing household costs. Using these factors all incomes within a household are adjusted such that they represent a separate one-person household. In this way the welfare level between households are made comparable. Because welfare is experienced on an individual level, a standardised income is assigned to each of the household members. The disposable income consists of gross income minus transfers of income such as alimony payments, premiums for social securities and taxes on income and wealth.
Source: Statistics Netherlands (2017$_{[12]}$).

The inflow rate into unemployment of employees on non-standard contracts is over five times that of workers on standard contracts, and the unemployment benefit inflow rate is roughly three times higher. The probability of leaving the job market entirely is also much higher: five times that of workers on standard contracts (Table 7.1). Separate data show that temporary workers are also four times as likely to move into the unemployment benefit scheme as regular workers (Table 7.2). The fact that non-standard workers are more likely to enter unemployment than the unemployment benefits scheme implies that non-standard workers are less likely to be eligible for unemployment benefit than standard workers once they become unemployed. This is probably due to their interrupted employment histories, which makes them less likely to meet the eligibility criteria. It is therefore not surprising that workers on non-standard contracts are roughly nine times as likely to move from employment into social assistance (see Table 7.1).

Temporary and agency workers are also more likely to flow into the WIA disability benefit scheme compared with standard workers. For on-call workers, however, this is less likely (Table 7.2). This may be due to their younger age, but possibly also to the eligibility criteria being harder to meet for on-call workers. These statistics do not necessarily imply that on-call workers are less likely to suffer from disabilities. Nor does the higher rate of temporary and agency workers moving onto disability benefit automatically imply that these non-standard contracts increase the probability that a worker becomes unfit for work. Possibly jobs often performed on such non-standard contracts are riskier, but it may also be the case that people who work on non-standard contracts are more likely to develop health problems. Another explanation may be that reintegration is more difficult when the public employment office is responsible for this, rather than the employer. The latter is the case for sick temporary workers after the end of their contract.

Table 7.1. Non-standard workers are more likely to transition into unemployment-related situations

	Inflow rate (yearly)[1]			
	Standard		Non-standard	
Unemployment	2.88%	(a)	15.64%	(a)
Non-participation	4.61%	(a)	22.60%	(a)
Unemployment benefit (WW)	2.43%	(b)	8.28%	(b)
Social Assistance (Bijstand)	0.15%	(b)	1.32%	(b)

1 Defined as the proportion of workers who were employed in the previous year, but who have transitioned to one of these outcomes in the current year.
(a) Source: data from Statistics Netherlands' Statline (link, downloaded on 13-11-2017). Own calculations: average yearly rate 2003-17; quarterly rate converted to a yearly rate: Py = 1-(1-Pq)^4.
(b) Source: Van der Werff, Kroon and Heyma (2016[4]), using Statistics Netherland's microdata. Own calculation: average rate 2009-14.

Table 7.2. Inflow rates into various benefit schemes are higher from non-standard contracts

	Inflow rate							
	Standard		Non-standard					
			Temporary		*Agency*		*On-call*	
Unemployment benefit (WW)	1.4%	(a)	5.9%	(a)				
Disability benefit (WIA)	0.32%	(b)	0.48%	(b)	0.70%	(b)	0.22%	(b)

(a) *Source*: UWV (2010[13]). Yearly rate in 2008.
(b) *Source*: De Beer & Verhulp (2017[3]), p.36 with own calculations. Average WIA inflow rate after 24-36 months based on three measurement dates: October 2007, 2008 and 2009).

7.5. Conclusions

In recent decades, the share of non-standard work in the Netherlands has grown substantially and it is now among the highest of all OECD countries. Currently, approximately one-third of all workers are employed on a non-standard work arrangement. The share of workers employed in temporary work, agency work and on-call work has risen from 14% in 2003 to 23% in 2017, while the share of own-account workers has increased from 8% to 12%. The probability of working in a non-standard employment relationship is mostly correlated with age. The probability of working on all types of non-standard employment contracts decreases with age, whereas the share of own-account work increases with age. There are differences between men and women, between educational groups and between ethnic groups as well, but these differences are smaller than those between the age groups. In some cases these differences appear to be driven by the variation in the age of the different groups.

In principle, all employees have the same rights under labour and social security law. However, exceptions exist: workers on temporary contracts do not have the same employment protection rights as standard workers. If their contract lasts less than two years, they have no rights to severance payments and the employer does not need to provide justification for their dismissal. In addition, once the contract ends, temporary workers also have different rights to sick pay and reintegration assistance.

Workers on variable hours contracts do not have the same rights as regular employees regarding working hours, and during the first six months they often do not have the same rights to sick pay. In principle their rights to employment protection are the same as for regular workers, so that employers cannot just stop calling upon a worker or reduce their monthly working hours. But one may doubt whether all workers are aware of these rights and whether they in practice enforce these rights, since they are in a dependent position and going to court is time consuming and expensive.

Since temporary agency workers fall under a different collective labour agreement than workers hired directly by the firms at whose workplace they are based, and their conditions – such as wages, fringe benefits and pension rights – may differ.

Despite the legal equality of the employment contracts, the position of workers employed in these different relationships is not 100% equal. The inflow into social security benefits such as unemployment benefits, social assistance and disability benefits, is higher among non-standard workers. We cannot exclude the possibility that this is partly due to reversed causality, e.g. that non-standard workers are less healthy. But it is also apparent that the rules lead to different outcomes for different groups of workers. Temporary workers are likely to have shorter and less stable employment histories than workers on open-ended contracts. The fact that entitlement to many social security benefits depends on employment history means that temporary workers often do not accrue benefit entitlements to the same degree as standard workers. The benefits received are therefore usually lower and have a shorter maximum duration.

The most pronounced difference in social protection is between employees (with an employment contract), who are covered by labour law, and own-account workers, who are not. Since own-account workers are not regarded as dependent employees, they are not covered by labour law or collective employee insurance regimes for sickness, disability and unemployment. Their social protection therefore differs substantially from that of all other workers.

The discussion on misclassification of workers is mostly focused on false self-employment. By hiring own-account workers instead of (temporary) employees, firms can save on social security contributions and avoid minimum wage regulations, which provides an incentive to opt for the former classification. On the other hand, workers can save on both taxes and social security contributions by performing a task as own-account workers instead of under a labour contract. Both firms and workers can therefore have an incentive to misclassify an employment relationship as own-account work. A report by senior civil servants from various Dutch ministries (2015[10]) showed that own-account workers at the higher end of the wage distribution can use their bargaining power to benefit from the lower costs, while firms profit from the tax advantages at the lower end of the wage distribution by negotiating low fees. There are concerns that, especially at the lower end of the wage distribution, workers are forced into own-account work in situations of dependent employment, with the result that social security rights are withheld from this vulnerable group of workers.

Recently, the Dutch government has tried to curb the growth in temporary contracts, because they view further growth of all kinds of flexible work arrangements as undesirable. In 2015, the WWZ law tightened the rules concerning a "chain of temporary contracts". The effectiveness of these measures in reducing the share of temporary work is not evident, however. There is no thorough study yet on the effects of the WWZ and a causal link between the introduction of the act and a lower share of temporary work is difficult to find. It does appear, however, that a sequence of three temporary contracts of seven and eight months each (23 months in total, which maximizes the total length and number of consecutive temporary contracts) has become much more popular since the introduction of the WWZ law. An attempt to combat false self-employment by clarifying the legal boundaries between own-account work and dependent employment (the so-called DBA law) did not have the desired effect, due to confusion about how strictly these new agreements would be monitored.

Despite these recent attempts to combat the growth of the various forms of flexible employment, and despite the economic upswing, its share is still increasing. This is probably due to the fact that the Dutch institutional setting provides firms with possibilities to save on social contributions, severance payments, reintegration obligations and laborious administrative procedures by hiring people as own-account workers or (to a lesser extent) on one of the flexible employment arrangements. By using temporary work arrangements, employers can circumvent employment protection legislation – i.e. severance payments and time-consuming procedures to obtain permission for dismissal – and sickness-related payments and reintegration obligations that end on the expiry of the contract. If policy makers wish to reduce the share of non-standard work arrangements, policy should be aimed at reducing incentives to hire workers on non-standard contracts and for workers to opt out of the social security system and pay lower taxes as own-account workers.

7.5.1. Policy options for reducing the share of non-standard contracts:

Combinations of several policy options offer ways of combating the further increase of non-standard work arrangements:

1. Stricter regulation of non-standard work, for example through:

- Minimum hourly compensation for own-account workers (proposed in the recent Dutch coalition agreement).
- Stricter rules concerning the use of temporary contracts (e.g. maximum duration and number of contracts, or the situations in which non-standard work arrangements are allowed).
- Stricter monitoring of the current rules concerning non-standard contracts (proposed in the recent Dutch coalition agreement).

A disadvantage of these policy options is that already existent incentives to avoid the use of standard (i.e. permanent) contracts will remain in place. So stricter monitoring is necessary in any event. However, in practice effective monitoring can be difficult and costly (see for example Eurofund (2015[14])).

2. Reducing differences in taxes and social security coverage between non-standard and standard work, for example by:

- Decreasing the difference in the tax wedge between own-account workers and standard workers, by reducing or abolishing the tax benefits of self-employment, or introducing an additional tax deduction for dependent employees.
- Increasing the rights of non-standard workers e.g. by expanding the right to severance payment to workers with short employment histories (less than two

years) and broadening social security laws to include all workers, not only dependent employees.

- Reducing the social security rights and employment protection of workers on open-ended contracts and the duration of sick payment and reintegration obligations for employers of workers on open-ended contracts.

Notes

[1] This category consists of temporary workers who indicate that there is a prospect of becoming a standard worker. Since this is an indication based on the perception of the worker, the certainty of this prospect is unclear.

[2] The combined share of temporary, agency and on-call workers among 15-24 year-olds increased considerably in the past decade, from 40% in 2003 to 65% in 2015. For 25-34 year-olds it rose from 12% to 25%. For all other age groups and for own-account work the prevalence of non-standard work was quite stable over 2003-15.

[3] Summary dismissal is possible in the case of gross misconduct by the employee.

[4] The wage used as a basis for the amount of benefit payment.

[5] An Internet search on the term "7+8+8 regel" gives 1 300 results, especially for HR consultancy firms.

[6] These two shares do not add up tot he overall share of 71%, because some CLAs have a seperate deviation from the chain rule for both specific groups and all employees.

[7] The temporary agency sector has two collective labour agreements. The biggest – the ABU CLA – does not extend the 26 weeks. The smaller one – the NBBU CLA – does extend the period to 78 weeks.

[8] By law, this clause can apply only for the first 26 weeks of the agency agreement, but deviation by CLA is allowed. In the NBBU CLA this period has been extended to 78 weeks.

[9] Since working hours vary in on-call contracts, the gross salary is based on the average monthly working hours for the calculation of the severance payment.

[10] Idem.

[11] This has been the case since 2012. Before then, only the rules concerning protection against the most severe dangers and creating dangerous situations to other people was in place for own account workers.

[12] Own-account workers who started from a situation of dependent employment have the right to continue their insurance at their previous insurance agency. This is an opt-in situation, not an opt-out, as a result of which only 2% use this option (Bosch, De Graaf-Zijl and Van Vuuren, 2015[9]).

[13] The following criteria must be met to be eligible for the IOAZ benefit: 1) Age between 55 and 65. 2) At least 10 years of working history as a self-employed person or three years self-employed after seven years as an employee. 3) At least 1 225 working hours per year as a self-employed person (this can be shared between partners of a household). 4) Income of no more than EUR 23 938 per year in the previous three years (including income of partners in a household). 5) Expected future income less than EUR 25 443 (as estimated by the municipality). In some cases partially disabled self-employed people are also eligible for the IOAZ, but this is determined on a case-by-case basis.

[14] Criteria for misclassification of self-employment are: 1) the worker in question cannot freely choose who actually performs the work; 2) the employer has authority over the worker; 3) the worker receives a wage, which is defined as compensation for his work exceeding cost reimbursement. If these three criteria apply, the worker is not classified as self-employed, but as an employee.

[15] The second criteria (the employer having authority over the worker) is the most diffuse, since the existence of authority is hard to objectively determine and context dependent. For example, the following situations suggest that the employer has authority over the worker: The employer

decides how, when and where the job is performed; the employer decides on the amount of working hours/days per week; if the job requires team work, the employer can influence this co-operation and the worker gets the same instructions as any other employees at the firm.

References

Berkhout, E. and R. Euwals (2016), *Zelfstandigen en arbeidsongeschiktheid*, CPB. [7]

Bolhaar, J., A. Brouwers and B. Scheer (2016), *De flexibele schil van de Nederlandse arbeidsmarkt: een analyse op basis van microdata*, CPB. [2]

Bosch, N., M. De Graaf-Zijl and D. Van Vuuren (2015), *Position paper t.b.v. 'IBO Zelfstandigen zonder personeel'*, CPB. [9]

De Beer, P. and E. Verhulp (2017), *Dertig vragen en antwoorden over flexibel werk*, Amsterdam Institute for Advanced labour Studies. [3]

de Graaf-Zijl, M. and E. Berkhout (2007), *Temporary agency work and the business cycle*, SEO Economic Research. [1]

Eurofound (2015), *New forms of employment*, Publications Office of the European Union. [14]

Ministerie van Financiën (2015), *IBO Zelfstandigen zonder personeel*, Ministerie van Financiën. [10]

PPMi (2017), *Study to Support Impact Assessment on the Review of the Written Statement Directive*, European Commission. [5]

SEOR (2013), *ZZP tussen werknemer en ondernemer*. [11]

Statistics Netherlands (2017), *cbs opendata*, https://opendata.cbs.nl/statline/#/CBS/nl/dataset/83686NED/table?ts=1518193405374 (accessed on 28 July 2017). [12]

Statistics Netherlands & TNO (2017), *Zelfstandigen Enquête Arbeid*, Ministry of Social Affairs and Employment. [8]

UWV (2010), *Groei van de flexibele arbeid en de gevolgen voor het beroep op WW*, Kenniscentrum UWV. [13]

Van der Werff, S., L. Kroon and A. Heyma (2016), *Beslag uitkeringen personen in flexibele schil 2006-2014*, SEO. [4]

Vermeulen, H. et al. (2016), *Uitzendmonitor*, KBA. [6]

Chapter 8. Sweden: Voluntary unemployment insurance

Jonas Kolsrud

There is an ongoing debate in OECD countries on how to provide social insurance coverage for non-standard workers. A possible solution is government subsidised voluntary social insurance. Such programs are common in Sweden. However, voluntary social insurance programs for non-standard workers – notably unemployment insurance – face several challenges that need to be addressed for such programs to function satisfactorily. The most salient is how the risk of voluntary quits is managed. This chapter reviews how Swedish social insurance programs square with non-standard work arrangements. It finds that the bar to access voluntary unemployment insurance is higher for non-standard workers, mainly since it is hard to establish that a job loss is involuntary. Non-standard workers are also not covered in collective bargained social insurance schemes, most notably occupational pensions, which account for 25% of total pensions. A further conclusion is that for voluntary programs to work, the rate of subsidies provided by the government must be sufficiently high. Data from Sweden show that otherwise premiums will be high causing insurance coverage to fall.

8.1. Introduction

The Swedish social protection system combines publicly funded and voluntary, union-run elements. Employers and employees jointly determine additional entitlements, most importantly occupational pension schemes, which are exclusively funded by employers and employees, as part of collective agreements.

This chapter studies how well this system tackles the challenge of providing social protection to non-standard workers with a focus on unemployment insurance (UI). The Swedish case may be of interest for other OECD countries since parts of the UI scheme are voluntary, and voluntary UI is one option to improve the social protection coverage of non-standard workers across the OECD.

Publicly provided UI in Sweden is organised around some 25 occupation specific UI funds, most of which are affiliated with a trade union. Workers pay membership premiums and the funds pay out UI benefits when members become unemployed. In November 2017, the government paid for 65% of total UI expenses, with membership premiums covering the remaining 35%.[1]

The self-employed in Sweden have their own UI fund.[2] Workers who provide services to clients through labour platforms – so-called platform, crowd or gig workers – may join a UI fund for standard workers; they have no separate UI fund.

However, important parts of Swedish social insurance do not cover the self-employed and gig workers. This pertains especially to employer contributions into collectively bargained occupational pension schemes which cover most standard workers. In 2010, around one-quarter of all pension payments came out of occupational pension schemes, and this share is expected to rise. As these contributions amount to around 5%, or more for high-income earners, of a worker's pre-tax wage, incentives for employers to use gig workers and the self-employed instead of traditional employees may emerge (Government of Sweden, 2011$_{[1]}$).

For standard workers to receive UI when unemployed in Sweden, the employer confirms the layoff to the UI fund. This is to ensure that only the involuntarily unemployed can collect benefits. Voluntary unemployed can get UI benefits but there is a nine-week waiting period. The self-employed and gig workers have no employer to certify that their unemployment is involuntary. The self-employed need to close their firm in order to receive UI. If the self-employed becomes unemployed again he or she must wait at least five years after the resumption of the business to receive UI. This check seems to work as the unemployment rate among self-employed UI fund members was lower (3.8%) over the 2004-16 period compared with the average unemployment among UI fund members (6.6%).[3]

In 2016, the average self-employed who received UI had daily UI benefits of about EUR 67 (SEK 637) while the average daily UI benefit was about EUR 76 (SEK 722) (IAF, 2018$_{[2]}$).[4] The lower unemployment rate and lower average UI benefit levels suggest that the cost of unemployment is lower for the self-employed compared to regular workers (data from the Swedish Unemployment Insurance Board (IAF)).

Gig-workers are technically eligible to receive UI benefits, but in practice, Swedish UI funds have been reluctant to pay them UI, because they find it hard to establish that their unemployment is involuntary, which is a prerequisite to receive UI benefits. Because UI rules are based on a standard employment relationship, UI funds can require claimants' employers to confirm that they have been laid off; because gig workers do not have employers, they can typically not fulfil this requirement. No clear practice on the payment of UI to gig workers is yet in place (Wallin, 2017; DIK, 2017). Designing an insurance which prevents gig workers from claiming UI when they become unemployed voluntarily or face a temporary shortage of job assignments is a key challenge for any voluntary UI scheme for gig workers. Such as insurance scheme should ensure that unemployed gig workers can get access to UI and that voluntary unemployment among gig workers does not result in a significant increase in UI costs.

A growing number of non-standard workers can be expected to increase UI-related costs not only from the supply side (workers' behaviour) but also from the demand side (employers' behaviour). Non-standard workers are likely to have higher unemployment risks compared with standard workers as they are not in a traditional employer-employee relationship. They also have larger income fluctuations, partly due to an increased unemployment risk but also due to them having less income protection from the employer. Employers mostly absorb much of the wage variation that would otherwise occur if firm-level shocks (drops in demand, higher input prices etc.) were transmitted to workers' wages (Guiso, Pistaferri and Schivardi, 2005[3]).

Given that employers provide their employees with income protection against firm-level shocks, non-standard workers should be compensated for their higher income uncertainty by receiving a higher wage (the theory of compensating wage differentials). This would also have the effect of increasing government tax revenues. Without these compensating wage differentials, employers using non-standard workers would shift costs they would normally incur themselves onto the public budget in the form of higher UI costs. That is, the public would effectively step in and provide non-standard workers with the income protection that employers normally provide to standard workers, but without compensation in the form of higher tax revenue from non-standard workers. Thus, an increasing number of non-standard workers can increase UI costs both due to workers' behaviour and due to employers' behaviour.

In 2016, gig workers made up 0.5-1% of total employment in Sweden. Thus, voluntary unemployment among gig workers is likely to have little impact on aggregate UI expenses. However, the number of gig workers has grown by a factor of 8.5 between 2011 and 2016 and is expected to increase further (Wallin, 2017[4]). The Swedish UI system needs to improve its way of checking that unemployment among gig workers is indeed involuntary. Otherwise UI costs may increase, or gig workers will run the risk of not receiving any UI, even though they are eligible for benefits.

Another takeaway from Sweden is that any voluntary UI scheme needs to be heavily subsidised by tax money for participation levels to be high. Two reforms in 2007 and 2008, which made UI fund premiums dependent on the rate of unemployed workers covered by each fund, raised UI fund premiums by 300% on average. When the reforms were launched, the UI fund density (the share of workers who are members of a UI fund) dropped by 10-15 percentage points. The reforms were rolled back in 2014 but UI fund density has yet to recover to its pre-reform levels.

Another reason why the Swedish system may find it hard to incorporate gig workers can be found in the way the system has treated actors and musicians. It has been common for actors and musicians, who often have temporary assignments, to register as unemployed and receive UI between jobs (SOU, 2003[5]). Until the 2010s actors and musicians had UI funds of their own. However, the reforms in 2007 and 2008, which linked the financial burden on each UI fund to its unemployment rate, sharply increased UI fund premiums in these two funds. As a result, the actors' and musicians' UI funds merged with other, larger funds, which mitigated the costs of their high unemployment rates.

To successfully incorporate gig workers within the current Swedish system they would probably need to join UI funds that mostly represent employed standard workers. In such funds the (presumably) higher costs of gig workers would be masked as they would constitute a small fraction of all members. However, this would depend on gig workers remaining a marginal group on the Swedish labour market and larger funds being willing to accept gig workers as members, even though this may lead to higher costs for the fund and its incumbent members.

This chapter is structured as follows: the next section provides an overview of the general structure of the Swedish unemployment insurance system, and Section 8.3 shows how non-standard workers are incorporated into this system. Section 8.4 discusses some theoretical concerns that arise in the provision of unemployment insurance for non-standard workers. The chapter then goes on to apply these theoretical concerns to the Swedish situation: how well does unemployment insurance work for these workers in Sweden (Section 8.5). It then discusses additional, union-run benefit schemes (Section 8.6) before showing trends in voluntary unemployment insurance coverage (Section 8.7). Section 8.8 concludes.

Box 8.1. Terminology on unemployment insurance in Sweden

This box summarises some key concepts mentioned throughout this chapter

Work condition: To receive UI benefits the unemployed must have worked approximately at least half time for six months before registering as unemployed at the Public Employment Service.

Basic UI: UI benefits paid for exclusively by tax money. This is a flat-rate benefit amounting to SEK 1 825 per week in 2017. To receive these benefits the unemployed must fulfil the work condition.

Voluntary UI: UI benefits which are both paid for by tax money and UI fund premiums. Voluntary UI is income related. To receive these benefits, the unemployed must fulfil the work condition and have been a member of a UI fund (which is voluntary) for at least 12 months before registering as unemployed at the Public Employment Service.

Publicly provided UI: The sum of basic UI and voluntary UI. Publicly provided UI grants the unemployed 80% of the pre-tax wage up to a ceiling. The maximum weekly benefit was SEK 4 550 in 2017. The term "publicly provided UI" is used as most expenses are paid for by taxes and the rules regulating benefits are statutory.

Union-provided UI: UI benefits function as a top-up to publicly provided UI. To receive these benefits, the unemployed person has to be member of a union that provides such UI *and* be eligible for voluntary UI.

UI fund premiums: The payment by UI fund members to UI funds. Paid on a monthly basis.

Financing fee: The contribution from UI funds to the public purse (paid out of UI fund premiums, amounting to about 25% of total expenditure of publicly provided UI).

Additional financing fee: An additional contribution paid by the funds to the public purse in 2007. It made funds with high unemployment contribute more and funds with low unemployment contribute less. It was replaced by the unemployment fee in 2008.

Unemployment fee: An additional contribution paid by the funds to the public purse in the 2008-13 period. It was also linked to a fund's unemployment rate.

8.2. The general architecture of the Swedish unemployment insurance system

Sweden – along with Denmark, Finland and Iceland – stands out among OECD countries as having a multiple-tier unemployment insurance system that combines compulsory, publicly provided elements with union-run schemes and collectively bargained elements, most importantly occupational pensions. The self-employed are covered by some elements of the system, but not all as they are neither covered by collective agreements nor have a union. This section sets out the basic structure of the system.

8.2.1. A brief history of the Swedish unemployment insurance system

In the late 19th century the growing labour movement in Sweden and other European countries started providing UI through trade unions. Union members paid in premiums to the unions' UI funds and received benefits when they lost their jobs. However, these voluntary UI schemes attracted workers with high unemployment risk while workers with low risk of losing their jobs abstained from membership. This led to insolvency among many UI funds, especially as many funds were industry specific: When an industry hit a trough, many of the UI fund members in that industry became unemployed, which made it hard for the fund to pay out benefits (Chetty and Saez, 2010[6]).

To improve risk sharing and to avoid adverse selection – of high-risk workers joining UI funds while low-risk workers abstain from membership – the governments of many European countries started to subsidise UI funds. This was effective in improving risk sharing and brought down premiums to a level where most workers joined a UI fund. This method of public subsidies to UI funds seems to have originated in the Belgian town of Ghent. The organisation of UI provision via union-affiliated UI funds is therefore referred to as the Ghent system (Holmlund, 1998[7]).

During the first half of the 20th century most industrialised countries made UI compulsory. The United Kingdom was the first country to provide compulsory UI in 1911. But in some countries, one of them being Sweden, the state continued paying subsidies to UI funds. The other Ghent countries are Denmark, Finland and Iceland. Belgium has a compulsory UI system but the benefit pay-outs are still administered through the unions (Holmlund, 1998[7]). The Swedish state has subsidised UI funds since 1935.

The Ghent system is bound to increase union density, as most unions run a UI fund and UI fund membership premiums are a part of union dues (Holmlund and Lundborg, 1999[8]). In 2013, union density was 68% in Sweden while it was 52% in Norway where publicly provided UI is compulsory (OECD, 2017[9]).

Since the early 1980s there has been an increase in the number of workers in Sweden who are members of a UI fund but not of a union. In 2010, 20% of all UI fund members were not union members (Kjellberg, 2010[10]). Typically, the UI fund premiums are small compared with union dues. If the UI benefits which fund membership provide are generous enough, it may therefore be attractive for some workers to only join a UI fund (Kjellberg, 2006[11]).

Figure 8.1. Voluntary UI provides higher replacement rates

Net-of-tax UI replacement rate in the public UI (in %) as a function of pre-unemployment monthly pre-tax wage, in 1 000 SEK

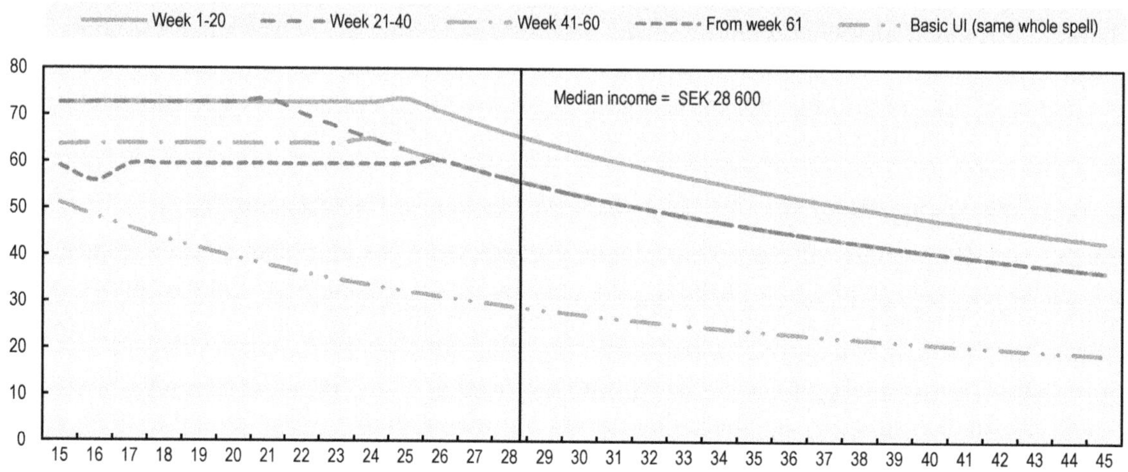

Note: The figure plots the relationship between monthly pre-unemployment wage in Swedish kronor and the net-of-tax replacement rate given by publicly provided UI benefits in the Swedish UI scheme as of July 2017; EUR 1≈ SEK 9.5. Publicly provided UI is basic UI plus voluntary UI. The UI scheme introduces time-dependent cut-offs at week 21, week 41 and week 61 of the unemployment spell. To receive benefits from week 61 onward the unemployed must participate in active labour market programs administered by the Public Employment Service. The basic UI is flat for all incomes and all unemployment spell durations. Sudden drops or increases in the replacement rate are due to differences in the personal allowance given for UI and the personal allowance given for wage. These differ as UI is less than the wage. All calculations use the 2015 median wage of SEK 28 600.
Source: The law regulating UI in Sweden (SFS, 1997[12]).

8.2.2. Benefit regulations in Swedish public unemployment insurance

Swedish publicly provided UI can be divided into two parts. The first is a basic benefit which is paid out to all unemployed workers who fulfil a work requirement of having worked approximately half time for at least six months prior to registering as unemployed at the Public Employment Service (PES), regardless of whether or not they are a member of a UI fund. The second part is a voluntary income-related benefit scheme. To receive voluntary UI the unemployed worker must have been paying premiums to a UI fund for at least 12 months and fulfil the work requirement. It is not possible to only receive voluntary UI without receiving basic UI.

In 2017 the basic unemployment benefit provided a flat-rate amount of about 30% of the median wage (see Figure 8.1).[5] Benefits are paid out for 60 weeks. To receive benefits after week 60, unemployed workers must participate in active labour market programmes (ALMP) offered by the PES. ALMP participants receive benefits at the same level for as long as they are unable to find a job – theoretically indefinitely. There are no time-dependent changes in the basic benefit during the course of an unemployment spell.

There are a number of time-dependent benefit cuts in Swedish publicly provided UI (basic UI plus voluntary UI). For the first 40 weeks of unemployment, the publicly provided UI amounts to 80% of the previous wage up to a ceiling of about two-thirds of the median wage. After week 21 the benefit ceiling drops to just over half of the median wage, but the replacement rate is still 80% of the ceiling. After week 40 the replacement rate drops to 70% of previous pre-tax income (with an unchanged ceiling, Figure 8.1).[6]

Publicly provided UI is paid out for 60 weeks, as is basic UI. After week 60 the unemployed person must participate in ALMPs to receive further benefits. These benefits amount to 65% of the previous wage and cannot exceed just over half of the median wage. Income-related ALMP benefits are paid out indefinitely, as are basic ALMP benefits.

The relationship between the pre-tax wage and the publicly provided UI replacement rate (the share of the net-of-tax wage replaced by UI benefits) is shown in Figure 8.1. The median worker received about 65% of the net-of-tax wage for the first 20 weeks of unemployment. From week 21 onwards the net-of-tax replacement rate is about 55%. Median workers who are ineligible for voluntary UI because they are not members of a UI fund get about 25% of the net-of-tax wage replaced by basic UI benefits. In February 2017, 36% of the unemployed had pre-unemployment wages above the income ceiling (Samorg, 2017$_{[13]}$).

There are about 25 different UI funds in Sweden, including one for the self-employed. Most funds are affiliated with a trade union and mostly cover the members of that particular trade union.[7] The UI funds are thus relatively occupational specific. But there is a significant degree of overlap between industries. About two out of five Swedish workers are members of a UI fund other than the dominant one in their industry (Swedish Fiscal Policy Council, 2011$_{[14]}$). As mentioned, UI fund membership does not require union membership. However, about 70% of workers were members of a UI fund in 2016, while 69.2% were union members (Figure 8.2).

Voluntary UI benefits are financed from both UI fund premiums and taxes. The financial burden imposed on UI funds by unemployment has changed over time. Since 2014, UI funds pay a financing fee (*finansieringsavgift*) to the Swedish state. The financing fees (paid out of UI fund membership premiums) cover about 25% of total voluntary UI outlays. The rest comes from government subsidies to the UI funds. From 2007 to 2013 the funds also paid additional fees depending on the relative cost of unemployed members in each fund. During this period the share of total UI expenses funded by membership fees was 40-60% annually (see Section 8.7).

This means that the (per member) financing fee depends on the average wage of the members in the fund. Thus, there is currently no "experience rating" in the UI funds in the sense that funds with a higher unemployment rate would also pay more to the public purse, as was the case in 2007-13 (Section 8.7).

Figure 8.2. Union- and Unemployment Fund membership are closely related

Union and UI fund density, as percentage of the labour force (ages 16-64), 2000-2016

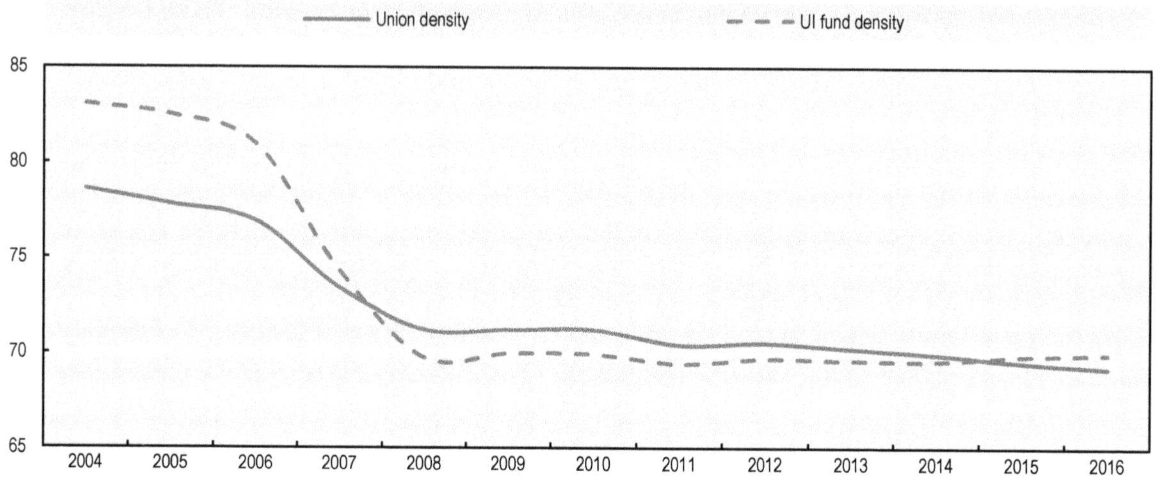

Note: Trade union density and unemployment insurance (UI) fund density in the labour force for workers aged 16-64 years. Students who are union members are excluded as they are not included in the labour force unless they actively search for work.
Source: Statistics Sweden's labour force survey (AKU) for the labour force and the Swedish Unemployment Insurance Board (IAF) for UI fund members. Union density from (Kjellberg, 2017[15]).

8.2.3. Other non-public unemployment insurance schemes

Most Swedish unions run additional UI benefit schemes, providing additional benefits funded exclusively by union dues. These programmes top up the publicly provided UI to 80% of the previous wage, removing the cap on publicly provided UI (as illustrated by Figure 8.1).[8] These top-ups are paid out for a period of 20 to 40 weeks, beginning at the onset of the unemployment spell. To receive union-provided UI the individual must be a union member, be a member of a UI fund and be eligible to receive publicly provided UI. Typically, these benefits cover all members of a union. Union-provided UI thus works as a group insurance (Lindquist and Wadensjö, 2011[16]). Some 70% of all employed workers in Sweden are members of a union and about 55-60% of the workforce are eligible for union-provided top-up UI via their union membership.[9] Swedish self-employed and gig workers have no union and therefore cannot receive union-provided UI.

About 90% of Swedish employees are employed under collective agreements. This means that employer associations and unions negotiate both wages and benefits. Many collective agreements include additional income insurance when individuals are laid off. For instance, government employees who are laid off always receive 80% of their previous wage, irrespective of wage level. Most non-standard workers are not covered by collective agreements and cannot receive such additional benefits if they become unemployed. The schemes in the collective agreements are not subject to any public funding. It should be noted, however, that many standard workers are unaware of the UI benefits available to them via collective agreements, which results in low take-up rates (Lindquist and Wadensjö, 2011[16]).

Table 8.1. Taxes and collectively bargained contributions for a yearly median wage

All entries in 2015 SEK and as percentages of the yearly pre-tax median wage in parenthesis

	Standard worker (private sector, blue collar)	Independent contractor	Gig worker	Small business owner
Labour cost	469 154 (136.70%)	442 625 (128.97%)	451 033 (132.14%)	451 033 (132.14%)
Social insurance contributions	-110 304 (32.14%)	99 425 **(28.97%)**	-110 304 (32.14%)	-110 304 (32.14%)
Collectively bargained contributions	-15 650 **(4.56%)**	0 (0%)	0 (0%)	0 (0%)
Pre-tax wage	343 200 (100%)	343 200 (100%)	343 200 (100%)	343 200 (100%)
Personal allowance	13 800 (4.02%)	13 800 (4.02%)	13 800 (4.02%)	13 800 (4.02%)
Taxable income	329 403 (95.98%)	329 403 (95.98%)	329 403 (95.98%)	329 403 (95.98%)
Income tax	-105 738 (30.81%)	-105 738 (30.81%)	-105 738 (30.81%)	-105 738 (30.81%)
Earned income tax credit	25 764 (7.51%)	25 764 (7.51%)	25 764 (7.51%)	25 764 (7.51%)
Net-of-tax wage	263 226 (76.70%)	263 226 (76.70%)	263 226 (76.70%)	263 226 (76.70%)

Note: The table shows how an average yearly pre-tax wage is divided into taxes and social insurance and contributions to collectively bargained schemes for four different worker types. Labour costs vary for the different worker types purely as a result of differences in social insurance and collectively bargained contributions. The income tax is the same: 32.1% of taxable income. Rate differences in social security contributions are highlighted in bold.
Source: Statistics Sweden, Swedish tax administration and Confederation of Swedish Enterprise.

8.3. Non-standard workers and the Swedish social protection system

There are four basic types of workers in Sweden: Standard workers (dependent employees), gig workers, independent contractors and small business owners. Gig workers are technically employees, since they are employed by an umbrella company for administrative purposes, although they are not subject to collective agreements (see below). Independent contractors and small business owners are self-employed.

All workers are included in the basic unemployment insurance system. The self-employed have their own unemployment fund, and gig workers may join a UI fund for standard workers. However, it is more difficult for non-standard workers to establish that they are involuntarily unemployed (Wallin, 2017[17]). Both since they, in practice, lack an employer to confirm it, but also since it can be hard for UI funds to determine if they should be considered as employed or self-employed.

As noted above, the self-employed have to close their business in order to receive UI. If they resume their business they cannot claim UI benefits for at least five years after the resumption of the business. Such a rule does not apply to gig workers who are considered as employed. This unclear treatment of gig workers can make it more difficult for them to receive UI, but it also makes it less favourable to be self-employed due to the business closure rule which do not apply to employed gig workers.

Workers in non-standard work arrangements are not covered by additional social protection provisions determined in collective agreements, most importantly occupational pensions. This makes them cheaper for employers (relative to dependent employees) but may put them at risk of old-age poverty.

8.3.1. Labour costs for different types of workers in Sweden

Employers withhold taxes and social security contributions for standard and gig workers (see below), while independent contractors and small business owners, being self-employed, are responsible for administering their own taxes.

Social insurance contributions (*arbetsgivaravgift*, including UI, sickness insurance, disability insurance, pensions etc.) are more than 2 percentage points lower for independent contractors than for other contract types (Table 8.1) because independent contractors do not have to pay employer social insurance contributions to schemes such as the wage guarantee (*lönegaranti*), which provides income replacement to displaced workers. Independent contractors are, however, covered for all publicly supported schemes (UI, disability insurance etc.) in the same way as other types of workers. While small business owners with no employees who are employed by their own firm have to pay contributions for the wage guarantee, they seldom receive payments in the case of bankruptcy, because of the moral hazard problem implied by being displaced by one's own firm.

For standard workers, the employer also pays around 5% in contributions for the collectively bargained pension and worker compensation schemes, including additional accident and illness cover. The contributions also cover expenses for collectively bargained UI and training for unemployed workers covered by collective agreements (see Section 8.3.4).[10]

Collectively bargained contributions are progressive. In some collective agreements, the contributions for wage shares above about 130% of the median wage can be 30% and more. This is mainly due to higher payments to collectively bargained pension schemes: as public pensions are capped at the same earnings threshold (both for contributions and for benefits), collectively bargained pension schemes help high-earning workers to reach higher net replacement rates upon retirement.

Gig workers are treated as employees as they are employed by so-called umbrella companies. The umbrella company handles their tax payments and pays their social security contributions. But the umbrella companies only function as employers from an administrative standpoint, the gig worker decides who to work for and how much to work, just like the self-employed. They are not subject to collective agreements, and thus are not subject to contributions to collectively bargained schemes (Table 8.1).

As a result, the total labour cost for an independent contractor is about 6% lower than that of a standard worker, while a gig worker costs 3% less (Table 8.1).

The income tax is the same for all four types. All workers are given a personal allowance which is smaller (both in absolute terms and relative to the pre-tax wage) the higher their income.[11] Taxable income is calculated by subtracting the personal allowance from the pre-tax wage. Table 8.1 shows that individuals pay the average (local) tax of 32.1%. All workers also receive an earned income tax credit paid out the same time the wage is paid out. The median worker keeps 78% of the pre-tax wage.

8.3.2. The self-employed in the Swedish unemployment insurance system

The self-employed have a separate UI fund (*Småföretagarnas a-kassa*). As with a UI fund for standard employees, the self-employed pay in premiums and receive UI if they become unemployed. To be defined as unemployed, the self-employed must shut down their firm. If, after receiving unemployment benefits, the firm is restarted, the self-employed person cannot receive unemployment benefits again for five years.

When an independent contractor starts a firm, the firm is not a legal entity separate from the independent contractor. This means that it is the independent contractor as a private citizen who bears the sole responsibility for the firm's operations. For instance, debt accumulated by the firm is also the independent contractor's private debt. As the firm is so tightly bound to the independent contractor, each independent contractor can only have one firm at a time. Small business owners, however, can have as many limited liability companies as they wish. But it costs about EUR 5 000 to set up a limited liability company.

There are about 200 000 independent contractors in Sweden aged 20-64, or 4-5% of total employment.[12] The self-employed UI fund has 120 000 members. However, individuals employed in small businesses (both owners and employees) may also be members of this fund, therefore the share of the self-employed who are members of a UI fund cannot be calculated using these numbers.

Since the self-employed do not have a union, they are less likely to be covered by union-provided UI. They are in general not covered by collective agreements either. As a result, many self-employed are not covered by additional, collectively bargained unemployment compensation.[13]

8.3.3. Gig workers in the Swedish unemployment insurance system

Gig workers are a growing category of workers. In 2011 there were about 4 000; in 2016 there were 34 000 (Wallin, 2017[4]). Gig workers are not defined as a special category in Swedish registry data nor in the Swedish labour force survey AKU. Gig workers are legally required to register with an umbrella company to handle their tax- and social security contributions (see below) and are considered standard workers in Swedish registry data. Therefore, it is hard to separate them from other employees and to study the kind of benefits that gig workers are able to access during unemployment and to what extent these benefits replace previous earnings. The number of gig-workers reported here comes from the umbrella companies' association (*Egenanställningsföretagen*).

An umbrella company is a private firm which essentially handles the paperwork for individuals who would otherwise be independent contractors or business owners. A gig-worker who is employed by an umbrella company is solely responsible for attracting clients. Once a job is done the client sends an invoice to the umbrella company which in turn pays a wage to the gig-worker. The umbrella company pays in social insurance contributions via the payroll tax. This means that the gig-workers receive pension contributions and get access to other parts of the social insurance system. The umbrella company charges 5-10% of the invoice amount for this service.

Some descriptive statistics on gig workers are provided in a report issued by the umbrella companies' association. Gig workers are predominantly young (50% are below age 30) and they are more often men (65% are men compared with 52% of all those in employment). About 40% work full time as gig workers while the other 60% have regular employment as well (Bjerke and Pettersson, 2012[18]). Individuals with regular employment can qualify for UI benefits via their regular employment. Note, however, that UI fund membership is voluntary.

To receive publicly provided UI the gig worker must fulfil the work condition and be a member of a UI fund. From an administrative standpoint it is important that the gig worker carefully reports the amount of time spent on each assignment to the umbrella company to fulfil the work condition. Otherwise it may be difficult to assess UI eligibility. However, there is currently no clear practice on how to establish whether gig workers are involuntarily unemployed in the Swedish UI system, given that they lack an employer (DIK, 2017[19]). Therefore, not all UI funds may consider gig workers as employed, which makes it difficult for them to receive voluntary UI. The extent of this problem cannot be quantified, however, because gig-workers cannot be identified in Swedish registry data.

There is no gig worker union, and therefore no union-provided UI. Gig workers do not receive any collectively bargained unemployment benefits either, as they are not subject to collective agreements.[14]

8.3.4. Pensions and other benefits for the self-employed and gig workers

The Swedish pension system consists of three tiers. The first is the public pension which the self-employed and gig workers are covered by. The second is the collectively bargained pension. And the final third tier is represented by private pension savings. Of all paid out pensions in 2014, 70% came from the public pension system with 25% coming from collectively bargained pensions. The relative importance of collectively bargained pensions is expected to rise in the coming ten to 20 years (SOU, 2011[20]). The self-employed and gig workers are (in general) not covered by collective agreements, and hence are not covered by the additional occupational pensions that are an integral part of the collective agreements.

One reason why collectively bargained pensions are expected to grow in importance over the next two decades is that public pensions grow more slowly than labour earnings. The Swedish pension system is a defined-contribution scheme. This means that pensions will reflect an individual's work history: the more the individual works, the higher their pension will be; at the same time, increasing life expectancy means that the balance in workers' individual accounts needs to be stretched out over longer periods of retirement. To keep the public pension system stable, a "brake" has been built into the system which automatically lowers pensions if pension liabilities exceed pension contributions. However, there is no corresponding "gas" that increases pensions when contributions exceed liabilities.

Another explanation for the expected growth in the relative importance of collectively bargained pensions is that income inequality has increased in Sweden (Bengtsson, Edin and Holmlund, 2014[21]), especially during the 1990s. Only wages below a fixed threshold – about 130% of the median wage in 2017 – count as pensionable income on which pension contributions and benefits are payable. The pensionable income threshold is indexed to the average wage. Thus, when wages of high-income earners grow faster than the average wage, the net replacement rate of the public pension system declines.

Finally, higher female labour force participation means that fewer individuals are relying solely on the basic public pension, and more are getting access to collectively bargained pensions (Hagen, 2017[22]).

The self-employed and gig workers are also excluded from collectively bargained sickness insurance and workers' compensation schemes. When workers become sick or have a workplace accident they receive publicly provided sickness insurance or workers' compensation. These benefits were capped at a threshold of about 160% of the median wage in 2017, which is indexed to inflation but not to wage growth.

Public sickness insurance and workers' compensation benefits thus are devalued over time as the income of more and more individuals exceeds the threshold. Therefore, being covered by collective agreements, and being covered by top-up benefits, become more important over time as public benefits become debased. As gig-workers are not covered by collective agreements they lose out from these top-ups that become more important over time.

Sick and injured workers who are covered by collective agreements receive top-ups on their public benefits. These top-ups are more important for individuals with work absences exceeding six months (Sjögren and Wadensjö, 2007[23]). In addition, the top-ups will also become more important over time due to the indexation of the caps on sickness insurance and workers' compensation benefits.

To sum up: gig workers risk to be left out of important social insurance schemes. They may not be eligible for voluntary UI and they are not covered by collective agreements, which reduces their future pensions and their protection against sickness and workplace injury. Employers pay less for gig workers compared with standard workers, especially when the worker receives a relatively high wage (above SEK 460 000 or EUR 50 000 annually). In these cases, collectively bargained contributions are above 30% for wage shares exceeding EUR 50 000 (Ekonomifakta, 2017[24]).

8.4. Theory on unemployment insurance and non-standard workers

The theory of optimal unemployment insurance – how the consumption smoothing effect of UI should be balanced against the distortive effect of UI on job search – builds on assumptions that may not be applicable to gig workers and the self-employed.[15] Typically the theoretical literature assumes that two conditions are met when designing UI programmes:

- UI benefits are lower than the present wage. The expected wage in a future job is not (significantly) lower than the present wage (and thus higher than the UI benefits) because of downward wage rigidity (at least in the short term, see below).
- Job separation is not a choice of the employee; the layoff risk is thus not affected by the UI benefit generosity.

These assumptions may not apply as much to gig workers and the self-employed as they do to standard workers for the following reasons:

- The self-employed and gig workers often have higher income variation than dependent employees (Hurst et al., 2010[25]). Moreover, they are more likely to have lower future than present earnings, because wage stickiness does not apply to the self-employed, and labour platforms often operate on very flexible prices. Thus, their present and future earnings may be lower than their UI benefits (which are based on current and past earnings). They could therefore choose to quit work based on a trade-off between UI benefits and the wage.
- The self-employed and gig workers cannot be monitored like standard workers; if they avoid work, they lose assignments but this information is hidden from the principal (in this case, the government agency) who pays out UI. Thus, assessing whether unemployment is voluntary or not is more difficult with the self-employed and gig workers.

The effect of the discrepancy between how theoretical models treat standard and non-standard workers laid out above can be described as follows: When the self-employed and gig workers both have private information about their future income and can quit work voluntarily without the UI fund being able to establish this, additional costs may be incurred to the UI system and to the public budget. The self-employed and gig workers may have private information on their future stream of income, and if they expect it to decrease, they have an incentive to stop working and receive UI instead.

For most regular employees, wages are sticky and do not fall when labour demand decreases. Economic theory predicts that downward wage rigidity instead leads to involuntary unemployment (Shapiro and Stiglitz, 1984[26]).

One way of dealing with the additional moral hazard created by the fact that it is difficult to establish whether a separation is voluntary or not is to simply reduce UI benefits. The more moral hazard an insurance scheme creates, the lower the UI benefit should be to maintain incentives to search for work. So if gig workers create additional moral hazard compared with standard workers, then their UI benefits should be lower. However, special rules for various types of workers may be hard to implement. If so, UI benefits would need to be lower for all workers.

Another solution is to tie benefits to workers' labour market history. Workers who have worked more are given more generous UI benefits while workers with a shorter labour market history receive lower benefits. This incentivises workers to qualify for more generous UI benefits by avoiding becoming unemployed regularly (cf. (Fredriksson and Holmlund, 2001[27])). In fact, this is done in Austria and Germany where older workers and workers with a long employment history are given more generous (public) UI benefits.

UI costs can also be expected to rise due to employer behaviour. An employment contract can be seen as a form of insurance for the employee: the employer, who maximises profits and therefore is neutral to risk, insures some of the employee's wage, since the employee is risk averse (Parsons, 1986[28]). In practice this means that the employer does not change the employee's wage to any large extent but instead absorbs the negative wage effects of various events such as unexpected decline in demand (Guiso, Pistaferri and Schivardi, 2005[3]). As gig workers do not have a standard employer-employee relationship, their services are not needed when demand drops. According to standard labour economic theory, the higher layoff risk should be compensated by a higher wage for non-standard workers. This is referred to as the theory of compensating wage differentials. Higher wages for non-standard workers also increase the public's tax revenues.

Unless compensating wage differentials emerge, the public will have to cover gig workers and the self-employed against some of the fluctuations in demand which employers normally protect their employees against (up to a certain point when personnel needs to be laid off). And this will not be offset by higher tax revenues from non-standard workers.

8.5. How does the Swedish UI system work for non-standard workers?

As mentioned in Section 8.4, an important difference between the self-employed and gig workers on the one hand and standard workers on the other is that the self-employed and gig workers are likely to have significantly higher income fluctuations. Therefore, if future pay is expected to be low it may be more profitable to register as unemployed. The Swedish UI system handles voluntary departures in two ways for standard workers. First, employers confirm to the UI funds that a regular employee has been laid off. Second, voluntary departures are associated with a waiting period of nine weeks for individuals who apply for benefits (SFS, 1997[12]). UI funds have the responsibility of checking whether the worker has been laid off or has departed from the job voluntarily.

From an employer perspective, employers have no incentive to report truthfully on whether a departure is voluntary or not. But for the employee it is important to have confirmation that they have been laid off involuntarily. Quitting voluntarily could also impede the employee's chance of receiving a severance payment as severance packages are negotiated between the union and the employers' association. Furthermore, severance payments are often paid by insurance funds that are jointly owned by employers' associations and unions. But cases where workers collude with the employer to be laid off are hard for the funds to detect.

UI funds' monitoring of voluntary versus involuntary unemployment does not detect all cases of voluntary departures. UI funds grant UI payments to some individuals they know have left jobs voluntarily. In the 2013-15 period, 12% of all registered unemployed had quit voluntarily. One in four (some 11 000 individuals) of those leaving employment voluntarily still received full UI and were thus not penalised by the nine-week waiting period which should follow in these cases (IAF, 2016[29]). Reasons as to why penalisation does not occur could be that the individual has left work due to sickness or when the individual has left work due to unequal, unfair or abusive treatment from co-workers or supervisors. The UI funds then give the applicant the benefit of the doubt.

Confirming that unemployment is involuntary is harder for UI funds when it comes to gig workers and the self-employed. For the self-employed there is instead a cost involved as the company must be down. If the self-employed resumes the business he or she cannot claim UI for the next five years. In 2016, 6 802 self-employed received UI benefits according to the Swedish Unemployment Insurance Board (IAF). This is about 3.5% of all self-employed aged 16-64. Gig workers do not incur such costs which may increase their incentives to take up UI during periods when work is scarcer.

Taking up UI during periods with few or no assignments may especially prove to be important in work with a high degree of seasonality. Like regular employees who lose their jobs, gig workers need to attend active labour market programmes at the Public Employment Service to receive UI benefit after 60 weeks of unemployment. But participation in these programmes is often required at an earlier stage of the unemployment spell. Non-compliance can lead to reduced UI benefits or even termination of benefit payments.

In general, being required to attend labour market programmes has been found to have an effect on unemployment durations; exit rates from unemployment have been found to rise just before individuals are required to participate in labour market training (Hall et al., 2016[30]).

The moral hazard created by the risk of not being able to establish whether or not job departures are voluntary has resulted in unclear treatment of unemployed gig workers (DIK, 2017[19]). UI funds may not pay out voluntary UI to gig workers, even though they are eligible (Wallin, 2017[4]). This means that gig workers who become unemployed involuntarily may lose out on their UI benefits as their involuntary unemployment status can be hard to verify. The umbrella companies are not likely to be able to verify whether the gig worker's unemployment is voluntary or involuntary, which is a requirement of unemployment benefit receipt.

There may be more administration involved when self-employed people file for UI, especially since the self-employed need to show that their firm is no longer active. This also needs to be established by the UI fund. The median time it took for a self-employed person to receive voluntary UI was six weeks in 2016 while the median time for all funds was five weeks. According to data from the Swedish Unemployment Insurance Board (IAF), the additional waiting time for the first UI pay-out for the self-employed is smaller compared to some funds covering regular workers such as the construction workers' UI fund (Byggnadsarbetarnas a-kassa) with a median waiting time seven weeks in 2016, and the fund which covers those employed in hotels and restaurants (Hotell- och restauranganställdas a-kassa) with a median waiting time of eight weeks.

8.6. The importance of union-run and collectively bargained benefit schemes

From a theoretical perspective, the generosity of publicly provided UI is related to the generosity of union-provided UI. If publicly provided UI decreases, union-provided UI can be expected to increase as union members wish to be insured against reduced consumption in the event of unemployment (Kolsrud, 2013[31]).

This effect can be illustrated by recent reforms of publicly provided UI in Sweden. Publicly provided UI is set in nominal terms. Thus, benefits decrease in real terms if they are not raised by active policy decisions. The nominal cap on publicly provided UI benefits was reduced by 7% in 2007, and then remained constant until the autumn of 2015 when it was raised by 33%. Between 2006 and 2011 the net replacement rate of publicly provided UI for median workers (the share of the net-of-tax wage replaced by UI) decreased by some 25 percentage points, from 80% to 55% (Figure 8.3, Panel A). The figure continued to decline until maximum UI benefits were raised in 2015.

Figure 8.3. Union top-ups counteracted cuts in publicly provided UI

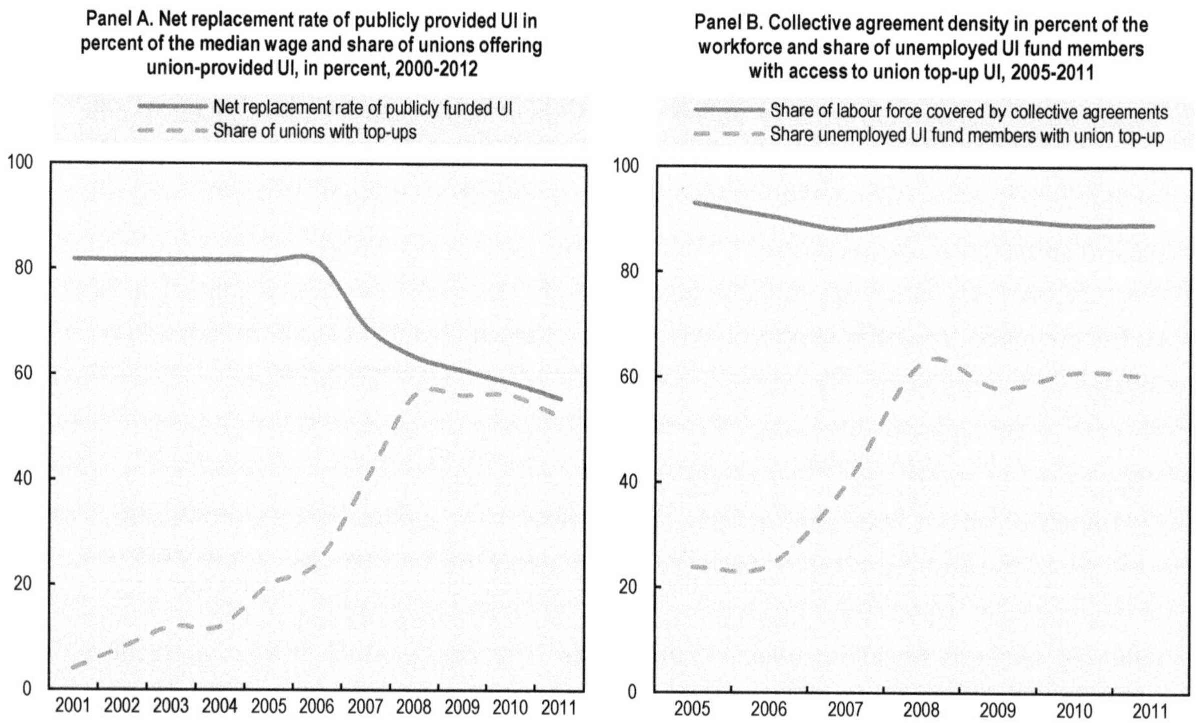

Source: Panel A: Statistics Sweden's labour force survey (AKU) for wages and the Swedish Unemployment Insurance Board (IAF) for union top-up UI provision. Panel B: Collective bargain density (Kjellberg, 2017[15]), the Swedish Unemployment Insurance Board (IAF) for union top-up UI provision.

The introduction of an earned income tax credit in 2007 further reduced the net-of-tax UI replacement rate by 5 percentage points for an average worker and slightly more for a median worker (Konjunkturinstitutet, 2016[32]). During this period, many unions who had not previously done so set up their own UI schemes to top up their members' income-related UI (Figure 8.3, Panel A).

The downward trend in the UI replacement rate has been partly offset by an increase in union-run UI. In 2011 half of all UI funds were affiliated to a union that had a top-up UI scheme, up from just one-quarter in 2005. About a third of all workers had access to union-provided top-ups in 2011. About 55-60% of union members had access to union-provided UI in 2011 and the union density was about 70%. This gives an approximate 40% coverage rate of union-provided UI top-ups in the labour force.

The self-employed and gig workers have no dedicated union, so it is less likely that they will be union members. Therefore, their income protection decreases if publicly provided UI benefits fall, without any replacement from other schemes. They are thus more vulnerable to benefit devaluation and benefit cuts compared with regular employees who are mostly union members.

The share of workers covered by collective bargains has been relatively stable during the 2000s (Kjellberg, 2018[33]) while the share of unemployed workers with access to union-provided UI has increased in line with the number of unions offering them, as indicated by Lindquist & Wadensjö (2011[16]), see Figure 8.3, Panel B.

8.7. Willingness to pay for UI in a voluntary UI system

UI funds pay a so-called financing fee to the Swedish government. The financing fee is the funds' contribution to government UI expenditure. In 2016, the financing fees covered about 25% of total UI costs. It is simply a function of the average wage among unemployed fund members and the total number of fund members – it does not depend on the unemployment risk of the members of a fund.[16]

In practice, there is a clear negative relationship between the unemployment rate of the members of a given UI fund and their per capita financing fee (Kjellberg, 2018[33]).That is, there is an inverted experience rating in voluntary UI, in which higher fund unemployment corresponds to lower per member financing fees (Figure 8.4). This means that low-risk funds subsidise high-risk funds, not only through tax payments, but also through UI fund premiums (which pay for the financing fees).

In an effort to moderate wage claims in sectors with high unemployment, in 2007 the government introduced an "additional financing fee" which brought an experience rating into the voluntary UI system, as well as raising the overall share of UI expenditures financed by UI funds. The additional financing fee also increased funds' and fund members' financing burden for income-related UI.

The resulting increases in UI fund premiums caused a large drop in the share of Swedish workers covered by voluntary UI, and may have increased adverse selection in the system. This indicates that voluntary UI schemes may require substantial public subsidies to produce high coverage rates. This section discusses the 2007 reform with a special focus on the self-employed.

Figure 8.4. Low-risk UI funds subsidize high-risk UI- funds

Per-capita financing fees (fund contributions to the government) of individual UI funds in SEK as a function of UI fund-level unemployment rates in percent, 2015/16

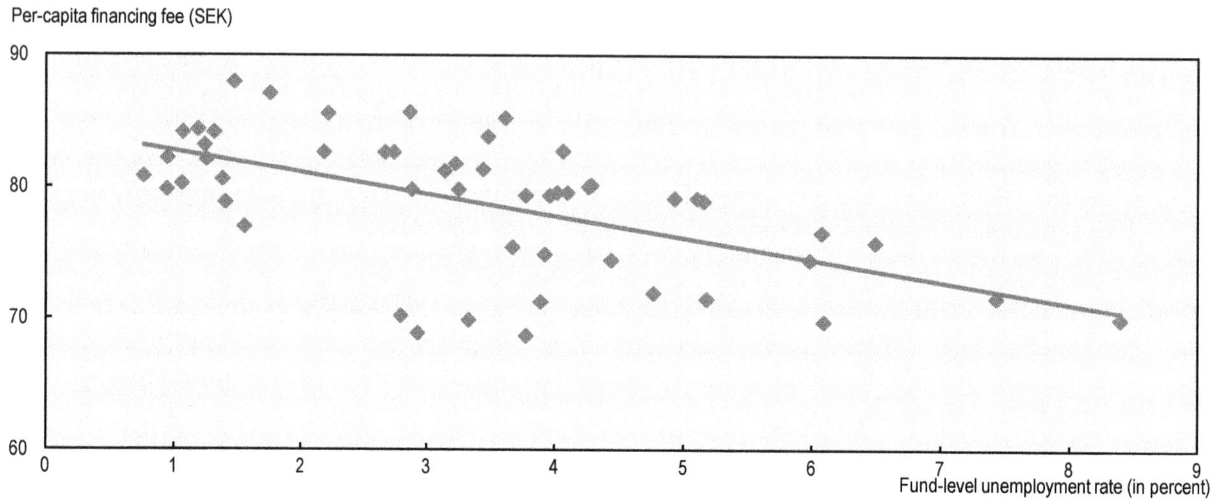

Note: The figure plots the monthly per fund member financing fee (in Swedish kronor) of the UI funds against the unemployment rate among UI fund members on the UI fund level for the years 2015-2016.
Source: The Swedish Unemployment Insurance Board (IAF).

8.7.1. The effects of raised UI fund premiums in 2007

The "additional financing fee", introduced in 2007 and replaced by an "unemployment fee" in 2008,[17] established a clear positive relationship between the UI benefit expenses of the funds and their payments to the state (see Figure 8.5).

It also substantially increased the share of UI expenditure borne by member premiums. Before the reforms in 2007 and 2008, about 10% of the costs of UI benefit expenses were covered by UI funds through the financing fees. After the reform 40-60% of the UI benefit expenses were paid for by UI fund membership premiums, even though 33% was set as a target value (Government of Sweden, 2007[34]). UI funds on average raised their premiums by 300% between 2006 and 2007.

After the reforms of 2007 and 2008 UI fund membership rates dropped by 10 percentage points, and unions also lost a large number of members (Figure 8.2). The decrease in union density is likely to be due to the fact that union membership and UI fund membership largely go hand in hand as UI fund premiums are a part of union dues.

Most of those who left were either younger (under age 25) or older workers (above age 60) and can therefore be described as low-risk or low-cost workers, which probably increased adverse selection. Young workers mostly have a high unemployment risk but they earn less, which results in lower UI benefits, and they find work rapidly, which results in lower total UI expenses. Older workers have lower unemployment risk compared with other age groups. The degree of adverse selection had only been small previously, as about 80-85% of all workers were members of a UI fund before 2007.

The unemployment fee was removed in 2014. But union and UI fund coverage rates have not yet recovered to their pre-2007 levels. The main lesson of the reform seems to be that increases in premiums, thought small in absolute terms, may cause large decreases in UI coverage. Most UI fund premiums rose by about 1% of the median net-of-tax wage between 2006 and 2008. The earned income tax credit, introduced in 2007, increased net-of-tax earnings by about 5% for the median worker. This means that workers increased their earnings after taxes and UI fund premiums had been paid. Governments should therefore be prepared to subsidise any voluntary UI scheme heavily if they wish to have high coverage rates and keep adverse selection low.

In 2016, after the unemployment fees had been removed, the funds paid about 25% of the UI expenses. The fact that this share is higher than the 2006 value, despite the abolition of the unemployment fees, was mostly to do with a lower number of UI remunerated days per UI fund member, caused by a tightening of eligibility requirements.

Figure 8.5. The 2007 reform introduced an experience rating via unemployment fees

UI-fund contributions to the government, per capita in SEK, as a function of the fund-level unemployment rate, in percent, 2008 – 2013

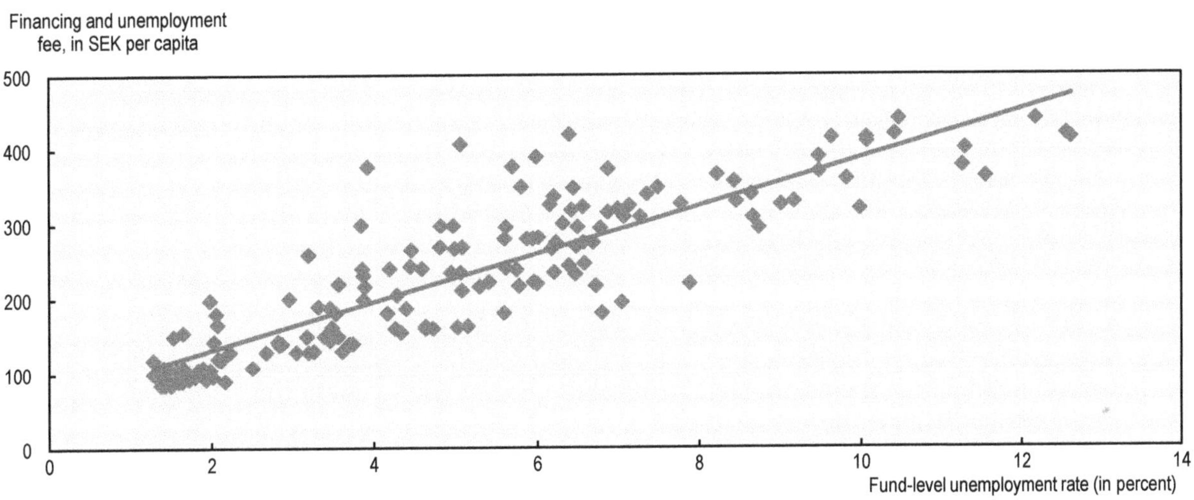

Note: The figure the per capita financing and unemployment fee (fund contributions to the government) against unemployment rates for each UI fund for the years 2008-2013. During the period each fund paid special unemployment fee to the Swedish state which was a function of its total UI expenses.
Source: The Swedish Unemployment Insurance Board (IAF).

UI fund density and union density (the share of the workforce who are members of a UI fund or union) have decreased during the 2000s (Figure 8.2) with a clear drop between 2006 and 2008 which corresponds to the introduction of an experience rating and higher fund premiums for UI funds. On average, UI fund premiums rose by 300% between 2006 and 2007. In addition, Table 8.2 shows some descriptive statistics to complement Figure 8.2 .

Those who left UI funds in 2007 and 2008 were mostly low-income earners, young workers (aged 16-24) and older workers (aged 60-64) (Kjellberg, 2016[35]). Kjellberg does not distinguish between low-income earners and young workers. It may be the case that dropouts were high among young workers who also earn less than the average worker. High-income workers, defined as having earnings above SEK 42 000 per month (about EUR 4 400) are under-represented in the dropout statistics compared with other earnings groups. In addition, Kjellberg finds that dropouts are more pronounced among individuals with no or negative net wealth and among individuals with net wealth above

SEK 1 million.[18] This again may very well reflect the fact that dropouts are more common among young workers (with low net worth) and older workers (with higher net worth).

Table 8.2. Descriptive statistics

Aggregate values for three different years

	2004	2010	2016
UI fund members (thousands)	3806.5	3370.1	3576.7
Union members (thousands)	3567.3	3403.4	3497.3
Labour force (thousands)	4538.6	4780.1	5053.9
UI fund density (%)	83.9	70.5	70.7
Union density (%)	78.6	71.2	69.2
Maximum daily UI (SEK)	730	680	910
UI remunerated days (millions)	56.4	30.5	18.6
Median monthly wage (2015 SEK)	21 000	25 300	28 600
Average UI replacement rate (%)	68	53	63
Collective agreement density among workers (%)	93	89	90

Note: Maximum daily UI refers to the publicly provided UI given during the first 20 weeks of unemployment. The number of UI fund members and the size of the labour force are reported for December each year. Collective agreement density for 2004 is not available; the figure for 2005 is used instead. For collective bargain density in 2016 the figure for 2015 is used. The median wage for 2016 is not available, the figure for 2015 is used instead. Median wages are given in 2015 prices.
Source: Statistics Sweden, IAF and (Kjellberg, 2017[15]).

While UI fund density has decreased, the share of workers covered by collective agreements remained relatively stable during the 2000s (Kjellberg, 2018[33]). The share of unemployed UI fund members who are members are entitled to union-run UI top-ups, has increased significantly during the 2000s.

The two additional UI systems – union-provided UI top-ups and UI via collective agreements – have therefore grown relatively in importance as the publicly funded UI has become less generous. This suggests that it has become harder for the self-employed and gig workers to insure against unemployment over the last ten years. The UI benefit increase of 2015 only partially compensated for the reduction in the UI replacement rate between 2007 and 2015 (see Table 8.2 and Section 8.6).

Figure 8.6. The UI fund membership among self-employed and the total workforce

UI fund density among the self-employed and in the overall workforce, in percent, workers aged 20-64, 2006-2015

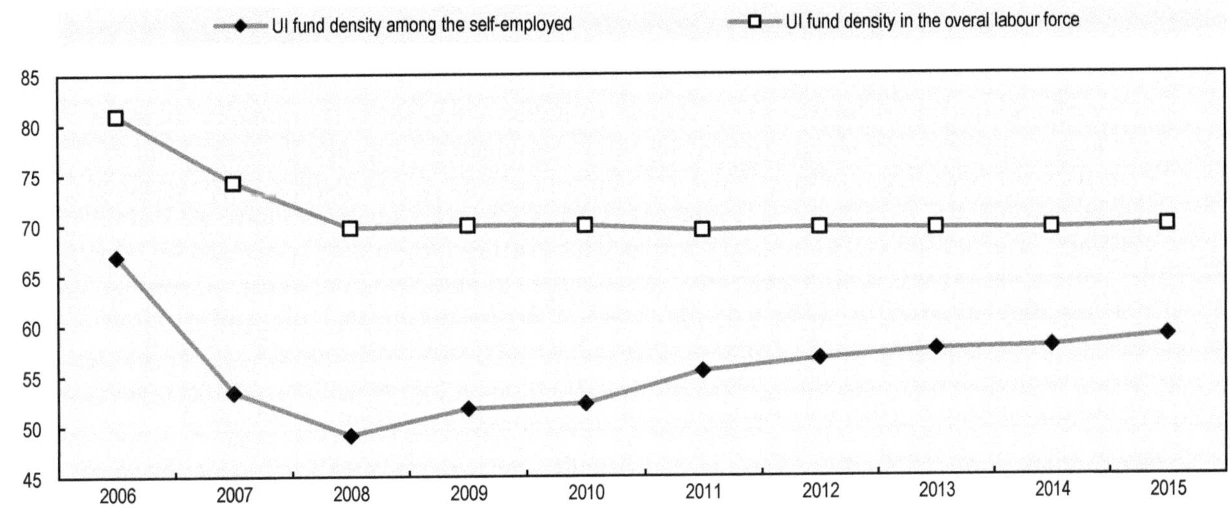

Note: The figure plots UI fund density in the total workforce and the number of members in the self-employed UI fund relative to the number of self-employed in the Swedish workforce. The individuals who are reported as being self-employed have their self-employment as their main income source. Data spans the years 2006-2015. Note that the self-employed UI fund also organise workers employed by small business owners. Therefore, actual UI fund density among self-employed is lower.
Source: The Swedish Unemployment Insurance Board (IAF) and Statistics Sweden (SCB).

8.7.2. The effect of higher UI fund premiums for the self-employed

The 2007 reform pushed up UI fund premiums for the self-employed fund more than for all other funds except one. Between 2006 and 2007 monthly UI fund premiums rose by 309% on average while premiums in the self-employed fund rose 337% between 2006 and 2007. After 2008, premiums for the self-employed – as well as for members in the other funds – decreased considerably (probably because the funds had overstated the effect of the unemployment fee when setting premiums). However, the reduction of premiums for the self-employed was larger than average: In 2009 the self-employed paid premiums that were 84% higher than in 2006 while the average increase in UI fund premiums between 2006 and 2009 was 161%.

The members of the self-employed UI fund were thus less affected by the reform than other funds, once the funds had got accustomed to the new pricing rule. This points towards a relatively lower unemployment risk among the self-employed. In fact, the average unemployment rate in 2004-16 in the self-employed UI fund was 3.8%. The average unemployment rate among all funds was 6.6%.[19]

When UI fund premiums rose in 2007 and 2008, UI fund density fell. However, the UI fund dropout rate appears to have been lower among the self-employed than for other groups. This is shown in Figure 8.6 which plots the evolution of UI fund density in the workforce and the number of members in the self-employed UI fund relative to the number of self-employed in the Swedish workforce. Note that the self-employed UI fund also includes individuals employed by small business owners. Therefore, the actual UI fund density among the self-employed is lower.

In contrast to the total workforce, UI fund density among the self-employed has increased since 2008, when the unemployment fee was introduced. This may be a result of premiums for the self-employed UI fund decreasing more after 2007 than average fund premiums.

8.8. Concluding remarks

In Sweden joining a UI fund to get access to voluntary UI benefits is voluntary. Being a member of a union and being covered by union-provided UI top-ups is also voluntary. And finally having a job where the wage and other benefits are collectively agreed is similarly voluntary. Effectively this introduces many voluntary elements into Swedish UI coverage. The self-employed and gig workers have access to publicly provided UI. But they do not have a union which can give them access to additional union-run UI top-ups. Nor are they covered by collective agreements, which means that they miss out on additional UI and severance payments granted by collective agreements. In addition, collective agreements contain important pension, sickness insurance and workers' compensation benefits that non-standard workers cannot benefit from.

A central feature of UI programmes is that benefits are paid out to workers who are laid off involuntarily. Swedish UI provides incentives for both regular employees and the self-employed not to quit work voluntarily: Swedish employers report to UI funds whether an employee's departure was involuntary or not, and voluntary quits result in a nine-week waiting period for UI. The self-employed on the other hand must close or freeze their company to receive benefits. If they resume their business after unemployment they cannot receive UI benefits the next five years.

However, Swedish UI regulation is less clear on how to establish whether gig workers have stopped work voluntarily. They are currently treated as standard employees but do not have an employer who can confirm that they have been laid off. This can introduce additional moral hazard in the UI system. UI funds have not yet solved this problem, and are hesitant to pay out UI benefits to gig workers, who may be uncovered as a result.

Collective agreements can provide incentives for employers to misclassify workers and to engage gig workers and the self-employed instead of regular employees. Swedish employers covered by collective agreements pay between 5% and 35% of wage costs, depending on the wage level, to a collectively bargained pension scheme. Such incentives can cause the aggregate insurance level in the Swedish labour market to decline as regular employees switch to become gig workers as employers seek to reduce labour costs. It can also increase the risk of old-age poverty, leading to higher public costs to counteract such poverty.

In voluntary UI systems, such as the Swedish one, coverage rates seem sensitive to the degree of public funding. When public funding is reduced, and UI fund members have to pay higher premiums, as caused by two reforms in 2007 and 2008, coverage rates can be expected to fall significantly. Even though public funding of UI funds has increased and UI fund premiums are close to what they were in 2006, coverage rates are still considerably lower than before the reforms. Other countries who consider voluntary UI schemes for gig workers and the self-employed should therefore be prepared to subsidise such schemes extensively if they are aiming for a high UI coverage rate.

As mentioned, subsuming gig workers into the UI scheme may prove difficult due to ambiguities regarding the involuntary nature of a gig worker's unemployment. But a takeaway from Sweden is that voluntary UI seems to work for the self-employed; adverse selection among the self-employed appears to be small, illustrated by relatively low unemployment among the self-employed. In addition, average UI benefits are only somewhat lower among the self-employed.

One remedy would be to require gig workers to set up firms of their own which they would need to close down to receive UI, a curb that seems to work for the self-employed. However, such a regulation would risk reducing gig worker employment as it involves more administrative duties for the individual worker. The trade-off in this case is between simplifying employment, and thereby increasing employment, and providing social protection by curtailing gig worker employment.

The key issue when it comes to providing gig workers with social insurance in general and UI in particular is the extent to which other workers should bear the costs of the increased moral hazard associated with gig workers, mainly due to the fact that it is hard to verify that their layoffs are involuntary. It is clear, from the case of the actors and musicians in Section 8.1, that workers with uncertain employment and large income variations are costly to a UI scheme. If the scheme receives heavy subsidies, it increases moral hazard (members using the UI during periods of voluntary non-employment). But if members need to bear a large share of their own costs, it increases adverse selection (high contributions will mean that low-risk workers opt out while high-risk workers remain members).

A voluntary UI fund exclusively for gig workers would face a high risk of becoming insolvent as low-risk workers opt out while high-risk workers remain members. Within the current Swedish system, a gig worker UI fund would most likely need to merge with a larger UI fund whose members have lower risks of being unemployed.

Giving high-risk and low-risk workers the same benefits within the current Swedish voluntary UI system would either result in higher UI fund premiums (since the administrative costs become higher when the fund's unemployment rate is higher) or require more redistribution via government subsidies. The downside of these two options is that higher fund premiums could prevent low-risk workers from joining and more redistribution increases the costs of the UI system as gig workers are likely to become unemployed more often.

Another possible way of incorporating gig workers into a voluntary UI system is to partially tie their benefits to their work history. Currently, the Swedish UI system is equally generous to workers who have worked six months as those who have worked 20 years without ever having been unemployed. Individuals who often register as unemployed could be given lower benefits compared with individuals who have been unemployed less often. There would still be redistribution from low-risk to high-risk workers but high-risk workers would bear their own costs.

Notes

[1] The calculation is based on data from IAF's database and is based on data from November 2017. The number of UI fund members where 3.6 million who paid in SEK 410 million UI fund fees. During the same period the average daily UI benefit was SEK 714 and the number of remunerated days where 1.67 million. Dividing UI fund fees with UI benefit payments gives 0.35

[2] Self-employed can be (and in many cases are) members of an unemployment insurance fund within their sector of activity and not necessarily with the self-employed UI fund. However, there are often certain educational or vocational qualifications that the applicant must meet, so not any worker can join any UI fund.

[3] The calculation is based on data from the Swedish Unemployment Insurance Board (IAF).

[4] The SEK/EUR exchange rate has had an average value of about 9.5 the last 10-15 years, this exchange rate is used throughout the paper.

[5] The monthly median wage was SEK 28 600 in 2015 (Statistics Sweden, 2017[38]).

[6] The maximum UI benefit is SEK 910 a day, paid out Monday to Friday, for the first 20 weeks of unemployment. From week 21 the maximum benefit is SEK 760 a day.

[7] The tie between trade unions and UI funds have weakened in recent years and there is no prerequisite to be a member of both a union and that union's affiliated UI fund. However, most unions do have a UI fund and members typically register with the UI fund affiliated to their union.

[8] While most programmes do have a cap, these tend to be high enough as to be irrelevant for most workers.

[9] See (Kjellberg, 2017[15]) for figures on union density and (Lindquist and Wadensjö, 2011[16]) for data on unions who provide additional UI.

[10] Table 8.1 refers to the costs associated with a private sector blue collar worker. Private sector white collar workers with an average wage have slightly higher contributions to collectively bargained schemes: 5.25% of the pre-tax wage.

[11] In fact, the personal allowance as a function of the pre-tax wage has a bell shape. It peaks in absolute terms at about one-third of average incomes. Thereafter it becomes smaller, both absolutely and relative to the wage (Skatteverket, 2017[36]).

[12] This is significantly below the share quoted in Chapter 1, Figure 1.1, because it only pertains to workers aged 20-64, while Figure 1.1 refers to the entire labour force, aged 15-74. Only those below the age of 65 are eligible for unemployment benefits, however.

[13] Independent contractors are both employers and employees at the same time which makes them ineligible. It is possible for small business owners with other employees to enter a collective agreement. If the business owner is also an employee of the company, then the collective agreement covers him/her too.

[14] Gig workers are not covered as the gig worker employers' organisation has not entered into collective agreements.

[15] For references, see for instance (Baily, 1978[33]), (Fredriksson and Holmlund, 2001[24]) and (Chetty, 2008[34]).

[16] It is calculated as 131% of the average daily UI benefit received by unemployed fund members, multiplied by the total number of members in the fund.

17 The "additional financing fee" resulted in the following method of calculating UI fund premiums for each fund j: $P_j = \bar{P}[1 + V(C_j - \bar{C})]$ where C_j=daily publicly provided UI times days unemployed divided by the number of UI fund members, i.e., publicly provided UI costs per fund member. The bar above P (UI fund premiums) and C denotes averages, $V = 0.000145$ is a weight (Government of Sweden, 2008[37]). Funds in which the cost of unemployment was relatively high were made to pay more to the state while funds with a lower relative cost for unemployment paid less. In 2008 the formula was simplified and the charge was renamed the "unemployment fee". The main reason for introducing the unemployment fee was that the additional financing fee did not raise UI fund premiums enough in the funds where unemployment rates were high. The new rule stipulated that each fund should pay 33% of its total publicly provided UI costs to the state (Government of Sweden, 2007[31]). That is $0.33C_j$. The new policy meant that high-risk workers no longer subsidised UI fund premiums for low-risk workers, which effectively was what the additional financing fee did.

18 Net wealth includes real estate holdings.

19 Note that the 6.6% is not the average unemployment rate among UI fund members, but rather the average unemployment rate of all funds. It is not weighted by the number of UI fund members in each fund at each point in time in 2004-16.

References

Baily, M. (1978), "Some aspects of optimal unemployment insurance", *Journal of Public Economics*, pp. 379-402, https://doi.org/10.1016/0047-2727(78)90053-1. [36]

Bengtsson, N., P. Edin and B. Holmlund (2014), *Löner, sysselsättning och inkomster - ökar klyftorna i Sverige?*, Swedish Fiscal Policy Council. [21]

Bjerke, L. and L. Pettersson (2012), , http://www.egenanstallning.org/rapporter/RAPPORT-EGENANSTALLDA_EN_VAG_IN_PA_ARBETSMARKNADEN_ALMEDALEN.pdf. [18]

Chetty, R. (2008), "Moral hazard versus liquidity and optimal unemployment insurance", *Journal of Political Economy*, pp. 173-234, https://doi.org/10.1086/588585. [37]

Chetty, R. and E. Saez (2010), "Optimal Taxation and Social Insurance with Endogenous Private Insurance", *American Economic Journal: Economic Policy*, Vol. 2/2, pp. 85-114, http://dx.doi.org/10.1257/pol.2.2.85. [6]

DIK (2017), *5 svar om egenanställningar*, https://www.dik.se/om-dik/nyhetsarkiv/5-svar-om-egenanstallningar/. [19]

Ekonomifakta (2017), *Sociala avgifter*, http://www.ekonomifakta.se/Fakta/Skatter/Skatt-pa-arbete/Sociala-avgifter/. [24]

Fredriksson, P. and B. Holmlund (2001), "Optimal unemployment insurance in search equilibrium", *Journal of Labor Economics*, pp. 370-399, https://doi.org/10.1086/319565. [27]

Government of Sweden (2011), *Tjänstepensioner och utträde ur arbetslivet*, Statens offentliga utredningar. [1]

Government of Sweden (2008), , http://www.regeringen.se/contentassets/85094a5214a84dc4b01587561286fe70/finansiering-av-arbetsloshetsforsakringen. [39]

Government of Sweden (2007), *En effektivare arbetslöshetsförsäkring*, Ministry of Labour, Governemt of Sweden. [34]

Guiso, L., L. Pistaferri and F. Schivardi (2005), "Insurance within the firm", *Journal of Political Economy*, Vol. 113/5, pp. 1054-1087, https://doi.org/10.1086/432136. [3]

Hagen, J. (2017), "Pension principles in the Swedish pension system", *Scandinavian Economic History Review*, Vol. 65/1, pp. 28-51, http://dx.doi.org/10.1080/03585522.2016.1269670. [22]

Hall, C. et al. (2016), *Screening through activation: differential effects of a youth activation programme*, IFAU. [30]

Holmlund, B. (1998), "Unemployment Insurance in Theory and Practice", *Scandinavian Journal of Economics*, Vol. 100/1, pp. 113-141. [7]

Holmlund, B. and P. Lundborg (1999), "Wage bargaining, union membership, and the organization of unemployment insurance", *Labour Economics*, pp. 397-415, https://doi.org/10.1016/S0927-5371(99)00010-X. [8]

Hurst, E. et al. (2010), "The importance of business owners in assessing the size of precautionary savings", *The Review of Economics and Statistics*, Vol. 92/1, pp. 61-69, http://dx.doi.org/10.1162/rest.2009.11500. [25]

IAF (2018), *Statistikdatabasen - Dagpenning - Ersättningstagare*, http://externastat.iaf.se/report.aspx?ID=29. [2]

IAF (2016), *När anställningen avslutats på egen begäran - granskning av giltiga skäl*, IAF. [29]

Kjellberg, A. (2018), *Kollektivavtalens täckningsgrad samt organisationsgraden hos arbetsgivarförbund och fackförbund*, Department of Sociology, Lund University. [33]

Kjellberg, A. (2017), *Kollektivavtalens täckningsgrad samt organisationsgraden hos arbetsgivarförbund och fackförbund*, Lund University. [15]

Kjellberg, A. (2016), *Vilka "hoppade av" a-kassan eller avstod från att gå med? En studie av a-kassornas medlemsras*, Department of Sociology, Lund University. [35]

Kjellberg, A. (2010), *Växande avgiftsskillnader i a-kassan - och utvecklingen därefter*, Department of Sociology, Lund University. [10]

Kjellberg, A. (2006), "The Swedish unemployment insurance - will the Ghent system survive?", *Transfer - European Review of Labour and Research*, Vol. 12/1, pp. 87-98. [11]

Kolsrud, J. (2013), *Insuring against unemployment*, Uppsala University. [31]

Konjunkturinstitutet (2016), *Lönebildningsrapporten*, Konjunkturinstitutet. [32]

Lindquist, G. and E. Wadensjö (2011), *Lindquist, Gabriella Sjögren, and Eskil Wadensjö. Avtalsbestämda ersättningar, andra kompletterande ersättningar och arbetsutbudet*, Ministry of Finance, Government of Sweden. [16]

OECD (2017), *OECD.Stat*, https://stats.oecd.org/Index.aspx?DataSetCode=UN_DEN. [9]

Ashenfelter, O. and R. Layard (eds.) (1986), *The employment relationship: Job attachment, work effort, and the nature of contracts*, North-Holland, https://doi.org/10.1016/S1573-4463(86)02004-7. [28]

Samorg (2017), *http://www.samorg.org/opinion-och-debatt/rapporter/*, http://www.samorg.org/wp-content/uploads/2017/05/2017-05-18-Sju-av-tio-sl%C3%A5r-i-a-kassetaket-kompensationsgrad-vecka-6-2017.pdf. [13]

SFS (1997), *Lagen om arbetslöshetsförsäkring, 1997:238*. [12]

Shapiro, C. and J. Stiglitz (1984), "Equilibrium unemployment as a worker discipline device", *The American Economic Review*, Vol. 74/3, pp. 433-444. [26]

Sjögren, G. and E. Wadensjö (2007), *Ett svårlagt pussel - kompletterande ersättningar vid inkomstbortfall*, Ministry of Finance, Government of Sweden. [23]

Skatteverket (2017), , https://www.skatteverket.se/download/18.3152d9ac158968eb8fd26ed/1481189766971/Grundavdragstabell+ej+f%C3%B6rh%C3%B6jt+grundavdrag.pdf. [38]

SOU (2011), *Tjänstepensioner och utträde från arbetslivet*, The Government of Sweden. [20]

SOU (2003), *Konstnärerna och trygghetssystemen*, Fritzes Offentliga Publikationer. [5]

Statistics Sweden (2017), *http://www.statistikdatabasen.scb.se*, http://www.statistikdatabasen.scb.se/pxweb/sv/ssd/START__AM__AM0112/TidsserieUtbinr/?rxid=f45f90b6-7345-4877-ba25-9b43e6c6e299.. [40]

Swedish Fiscal Policy Council (2011), *Swedish Fiscal Policy*, Swedish Fiscal Policy Council. [14]

Wallin, P. (2017), "Därför ökar antalet egenanställda i rasande fart", *Civilekonomen*. [17]

Wallin, P. (2017), *Egenföretagare vs egenanställd*, pp. 28-32. [4]

ORGANISATION FOR ECONOMIC CO-OPERATION AND DEVELOPMENT

The OECD is a unique forum where governments work together to address the economic, social and environmental challenges of globalisation. The OECD is also at the forefront of efforts to understand and to help governments respond to new developments and concerns, such as corporate governance, the information economy and the challenges of an ageing population. The Organisation provides a setting where governments can compare policy experiences, seek answers to common problems, identify good practice and work to co-ordinate domestic and international policies.

The OECD member countries are: Australia, Austria, Belgium, Canada, Chile, the Czech Republic, Denmark, Estonia, Finland, France, Germany, Greece, Hungary, Iceland, Ireland, Israel, Italy, Japan, Korea, Latvia, Lithuania, Luxembourg, Mexico, the Netherlands, New Zealand, Norway, Poland, Portugal, the Slovak Republic, Slovenia, Spain, Sweden, Switzerland, Turkey, the United Kingdom and the United States. The European Union takes part in the work of the OECD.

OECD Publishing disseminates widely the results of the Organisation's statistics gathering and research on economic, social and environmental issues, as well as the conventions, guidelines and standards agreed by its members.

OECD PUBLISHING, 2, rue André-Pascal, 75775 PARIS CEDEX 16
(81 2018 75 1 P) ISBN 978-92-64-30693-6 – 2018

www.ingramcontent.com/pod-product-compliance
Ingram Content Group UK Ltd.
Pitfield, Milton Keynes, MK11 3LW, UK
UKHW051500290926
15471UKWH00008B/1323

9 789264 30693